W9-ANN-433

Revolutionary
Breakthroughs
and
National
Development

Revolutionary Breakthroughs and National Development

The Case of Romania, 1944-1965

KENNETH JOWITT

University of California Press
Berkeley and Los Angeles, 1971

University of California Press
Berkeley and Los Angeles, California
University of California Press, Ltd.
London, England

Copyright © 1971, by
The Regents of the University of California
International Standard Book Number: 0-520-01762-5
Library of Congress Catalog Card Number: 71-123625

Designed by Eleanor Mennick
Printed in the United States of America

For my father, Kenneth Jowitt, Sr.,
my wife, Rebecca Jowitt,
and especially to the memory of my
mother, Elizabeth Jowitt.

Acknowledgments

INTELLECTUALLY, the major influences on the arguments presented in this work are contained in the writings of Max Weber and Philip Selznick. However, there is a much broader range of individuals and works that have shaped and continue to shape my interests and perspectives.

My interest in national development was in large part stimulated and partially defined by Ernst Haas, while my decision to devote my efforts to the comparative analysis of Marxist-Leninist systems was encouraged by the work and example provided by Chalmers Johnson.

I have benefited greatly from writings of Robert Tucker, Alfred Meyer, Zbigniew Brzezinski, Richard Lowenthal, and T. H. Rigby and from the writing and encouragement of R. V. Burks. Two individuals in particular have in different ways contributed to this work and to my intellectual development, not least of all by providing me with personal models to emulate: Gregory Grossman and John Michael Montias.

There are also certain institutions to which I am indebted, particularly the Institute for International Studies, the Center for Slavic Studies, and the Department of Political Science, all at the University of California, Berkeley. To the first two I am grateful for having sponsored the work that is presented here. To the University of California at Berkeley and the Department of Political Science I am grateful for having offered me as stimulating and rewarding a learning experience as I could have hoped for.

I also wish to recognize the contribution made by my editor, Mrs. Shirley Taylor.

As for my wife Rebecca's contribution, only I can appreciate how essential it was and continues to be.

Contents

Introduction

As an explanation of my motivating concerns, perspectives, and assumptions, I would like to repeat Harry Eckstein's prefatory remark in his study of Norway: "My overriding interest as a political scientist is not in any particular polity but in the comparative study of political systems and in problems that can be dealt with only through such study."[1]

This study, like Eckstein's, is an exercise in comparative analysis. The major problem studied in this work is different, but the rationale behind the comparative focus is similar. Like Eckstein, I share the conviction that "the theoretical fruits of broader studies can sharpen one's understanding of particular cases,"[2] and that reciprocally, intensive analysis of a given case can contribute to the refinement of the theoretical constructs one

---

[1] Harry Eckstein, *Division and Cohesion in Democracy: A Study of Norway* (Princeton, 1966), p. v.

[2] *Ibid.*

is interested in elaborating. Without comparison there is the danger of having processes, events, and structures incorrectly perceived and conceived as either unique or identical. Comparison is necessary to appreciate the distinctive character of such phenomena. Rather than slighting the particular qualities of the units it examines, comparative analysis is capable of specifying the distinctive aspects of a given unit (i.e., nation-state) as they relate to a conceptually defined problem area, whereas an "area study" tends to stress the uniqueness of the units it focuses on.

The assumption of this study is that without a comparative framework (and most of us employ them implicitly if not explicitly) the observer is likely never to get beyond his data and possibly his own value preferences. The danger is greater that social reality will appear to have a self-evident meaning rather than one that should be questioned and studied.

The problem area around which this study is oriented is the process of nation building: the elements that define it, their relationships, and the conditions and factors that shape the quality of these relationships. Part I consists of a theoretical elaboration of the nation-building process and an initial testing of this formulation through the comparative analysis of several national units. The remainder of the study, following Eckstein's concept of a "theoretical case study,"[3] is an attempt to arrive at "a more satisfactory treatment of [a] problem through a combination of the genres of specialists and generalists." The case selected is Romania. There are several reasons for this selection. One of my major interests as a political scientist is Leninist ideologies, elites, and systems. In particular, I am interested in answering the question: What is distinctive about Leninist political systems and communities as arrangements of political leadership and opportunities for the political actualization of those who are members of such systems and communities? To word it somewhat differently, I am interested in ascertaining the distinctive strengths and weaknesses (competence and incompetence) displayed by different types of Leninist regimes in dealing with the nation-building process. As a polity with a Leninist regime Romania is an appropriate focus

---

[3] *Ibid.*, p. viii.

for such a set of concerns. As a polity that has redefined its status from a "satellite" to a largely self-directed political entity, self-consciously dealing with the question of a Leninist elite's relation to the nation both on ideological and political grounds, the Romanian experience offers a promising context within which to study the process of nation building. It is promising on several levels: at the highest level it provides a context for the refinement, testing, and generation of hypotheses concerning nation building as a universal process; at a slightly lower level it provides data for an increased understanding of the distinctive form and substance this process assumes in Leninist settings. At an even more specific level it offers the analyst of national development valuable material in attempting to understand the elements and processes of the growth of political integrity and the redefinition of political status. Finally, Romania like any other polity deserves to be studied precisely because it is a distinct political entity, a reflection of and a shaping influence on the social and personal character of those collectivities and individuals who make it a political, cultural, social, and economic reality.

The various components of this study — theoretical, comparative, and "case study" — are by intention interdependent and overlapping, because I think that such an approach is most likely to increase our understanding of the nation-building process and the particular quality of political events and processes in Romania since 1944.

PART I

A Comparative Analysis
of Nationalist and Leninist Ideologies
and Nation-Building Strategies

Nation-Building Strategies

NATION BUILDING consists of two major tasks: breaking through and political integration. Related to each of these tasks are two processes — industrialization and the institutionalization of an effective leadership organization — whose definition is critical to the way in which the tasks of breaking through and political integration are dealt with.

Breaking through means the *decisive alteration or destruction of values, structures, and behaviors which are perceived by a revolutionary elite as comprising or contributing to the actual or potential existence of alternative centers of political power.* Political integration means the creation of a new political formula, new political institutions, and new patterns of political behavior: a new community based on norms of reciprocity, on shared sentiments, and on mutual (political-civic) recognition, all of which receive some institutional expression. The analysis in this book will focus mainly on the first task. A future work will consider the task of political integration and community building.

Breaking through may be viewed as a problem, a process, and an outcome. It is a task which an objective observer can posit as confronting all nation-building elites; it is an empirical question whether or not, and in what ways, different nation-building elites perceive such a task as existing. It may be conceived of as a process extending over time, affecting different social domains and resulting in a mixed set of outcomes. The notion of decisive breakthrough refers to a situation where those values, structures, and behaviors perceived by a nation-building elite as threatening have been effectively constrained or eliminated.[1] It is of major analytic interest that different nation-building elites will have different definitions of what a decisive breakthrough involves. The character of the breakthrough reflects and is shaped by the strategy (or strategies) that a nation-building elite employs. Similarly, the premises supporting it and the strategies employed directly affect the character of political integration, that is, the type of political community that is created. For the analysis of nation-building presented here, I shall refer to two major strategies,[2] Reformism and Revolution. It is my contention that the nation-building process is dependent for its success on an initial strategy of revolution.

Each of these approaches, reformist and revolutionary, emphasizes different procedures for effecting change. Reformism stresses the value of "muddling through" and shifting alliances.[3] The rationale for "muddling through" is that the "test of a 'good' policy is typically that various analysts find themselves directly

---

[1] Otto Kirchheimer ("Confining Conditions and Revolutionary Breakthroughs," *American Political Science Review*, 59 [December 1965]: 964–974) notes (p. 967) that a revolutionary breakthrough may occur with the "old data" (i.e., antirevolutionary institutions) remaining, "though absorbed in a new context and thereby deprived of its confining nature." Such an outcome involves the decisive alteration as opposed to elimination of elements in a society which are seen as threats to the nation-building program.

[2] Strategies here are conceived of as "the links between the intentions and perceptions of . . . officials and the political system that imposes restraints and creates opportunities for them" (Aaron Wildavsky, *The Politics of the Budgetary Process* [Boston, 1964], p. 63).

[3] See Charles E. Lindblom, "The 'Science' of Muddling Through," *Public Administration Review* 19 (September 1959), 79–88; and Albert O. Hirschmann, *Journeys Toward Progress* (New York, 1965), pp. 327–386.

agreeing on a policy (without their agreeing that it is the most appropriate means to an agreed on objective)."[4] Shifting alliances are seen as an adaptation of the "muddling through" procedure which is relevant to social systems characterized by the existence of more than one principle of political legitimacy, economic orientation, and/or life style. "Muddling through" is logrolling in homogeneous, secular cultures, but in heterogeneous or fragmented cultures, where the major political actors have extensive and intense concerns about all issues, "muddling through" takes the form of shifting alliances. Both "muddling through" and shifting alliances have been defended in terms of their "realism and relevance." Ideally, "muddling through" and "shifting alliances" possess the virtue of allowing "the several problems that are before [a] country to be tackled sequentially rather than simultaneously."[5]

Viewed as an alternative strategy, revolution directly confronts what are conceived to be obstacles to change. Such obstacles are also viewed from a perspective which stresses their interdependence. It is the consideration of issues in terms of their interdependence, not the automatic attempt to solve all issues simultaneously, that characterizes revolutionary regimes. Revolutionary elites may also approach issues sequentially. A revolutionary approach is distinctive in its urgency, systemic focus, and purposeful use of violence — in some form — to minimize the number of commitments to the existing society and also the possibility of counterelites' defining their opposition in politically relevant terms.

A revolutionary strategy involves "the conscious espousal of a new social order" and impinges on the most general (and basic) level of socio-political organization, the community. The main instrument that gives revolution its distinctive competence is violence. Violence in the form of coercion and terror "informs" the orientation and behavior of revolutionary elites engaged in

---

[4] Lindblom, p. 81.

[5] Hirschmann, pp. 376–377. For a discussion and definition of homogeneous secular cultures see Gabriel Almond, "Comparative Political Systems," in *Comparative Politics: Notes and Readings*, ed. Roy C. Macridis and Bernard E. Brown (Homewood, Ill., 1961), pp. 439–454.

nation building. No matter which strategy, or combination of strategies, is employed by political elites, political parties are often the critical organization units in a system undergoing change. In discussing political parties Blau makes a point that is widely acknowledged:

> A political party does not remain a social unit distinct from other social units whose support it attracts but becomes interpenetrated by them. Initially, the party may be conceived of as a separate social group that modified its ideology in accordance with the interests of various social segments of the society in exchange for their social support. Success in this endeavor, however, destroys the boundary between the party and the other groups, since the party is now largely composed of important elements of these groups. It is no longer meaningful to speak of social exchange between the party and other groups. The appropriate conception is that competition and exchange occur among the elements within the party that represent the interests of various segments of the society, and their objective is to win dominant influence over the party's program and conduct of affairs.[6]

This conception of party can be related to the strategy of "muddling through"' and placed in the context of nation building through reference to what Apter has termed the "reconciliation system." Within the latter, "the 'party of representation' views politics as an elaborate system of bargaining for support. It is based on compromise. It corrupts ideologies by not taking them too seriously. It can stand competition and, indeed, requires it. It defines the character of the reconciliation system."[7]

Not all political parties fit the "representation" model, however. Some parties consciously attempt to avoid or contain the process Blau describes and the mode of behavior Apter depicts. Such parties aspire to be "organizational weapons," because they want to minimize the number of commitments they make. This does not suggest that interests which exist in the larger social system are not formulated and defended within these parties; rather, it is to say that such formulation and defense as occurs

---

[6] Peter Blau, *Exchange and Power in Social Life* (New York, 1964), p. 249.
[7] David Apter, *The Politics of Modernization* (Chicago, 1965), p. 215.

is not institutionalized. The alternatives, therefore, are not necessarily either a party with an attenuated identity and institutionalized aggregation of social interests within its boundaries, or a party with a well-defined identity completely divorced from its environment.[8] If in the context of nation building one believes that both representation and leadership are critical functions which political parties must perform, than one might argue that the "party of representation" seriously endangers the leadership function. Engrossed in compromise and aggregation, it often makes a series of incompatible commitments, which have a definitive impact on the nature of the organization. Given this character, the "party of representation" is often mainly concerned with sheer organizational survival, and as Selznick has so well stated, "the leadership of any polity fails when it concentrates on sheer survival. Institutional survival, properly understood, is a matter of maintaining values and distinctive identity."[9]

On the other hand, the "organizational weapon" type of party faces the danger of failing to perform a representative function. This is a concern of a revolutionary elite to the extent that it requires a minimum of support and information from its environment. But during the breaking-through phase of nation building it may not be desirable to represent certain interests. This is especially true when such interests may be capable of and concerned with preventing the adoption and/or implementation of policies considered critical by the ruling party. These are often policies directly related to the process of secularization and industrialization.

An awareness of the negative outcomes of a reformist strategy is not limited to critics of this strategy. For example, Lindblom, the most consistent exponent of the "branch" or muddling-through model, in an earlier work with Dahl observed that "the need for

---

[8] Apropos the proce⸴ of institutionalization, Clement Henry Moore has some interesting comments in his study, "Tunisia After Bourguiba: Liberalization or Political Degeneration?" Reprint, Department of Political Science, University of California, Berkeley (originally published in *Political Modernization in the Near East and North Africa*, Princeton University Conference, 1966).

[9] Philip Selznick, *Leadership in Administration* (White Plains, N.Y., 1957), p. 62.

widespread acceptance among the politically active often produces irrational agreement through logrolling."[10] Muddling through, in other words, with its emphasis on bargaining, compromise, and shifting alliances, can be unrealistic, irrelevant, and irrational, even in a homogeneous-secular context such as the United States. It may well be that even in this context reformism has entailed higher costs than are generally allowed. In fact, "the moral may be that the United States is a politically underdeveloped society, which, because of development in other areas, can afford such conditions."[11]

Dahl and Lindblom provide a second cirticism of the muddling-through model or reformist strategy when they point out how "the prevalence of bargaining results in public policies shaped to fit the demands of those who are highly organized":[12] parties of representation may not be so representative after all. Speaking of the Parti Démocratique du Côte -d'Ivoire, one scholar notes that "ever since it became a government party the P.D.C.I. has maintained itself through a distributive capacity. Many new political offices have been created to accommodate demands for representation." So far one might agree that while not approximating a rational-legal model of development, the P.D.C.I. — unquestionably a "party of representation" — is acting in a representative, community-building fashion. However, it seems that "at the same time the regime has gained complete control over the allocation of these offices and has reduced government accountability to representative organs."[13]

A third criticism of reformism relates to the supposed utility

---

[10] Robert A. Dahl and Charles E. Lindblom, *Politics, Economics, and Welfare* (New York, 1953), p. 339.

[11] Frederick Frey, "Political Development, Po⸱ ⸱r, and Communications in Turkey," in *Communications and Political De⸱ lopment*, ed. Lucian Pye (Princeton, 1963), p. 325. On this point the argu⸱ ⸱nents presented by Grant McConnell (*Private Power and American Democracy* [New York, 1966]) are also relevant.

[12] Dahl and Lindblom, *Politics*, p. 340.

[13] Aristide Zolberg, "Ivory Coast," in *Political Parties and National Integration in Tropical Africa*, ed. James S. Coleman and Carl G. Rosberg, Jr. (Berkeley, and Los Angeles, 1966), p. 88.

of shifting alliances à la Hirschmann. In a situation where there are four political actors and a similar number of issues, it may be that actors A, B, and C agree on issue 1 and effect a policy change with regard to it. A, B, and C then dissolve their coalition because only issue 1 has brought them together. Before they can turn to the three remaining issues, however, issue 1 quickly reappears. It may be inevitable that problems seldom stay permanently solved or resolved.[14] One can thus explain the reappearance of issue 1 as a result of the fact that a new coalition of B, C, and D agree on issue 3; D is vital to C and B, but D is completely against the policy agreed on by A, B, and C over issue 1. Assuming that B and C have low preferences on issues 2 and 4, and that issue 3 is more important to B and C than issue 1, we have the reappearance of the first issue. This sequence could perhaps occur in any context, but it is more likely to occur when all or most of the major actors are concerned and involved with all the major issues. In other words, when political actors assume such a posture in heterogeneous or poly-normative political environments, shifting alliances may be more necessary than logrolling, and even more effective, but not effective enough. In such a political context logrolling may be impossible, and the results of shifting alliances may be extremely fragile.

A fourth criticism of reformism as it relates to the leadership function has already been mentioned. To state it briefly: politics and vision are necessary components of all nation-building strategies — and reformism, particularly in heterogeneous, nonsecular, political environments, can result in an unending concern with politics and a loss or lack of political vision on the part of the leaders.[15]

Criticisms have also been made of revolutionary strategies involving coercion, violence, terror, direct confrontation of obstacles, simultaneous consideration of problems, and "decisive breakthrough." Apter, for instance, holds that the "mobilization sys-

---

[14] As suggested by William J. Gore and J. W. Dyson, eds., *The Making of Decisions* (New York, 1964), Introduction, p. 16.

[15] The use of this particular set of terms was suggested by the title of Sheldon Wolin's work, *Politics and Vision* (Boston, 1960).

tem tends to be a higher coercion system than the reconciliation system with a consequent loss of information."[16] Mobilization systems are characterized by parties whose ideal is the organizational weapon and whose strategy, if not involving a decisive breakthrough, is nevertheless antithetical to "reformmongering." However, one might argue that within a poly-normative context[17] coercion is useful as a means of eliciting one type of information and suppressing another. In short, policy makers may not want "particularistic" information.

Apter's argument runs thus: "Mobilization systems, because they rely on coercion create uncertainty, which makes coordination of the modernization process difficult. In the long-run the mobilization system will become increasingly inefficient because it loses sources of information."[18]

But if in the short run or breakthrough phase the use of coercion is effective in depressing certain responses, it may not be necessary for the mobilization regime to maintain the coercion at the same levels, or to continue the same type of coercion.[19]

---

[16] Apter, *Politics of Modernization*, p. 387.

[17] A poly-normative system is one that is characterized by the antagonistic coexistence of qualitatively different orientations toward the world and political life; Fred Riggs, *Administration in Developing Countries: The Theory of Prismatic Society* (Boston, 1964), p. 176. Almond's notion of "mixed cultures" is a statement of essentially the same condition.

[18] Apter, *Politics of Modernization*, p. 421.

[19] The concept of political coercion demands greater analytic specification. As a first step in this direction it may be useful to differentiate between two forms of coercion: political violence and political terror. Political violence involves the intense and directed use of force against collectivities in accordance with a program of social transformation. Political terror involves the intense and arbitrary use of force to maintain an unstructured social situation, ideally to atomize society and to break through informal social relations rather than formal institutions. With this analytic distinction in mind, one is in a position to differentiate mobilization from totalitarian regimes, a task that so far no one has adequately dealt with. For example, employing this distinction between political violence and political terror and their relationship to the concepts of mobilization and totalitarian system, one can differentiate major shifts over time in the political character of a revolutionary regime (such as the Soviet) in terms of: (*a*) changing targets, from collectivities (re: political violence and mobilization orientation) such as kulaks to the more nebulous

Moreover, coercion often characterizes the reformist strategies of "parties of representation" in reconciliation systems. In referring to the reform-oriented regime of the Ivory Coast, one student of West African parties has written that "large waves of arrests are at least as common . . . as in Ghana, but they are not made public."[20] It solves nothing to say that the party of representation "cannot utilize much coercion [for] if it does, it will be transformed into a mobilization system."[21]

A second criticism of revolution as a strategy emphasizes the loss of support that a revolutionary elite usually incurs. Once again, however, one must ask not only how much support a nation-building elite requires for policy innovation and implementation, but also how much it desires, from whom, and at what price? The argument here does not deny that there are real and potential costs associated with a revolutionary strategy such as the decrease in information, the loss of support from certain sectors, the danger of a police apparatus, and the irrational extension of terror which may jeopardize the gains of a rational use of violence. Rather, the point I stress is that in poly-normative contexts the costs associated with a reformist policy are at least

"class enemy" or "hostile elements" (re: political terror and totalitarian orientation); (*b*) relationships between and within elite organizations, i.e., from some form of collegial rule to patrimonial, from purges to liquidations, from a politically directed security apparatus to a security apparatus unchecked by a political organization; (*c*) elite-public relations, i.e., it may be hypothesized that random terror produces greater regime-legitimacy problems than does the political violence that occurs in a mobilization system and is directed against specific announced targets such as the industrial bourgeoisie or rich peasant. Similarly, working with this more refined set of concepts the analyst may become more sensitive to questions of linkage: under what conditions does a mobilization regime become totalitarian?

One recent work that deals with the question of political terror is by Alexander Dallin and George Breslauer: "Political Terror," in *Change in Communist Systems*, ed. Chalmers A. Johnson (Stanford, 1970), pp. 191–215. In most respects this is very sophisticated, but it fails to distinguish between political violence and political terror, and thus it cannot differentiate the mobilization phase of Soviet development from the totalitarian phase.

[20] Aristide Zolberg, *Creating Political Order* (Chicago, 1966), pp. 84, 86.

[21] Apter, *Politics of Modernization*, p. 417.

equal to and probably greater than the costs attached to a revolutionary strategy.

By examining the notion of commitment and the nature of violence, one can explain the difference between reformism and revolution as nation-building strategies, between the effectiveness of "parties of representation" and parties as organizational weapons in pursuing these strategies, and between the different types of problems and achievements that characterize these approaches. With a few minor substitutions, Becker's statement expresses the definition of commitment that I use here. What interests Becker about commitment "is the possibility of using it to explain situations where an [elite] finds that [its] involvement in social organization has, in effect, made side bets for [it] and thus constrained [its] future activity." [22] In terms of commitments, when the "party of representation" forsakes coercion it must engage in widespread bargaining in order to secure compliance. But bargaining reduces flexibility to the extent that it involves an "elaboration of commitments — ways of acting and responding that can be changed if at all only at the risk of severe internal crisis." [23] A policy of shifting alliances often creates an atmosphere in which issues can rarely be dealt with decisively; moreover, a reformist "party of representation" strategy of bargaining and compromise can result in the default of leadership because of commitments that seriously limit an elite's ability to deploy resources. This limitation is particularly significant because after nation-building elites assume power, they are almost immediately presented with the question or problem of achieving a decisive breakthrough. Herein lies the virtue of a revolutionary strategy: it consciously attempts to minimize constraining commitments. To accomplish this end, violence is employed. Skillfully handled, violence can help the elite's leadership position and goal achievement in several ways. It can act as a check or restraint on certain undesirable behavior patterns, particularly when these are associated with strategic but intransi-

---

[22] Howard S. Becker, "Notes on the Concept of Commitment," in *The Making of Decisions*, ed. Gore and Dyson, p. 281.

[23] Selznick, *Leadership*, p. 40.

gent elements in the political-social system. It can also help to protect the elite's political organization from antiregime elements (though as we shall see, it can also make the "party" vulnerable to the demands of other elite organizations such as the secret police). In addition, violence can increase a party's flexibility in adapting to new conditions. In a democracy, such flexibility is ideally related to the existence of multiple centers of information and power as well as to the responsiveness of democratic elites; but in a revolutionary context characterized by competing principles of legitimacy and ways of life, and by intense political conflict, the same sort of deployment would mean permanent crisis and near-paralysis.

Thus, by the use of violence,[24] nation-building elites with a

---

[24] Huntington has offered an interesting argument related to the revolutionary's use of violence. He suggests that the reformer's problems are more difficult than the revolutionary's in three respects: (*a*) the reformer must fight a two-front battle, against both the conservative and the revolutionary, and since the revolutionary stresses rigidity in politics, his task being to polarize and cumulate cleavages, he requires less skill than the reformer, who must promote fluidity and adaptability; (*b*) because the reformer's goal is partial, not total, change, he "must be more sophisticated in the control of social change"; (*c*) the reformer has to balance two goals — participation and social-economic reform — whereas the revolutionary can deal with his goals sequentially. See Samuel P. Huntington, *Political Order in Changing Societies* (New Haven, 1968), pp. 344–345.

It seems to me, however, that the revolutionary's task is no easier than the reformer's. To begin with, an individual or a political group attempting to come to power through a revolution must be differentiated from a political regime attempting a revolutionary transformation of society. An individual or group in the former position is almost always fighting a two-front war against conservatives and liberals (moderates), particularly during the initial and early stages of the struggle, when it has the fewest resources in terms of members, funds, and following. Second, and again referring to a revolutionary or revolutionary group out of power, the political skill demanded if broad social forces are to be mobilized is very rare, as the number of unsuccessful attempts to polarize and cumulate cleavages in a society demonstrates.

The critical role and presence of political skill can be easily appreciated if one entertains the hypothesis that the use of manipulation and force by revolutionary groups — aspiring to or in power — does not adequately explain revolutionary movements. There is little doubt that manipulation and coercion are used and often irrationally, but one cannot ignore the political skills of a Mao, a Castro, a Tito and even a Kim-Il Sung in *eliciting support* (of dif-

marked sense of urgency about initiating a comprehensive program of qualitative change can reduce their commitments to established elements within their environment and increase the probability that their programs will be implemented in a manner that
accords with their intentions and preferences.

By way of example, consider the T.V.A. as compared with
Soviet collectivization. Under the latter program, production has
suffered, but control of the peasantry has been accomplished,[25]
delivery of goods ensured, and integration into the economy carried out. In Aron's terms, violence with respect to these goals
might be characterized as "rational if not excusable."[26]

---

ferent types, at different times, from different groups for different policies).
Third, the argument that the revolutionary stresses rigidity in politics is both
too absolute a statement, as anyone familiar with Lenin's work on "Left-Wing
Communism" realizes, and too value-laden. An analyst with an "appreciation"
of revolution equal to Huntington's appreciation of reform might have re-
phrased Huntington's statement that "the revolutionary promotes rigidity in
politics, the reformer fluidity and adaptability," to read: "the revolutionary
promotes clarity in politics, the reformer confusion and opportunism."

As for Huntington's second argument concerning sophistication in the
management of social change, it is true that the reformer is interested in the
quantity of change; but it is equally true that the revolutionary trends to be
interested in the type of change and the direction it will take. It is an open
question as to which is more difficult, controlling the degree of change without
recourse to certain types of violence or in a situation of wide-scale mobilization
defining the direction of social change so that it corresponds in decisive aspects
with the political program one is committed to.

This brings us to Huntington's third point: that the revolutionary is not
called on to balance the goals of participation and social-economic reform.
Again it seems to me that the revolutionary concerned with the direction and
nature of change would because of the emphasis on mobilization have to be
intimately and immediately concerned with the issue of assimilation (i.e., with
the construction of a social-economic-ideological environment capable of sus-
taining, defining, and controlling the changes that had been stimulated). Just
what types of revolutionaries demonstrate how much and what type of concern
with the task of assimilation is, of course, an empirical question and a base
for comparative analysis.

[25] See Roy D. Laird, "Some Characteristics of the Soviet Leadership System: A Maturing Totalitarian System," *Midwest Journal of Political Science*
10 (February 1966): 30.

[26] Raymond Aron, *Démocratie et totalitarisme* (Paris, 1965), pp. 265–285.
The chapter entitled "Social Cost of Development" in Charles K. Wilber's ex-

It is legitimate to conclude that if there was to be a qualitative and purposeful redefinition of Russian political, social, and economic life, a set of policies based on a widespread use of coercion was necessary to accomplish a "decisive breakthrough." Such a conclusion is strengthened when one notes the extent to which a reformist T.V.A. approach in the homogeneous-secular American context failed to bring about a decisive breakthrough,[27] and when one appreciates that a program of coerced collectivization can be accomplished without the high incidence of irrationality which accompanied the Soviet effort (the Romanian effort in the late 1950s and early '6os seems to provide support for such a contention). Perhaps with a statement from Kirchheimer, I can sum up what I have said about the relation between commitments and violence and the difference between revolutionary and reformist strategies. Referring to Stalin (and Hitler), Kirchheimer noted that "both were acting outside the frame of the traditional conceptual apparatus of politicians. They made only short-range compromises, which they revoked as soon as the slightest margins of safety allowed them to do so."[28] Though the examples of Stalin and Hitler certainly emphasize the risks associated with a revolu-

---

cellent work, *The Soviet Model and Underdeveloped Countries* (Chapel Hill, 1969), provides the best single discussion I have seen on the cost of alternative strategies of development. Wilber addresses himself to the question (p. 109): "how high is the cost of development in the Soviet model in terms of living standards, excess mortality, and human values (freedom, dignity, etc.)?" A full reading of this chapter is more than warranted, but one of Wilber's summary statements (p. 131) is worth noting here: "The social cost of development in the Soviet Union was high indeed — purges, Stalinist terror, forced labor, famine, and lack of freedom. The cost of capitalist development was high also — slavery, colonialism, genocide of native races, and lack of freedom. The extent of a cause and effect relationship is probably impossible to establish. It would seem, however, that particular historical circumstances, rather than the development process itself, account for the major share of the human costs. The human cost of either capitalist or Communist development appears less than the cost of continued underdevelopment." The chapters on the "Cost of Underdevelopment" and "Social Costs and the Soviet Model" are particularly worthy of attention.

[27] On T.V.A. see Philip Selznick, *T.V.A. and the Grass Roots* (New York, 1966), *passim*, and p. xiii.

[28] Kirchheimer, "Confining Conditions," p. 967.

tionary strategy they do not warrant the conclusion that systematic murder is an integral part of a revolutionary strategy. One conclusion that does seem warranted, however, is that an effective nation-building strategy depends on an elite's minimizing the number and character of its commitments, holding certain issues as resolved, and preventing their continuous espousal by counterelites. In short, nation-building elites must achieve a decisive breakthrough and to do so they may be forced to use a revolutionary strategy.

2

Background Factors
and National Profiles

THE IMMEDIATE TASK is to define and weigh those factors that shape an elite's choice of nation-building strategies and the outcomes associated with these choices. Eight factors appear to determine the strategy; they may be grouped under three main headings: Organizational, Situational, and Historical. Organizational factors are: (1) ideology, (2) leadership, and (3) party structure. Situational factors are: (1) extent of social disorganization or disintegration, (2) resource level, (3) mode of coming to power, and, (4) level of development. As used here, the Historical factor refers to the degree of domestic and international autonomy a political system has enjoyed.

These factors can be broken down further. *Ideologies* may be differentiated as either consensual or cooperative. Cooperative ideologies are tolerant of differences and necessitate agreement only on the form of behavior; cooperative ideologies "make no demands on role uniformity but only upon procedural rules. Cooperation concerns the settlement of problems in terms which make possible the continuation of differences and even fundamental disagreement."[1] Consensual ideologies, on the other hand, demand internal agreement in terms of shared perspectives, the content of behavior, and the abolition of differences. (For these reasons it is difficult to imagine a cooperative breakthrough ideology.) *Leadership* can be exercised by middle class elements such as in India, by *déclassé* elements as in Cuba, by professionally organized revolutionaries, as in the Soviet Union (in 1917), or by military leaders as in Egypt. *Party structure* involves the composition of party personnel, control(s) exerted over the latter, the nature of commitments built in to the party organization, and the resulting distinctive competence or incompetence that characterizes the organization.

Social disorganization and disintegration refer to the viability of such major societal institutions as the family, the market, and the military. The important question here is whether the institutional incoherence of a society is one of degree or of quality. It is not always easy to say whether the situation is one of disintegration or only disorganization, but there are some indicators of quality that are helpful in the analysis. Certain phenomena can be viewed as indicators of disintegration. Levels of desertion, divorce, and child slavery, for example, which are abnormally high by the standards of a given society are useful indicators in analyzing the strength of the family; an unusually high proportion of a society's commerce channeled through a black market, and the inability of a market to distribute goods where they are most needed are useful indicators of a disintegrating market; high levels of mutiny, desertion, and refusal to obey orders can be seen as indicators of military disintegration. *Resource level* refers to the existence or nonexistence of educated cadres, specifically bureaucratic, technical, and political personnel. *Mode of coming to power* is more or less self-explanatory, but it can be broken down into the specific forms of revolution, such as the coup d'état or "mili-

---

[1] This definition and the one of consensual ideology are taken from Irving Louis Horowitz, "Consensus, Conflict, and Cooperation: A Sociological Inventory," *Social Forces* 41 (December, 1962), 177–188.

tarized mass insurrection,"[2] and according to the length and intensity of the revolution. *Level of development* refers to the potential and real resource base on which an elite can draw as well as to the extent and character of industrialization.

Using these factors of analysis, then, let us look at our nation-building sample: the Soviet Union, China, Yugoslavia, Cuba, India, Mexico, Turkey, Ghana, and Egypt. The procedure will be to present a "profile" for each country and to explain its content; I shall then engage in a series of comparisons in order to locate and explain differences between and within the categories "reformist and revolutionary." Obviously, these profiles are selective in terms of the information presented. I should add that the attempt to draw such profiles inevitably involves some trespassing on a number of special fields, but I hope my position is justified, on three grounds: (*a*) like Weber, I hold that "however objectionable it may be, such trespassing on other special fields cannot be avoided in comparative work," (*b*) that one rationale for a community of scholars is to allow its members to take advantage of the work done by others in specific fields in an attempt to cumulate and relate bits of knowledge, and (*c*) that in so doing I can only hope that the specialist "will find nothing definitely wrong in points that are essential."[3]

Soviet Union

In the case of the Soviet Union the organizational factors are internally consistent, and when viewed together, all seem to lead in the same direction. The leadership consisted of professional revolutionaries with a consensual ideology (Marxism–Leninism) that demanded a decisive breakthrough,[4] and the party structure ap-

---

[2] See Chalmers A. Johnson, *Revolution and the Social System* (Stanford, 1965), *passim.*

[3] Max Weber, *The Protestant Ethic*, trans. Talcott Parsons (New York, 1958), pp. 28–29.

[4] There is no intention here of denying the openness that existed within the Soviet elite as to the definition of the breakthrough process. For one critical instance of such openness see V. Erlich, *The Soviet Industrialization Debate: 1924–1928* (Cambridge, Mass., 1960).

proximated that of an organizational weapon to the extent that it emerged from the civil war with a significant number of political cadres who could be considered "deployable agents."[5] The Bolsheviks were faced with a totally disintegrated environment. After seven years of international war, revolution, and civil war, both the social and political order were in a state of chaos. Agriculture and industry were nearly ruined. Industrial production was only one-seventh of the prewar figure: "Most factories lay idle . . . In 1921, pig iron production was only 3% of pre-war. . . . The most essential things, food, consumer goods, and fuel, were lacking."[6] The disintegration of society had of course made it possible for the Bolshevik Party to attempt a revolutionary breakthrough, but it also threatened the party's capacity for political leadership and even for survival.[7] The fact that the party's mode of coming to power included not only a coup d'état but also a successfully fought internal war resulted in the already mentioned possession of a number of trained cadres and a reliable military force; and the rapid economic development that Russia had undergone prior to the World War presented the Bolsheviks with technical and bureaucratic cadres which they could draw on.[8]

---

[5] See Philip Selznick, *The Organizational Weapon* (New York, 1960), pp. 20–21. Once again one must recognize in equal measure the existence of a significant number of tested political cadres capable of providing coherence and direction for the regime, and the difficulty in distributing these cadres, controlling the socialization of additional cadres, and ensuring their performance. On this latter set of considerations see Merle Fainsod, *Smolensk Under Soviet Rule* (New York, 1963), *passim*.

[6] Georg Von Rauch, *A History of Soviet Russia* (New York, 1967), p. 124.

[7] Fainsod, *Smolensk*, p. 38.

[8] Concerning the availability of bureaucratic cadres see Merle Fainsod, "Bureaucracy and Modernization: The Russian and Soviet Case," in *Bureaucracy and Political Development*, ed. Joseph LaPalombara (Princeton, 1963), pp. 233–267. For a discussion of how successful the Soviets were in securing the aid of and controlling these products of the old regime see Jeremy Azrael, *Managerial Power and Soviet Politics* (Cambridge, Mass., 1966), *passim*. For a brief comment on Russian economic development prior to 1917 see Alec Nove, "Soviet Political Organization and Development," in *Politics and Change in Developing Countries*, ed. Colin Leys (Cambridge, Mass., 1969), pp. 65–67.

China

So far as the organizational factor is concerned, the main difference between China and the Soviet Union is the military aspect
of the Chinese Party. Indeed, as Johnson says, a "large, Party-led
Revolutionary Army came to power." [9] The situational circumstances may be described as follows: the level of disintegration
was very high, and as Schurmann notes, it was so extensive that
"by the 1930's it was evident that more had crumbled than the
political system alone": "The social fabric had disintegrated in
much of rural China, yet the new patterns in the cities were too
weak to exercise a commanding force over the country. The disintegration of the traditional economic system . . . continued without interruption, yet the modern sector could not constitute an
effective substitute. In the world of ideas and values, Confucian-
ism was dying." [10] In addition, the war "totally destroyed the traditional rural social order and sensitized the Chinese peasantry
to a new spectrum of possible associations, identities, and purposes." [11] The mode of coming to power was of course a prolonged,
intense, revolutionary struggle against a highly intransigent elite.
Moreover, the Chinese Communist Party enjoyed a period of "isolation" before coming to power; during its Yenan period Mao was
able to "build up a homogeneous leading staff . . . where detailed
observation was almost impossible for Moscow, and to strengthen
the loyalty and cohesion of [its members] in a prolonged struggle
amidst great danger and hardship." [12] In terms of the relevant experiences and memories of the Party elite, China's history was that

[9] Chalmers A. Johnson, "Building a Communist Nation in China," in
The Communist Revolution in Asia, ed. Robert A. Scalapino (Englewood
Cliffs, N.J., 1965). For a stimulating discussion of the possible relations between
revolutionary army and vanguard party, and of the import of the Cuban ex-
perience in this connection, see Regis Debray, *Revolution in the Revolution?*
(New York, 1967), pp. 95–126.

[10] Franz Schurmann, *Ideology and Organization in Communist China*
(Berkeley and Los Angeles, 1966), p. xxxvi.

[11] Chalmers A. Johnson, *Peasant Nationalism and Communist Power*
(Stanford, 1966), p. 5.

[12] Richard Lowenthal, *World Communism: The Disintegration of a Secular Faith* (New York, 1964), p. 252.

of a semicolony for the control of which, as Mao has stated, "many imperialistic powers [were] contending."[13] Leninism was a meaningful ideology for the elite because it explained what had been happening to China and pointed to the ways in which solutions could be found.

China's level of development was low. Its resource level was mixed; an example is the relatively greater supply of party as opposed to technical cadres.

Yugoslavia

In many ways the Yugoslav configuration resembles the Chinese.[14] The leadership was composed of professional revolutionaries whose commitment to a consensual-revolutionary ideology had been tested in the course of a four-year war against foreign invaders (the Nazis and Italians) and domestic opponents (the Chetniks under Mihailovic and the Croatian Ustashe). As in the Chinese case, a Party-led guerrilla army came to power. By 1945 this army numbered 800,000, and the party had grown from 12,000 members at the beginning of the war to 140,000.[15] The Party elite consisted of professional revolutionaries imbued with a consensus ideology and in control of a well-articulated organizational weapon. The environment, also as in China, was marked by political, economic, and social disintegration, the invasion by the Germans in April,

---

[13] Stuart R. Schram, *The Political Thought of Mao Tse-tung* (New York, 1964), excerpt from "On the Tactics of Fighting Japanese Imperialism," p. 155.

[14] The Yugoslav case provides a good example of the different orientation of specifically nationalist and Leninist (or transnationalist) elites toward a "decisive breakthrough" as well as the nature of the constraints that act on the former. In his book *Tito* (New York, 1957), Fitzroy Maclean makes a comment with reference to Tito and his rival Mihailovic that might also hold for Mao and his rival Chiang: "Though a brave and a well-trained, experienced soldier, Mihajlovic lacked the ruthless determination, the unwavering singleness of purpose of his rival. . . . In character their [Chetnik] movement was static rather than dynamic . . . In their anxiety to avoid casualties *to prevent the disruption and destruction of the old, established way of life*: they lost sight of what they had originally set out to do." [p. 224; my italics.]

[15] See George W. Hoffman and Fred Warner Neal, *Yugoslavia and the New Communism* (New York, 1962), p. 73.

1941, having resulted not simply in military defeat for Yugoslavia but in the "total disintegration of a ruling system, a disintegration after which it looked as if the Yugoslav state as a unified political entity would never recover."[16] The Partisans assumed power, however, just as the Chinese did, with a set of tested programs and organizations designed to provide political coherence and bring order out of chaos. Four years of war, during which 11 percent of the Yugoslav people "were killed, fled or were expelled, or refused repatriation," had resulted in large-scale disruption and uprooting of significant portions of the population, and the Yugoslav Communist elite was faced with the major task of assimilating these elements by providing them with new identities and securing their loyalty.

Yugoslavia had entered the Second World War with an underdeveloped economy, being still "predominantly agrarian, exporting food products and raw materials and importing machinery and finished goods." On the other hand, it "could boast an industrial base suitable for rapid growth. . . . Economic production had expanded noticeably and so had the volume of domestic and foreign trade. Modernity reached even the most isolated communities, and there was a more rapid shift of population from rural communities to cities."[17] The war brought "devastation and destruction of unprecedented magnitude. The economic impact was apparent in loss of manpower, destruction of productive facilities, exploitation by the occupying powers and disintegration of the country as an economic unit."[18]

In the attempt to deal with the chaos created by the war and to initiate a program of economic development, the Yugoslav elite

---

[16] Jozo Tomasevich, "Yugoslavia During the Second World War," in *Contemporary Yugoslavia*, ed. Wayne S. Vucinich (Berkeley and Los Angeles, 1969), p. 74.

[17] Wayne S. Vucinich, "Interwar Yugoslavia," in *ibid.*, pp. 36–37, 57.

[18] Hoffman and Neal, *Yugoslavia*, p. 86. Destruction and devastation were not equally distributed, however. According to Tomasevich ("Yugoslavia," p. 107), at the time of Serbia's liberation by the Partisans it "had large manpower reserves and its economy was in relatively good condition." By 1947, the Yugoslav regime had attained a level of industrial production equal to that of the prewar level; see Hoffman and Neal, pp. 299–303.

could draw on a well-developed political cadre and also on one of interwar Yugoslavia's major achievements — a stratum of educated personnel, which had in good measure oriented itself in radical and revolutionary directions.[19]

As for the Yugoslav elite's appreciation of the interwar period, it was oriented around two "memories": the lack of domestic political coherence best evidenced by the failure to establish ethnic reciprocity and to include and represent the peasantry in the political system,[20] and the gap between the formal claim to sovereignty and the actual infringements on that sovereignty which occurred at the hands of Germany and Italy — infringements which were a consequence not only of these nations' greater power but also of the internal regional-ethnic fragmentation and the gap between the elite and the masses.

Cuba

The Cuban case differs from the preceding Leninist cases in a number of ways. The Cuban leadership might be characterized as *déclassé* revolutionaries. Unlike the other Leninist elites so far discussed, the Cuban elite lacked an organizational weapon party before coming to power and it has had considerable difficulty trying to create one. This has had several consequences for nation building: (a) legitimacy is more closely tied to an individual than to an organization or institution; (b) the army has occupied the central position in political life; (c) more tentatively, it would appear that to date the regime has lacked a coherent political institution to serve as the political nucleus of a new national commu-

---

[19] In this connection see the comments by Vucinich, "Interwar Yugoslavia," p. 57, and in particular Hugh Seton-Watson's analysis of the Yugoslav youth in his *Eastern Europe Between the Wars, 1918–1941* (Hampden, Conn., 1962), pp. 229–230, 241.

[20] See Seton-Watson, pp. 216–241 and *passim*. Stated in terms consistent with this analysis, during the interwar period the effective national community in Yugoslavia was by no means coterminous with the state boundaries of that entity. For a discussion of Yugoslavia's position in the international arena see the aforementioned works by Seton-Watson and Vucinich as well as C. A. Macartney and A. W. Palmer, *Independent Eastern Europe* (New York, 1962).

nity;[21] and (d) aside from the military, there has been no organizational context that would provide for the creation of deployable cadres. The Cuban leadership's political and administrative orientation does, however, resemble the other examples thus far cited in that the "declasse revolutionaries who have determined Cuba's fate have used one class or another, or a combination of classes, for different purposes at different times. Their leader functions above classes, cuts across classes, or maneuvers between them."[22] Indicating its revolutionary posture, the Cuban leadership has minimized its commitments, using violence to do so, and has manipulated alliances.

Castro's ideology may appropriately be described as a root-and-branch ideology: he wants to redefine, not reform, the Cuban political system. In effect, he is determined to "complete" the Cuban revolution of the late nineteenth century, which he and other nationalists feel was interrupted and deflected by the United States. He wants comprehensive and direct change of the political community. It is true that when Castro came to power he possessed a "mentality" rather than an "ideology," but it was a revolutionary not a conservative mentality, and it was basically compatible with the principles of Leninism: it included a refusal to compromise as a matter of principle (though survival and expansion of power might require it as a tactic), an extreme distaste for "economism," and a continual fear of "restoration," "backsliding," and binding commitments.[23] The unintended consequences of commitments were to be prevented by minimizing the number of

---

[21] Two quite different works that deal with the question of political organization in Cuba are Jose Iglesias, *In the Fist of the Revolution* (New York, 1969), and Richard Fagen, *Transformation of Political Culture in Cuba* (Stanford, 1969).

[22] Theodore Draper, *Castroism: Theory and Practice* (New York, 1965), p. 133.

[23] On these points see Richard Gray, *Jose Marti: Cuban Patriot* (Gainesville, Fla., 1962), p. 79; Che Guevara, *Guerilla Warfare* (New York, 1961), pp. 112, 116–117; C. Wright Mills, *Listen Yankee* (New York, 1960), p. 50; Jules DuBois, *Fidel Castro* (New York, 1959), p. 345; Henry Roberts, *Russia and America* (New York, 1956), pp. 48–50; V. I. Lenin, *State and Revolution* (New York, 1932), pp. 9, 83, 92, 96.

new commitments and by breaking any that already existed (i.e., Castro's dissolution of the July 26th movement). To quote Guevara: ". . . the most important distinctive characteristic is the decision to carry Cuban reform all the way, without concessions of any kind."[24] The Cubans adopted Leninism in order to secure Soviet aid and protection, to provide a more specific action orientation for policy making, and to create an appropriate organizational form for decision making. Following Batista's second coup in 1952, the Cuban social system was highly disorganized, but the system itself had not disintegrated. Furthermore, the resource level and level of development were fairly advanced in comparison with the rest of Latin America, even to the point of mechanized agriculture.[25]

As for Cuba's political history, it was clearly neocolonial (see pp. 53–55), since political life was shaped with reference to one "significant other," the United States; and it was this circumstance that determined much of Castro's orientation and in part motivated his choice of Leninism as a universal ideology.

Finally, it was by means of revolution that power was obtained. Even though the revolution was not of great duration and was most intense in urban areas, it nonetheless made possible not only the means for a "decisive breakthrough" — an armed and devoted force — but also a revolutionary myth to protect and identify with.

India

The case of India is quite different from any thus far examined. The leadership of the Congress Party is complex: it contains "intellectuals with a leaning towards socialism; solid businessmen to whom such notions were poison; journalists, politicians, and lawyers who gave articulate expression to a wide variety of ideas —

---

[24] Guevara, pp. 116–117.

[25] In this connection see Dudley Seers, ed., *Cuba: The Economic and Social Revolution* (Chapel Hill, 1964), pp. 65–100 and *passim*; Wyatt MacGaffey and C. Barnett, *Cuba: Its People, Its Society, Its Culture* (New Haven, 1962), *passim*.

the whole resting on a peasant base newly awakened by Gandhi, who had in his makeup rather more of the traditional Indian holy man than of the modern politician." [26] The Congress ideology has been and is still one of reformism, assimilation, and bargaining — a "cooperative ideology" — and the party structure reflects this ideology in that it has chosen comprehensiveness over discipline, to use Kothari's words. The Congress, though not open to every interest, is essentially a coalition organization representing different ideological orientations and social bases. [27]

In 1946 India appeared to have experienced a good deal of system disorganization rather than disintegration. One reason for this is the Congress Party's mode of coming to power, a process that is highly relevant to the strategy and outcomes which have thus far characterized the Indian attempt at nation building. In particular, this had to do with the relative receptiveness of the colonial power and the way in which the country was mobilized against the British. Emerson has pointed out that "Britain's mode of leaving India made it possible to remember some of the best of the long relationship and forget some of the worst"; while it has been argued about the second that "Gandhi struck a responsive chord in Hindu culture, and stuck it in such a way as to galvanize the country into opposition against the British without threatening vested interests in Indian society." [28] In 1946, the level of development in India was low, but for an underdeveloped nation its resource level was very high. There were significant numbers of Western-educated Indians. An Indian press existed "which spent most of its time building up the national cause." There were the Congress and the Moslem League, and "the creation at various levels of councils and administrative bodies in which Indians increasingly took the lead." [29]

To complete our profile of India it is sufficient to note that

---

[26] Barrington Moore, *Social Origins of Dictatorship and Democracy* (Boston, 1966), p. 388.

[27] See Rajni Kothari, *India* (Boston, 1970), p. 156.

[28] Rupert Emerson, *From Empire to Nation* (Boston, 1960), p. 78; Barrington Moore, p. 373.

[29] Emerson, p. 78.

with respect to domestic and international autonomy, prior to its independence in 1947 India for approximately a century had been a colonial dependency of Great Britain.

Mexico

The leadership of the Mexican revolution over the past five decades has been mixed. There have been landowners like Madero, middle class elements such as Obregon and Calles, military men such as Obregon, and bureaucratic-politicos such as Cortines, Mateos, and Ordaz. The most distinguishing characteristic of this leadership is its bifurcation into "revolutionary" and "reformist" elements: the two have always been present, and in conflict, sometimes between individuals such as Calles and Cardenas, sometimes between or among different elements within the elite. But the overriding commitment to the "revolution," particularly to the goal of national sovereignty along with structural arrangements within the Partido Revolucionario Institucional, has effectively contained the strain between revolution and reform.

The ideology is thus revolutionary or consensual primarily (though not solely) on the issue of national autonomy, whereas on social, economic, and domestic political issues — other than the as yet undisputed place of the Presidency, and the importance of attempting to secure "voluntary" agreement — it has tended to be cooperative and reformist. Since the end of Cardenas' rule, the reformist orientation has predominated, but the "revolutionary" aspect still exists as myth and even in fact in certain sections of the P.R.I. Carlos Madrazo's actions after becoming head of the P.R.I. in 1965 may be seen as an attempt to restore the party's revolutionary character.[30]

---

[30] It is worth noting Madrazo's fate in the P.R.I. I quote from a recent article by John Womack, Jr., "The Spoils of the Mexican Revolution," *Foreign Affairs* 48 (July 1970): 683. "In 1964 the incoming . . . president named Madrazo to run the PRI, and bade him, friend of the family, ardent political ally, and past master of intrigue, to reform the party. Madrazo promptly advertised several shocking promises — open party primaries (rather than gubernatorially rigged rituals) to nominate candidates for municipal elections, university students in prominent party posts . . . ; a Commission for Honor and Justice, to

The "cooperative" orientation of the P.R.I. is evident in its pluralistic structure, a structure which arose out of the "need for stabilization of relationships among competing groups."[31] The nationalist elite originally came to power through the revolution of 1910, and the revolution was associated with and contributed to social breakdown and disintegration. It affected the level of development negatively by bringing most of the industrial activity to a standstill: "There was widespread destruction of capital equipment, and a net loss for the industrialization process resulted."[32] The resource level was low, and Mexico's historical experience was one of continual fighting against Spain, France, and the United States in an effort to achieve national sovereignty. Mexican political elites perceived their experiences in colonial-neocolonial terms.

Turkey

The political leadership of the Turkish revolution was also heterogeneous, but the military and Ataturk dominated. Ataturk's ideology focused on national independence and involved what might be termed a policy of "differentiated cooperation." He would compromise only on certain issues at certain levels. Thus, the caliphate was abolished at the national level, but at the local level the power of the religious elites was maintained. Shifting alliances were accompanied by diminishing alliances up to a point. Ataturk shifted and diminished alliances (and commitments) with regard to "mili-

---

expel racketeers from the party; the formal registration of party members, to indicate how much patronage each sector of the party deserved; the collection of individual financial pledges, to build the party's own resources and release it from reliance on official subsidies. In prospect was the removal of the PRI from official control, the construction of an independent party. Even more shockingly Madrazo acted to fulfill his promises. At once he outraged the establishment and embarrassed the president, and in 1965 had to resign. But he would not properly retire. Continuing to politick publicly around the country, flattering the youth, bewailing economic inequities, finally fishing for a following among student rebels in 1968, Madrazo became a trial to the regime. He died in a suspicious plane crash near Monterrey last year."

[31] L. Vincent Padgett, *The Mexican Political System* (Boston, 1966), p. 48.
[32] *Ibid.*, p. 203.

tary defense of independence (1919–1922), establishment of a new state (1923–1928), legal and cultural reforms (1926–1933), and state-sponsored industrialization (1930 ff.)."[33] He did not, however, create a party of deployable agents, because "the party did not impose upon its members a strict adherence to its program. Disparate tendencies and affiliations were allowed to develop within manageable limits. This situation facilitated the emergence of future political leaders and contributed to plurality within the unique party."[34]

Ataturk took power during a period of significant disintegration associated with the defeat of the Ottoman Empire in the First World War and the discrediting of the Young Turk Movement. His assumption of power was revolutionary in nature and based on a "comprehensive" nationalist-military movement.

At this time, the level of Turkish development was not at all favorable: "After 13 years of almost uninterrupted warfare, the country was disorganized and practically bankrupt." According to one expert, the only meaningful economic development that occurred during Abdulhamid's reign was the construction of railroads, and the profits from this endeavor flowed out of the country. Finally, although the planning and execution of economic construction began on a respectable scale under the Young Turks, in 1924 Turkey's economic situation was still "bleak," with its communication and industrial establishment limited.[35]

The resource level, however, was more developed. Political cadres existed as a result of the New Ottoman, Union and Progress, and Defense of Rights movements. Bureaucratic personnel had been trained and created during the one hundred years 1808–

---

[33] Dankwart A. Rustow, "The Development of Parties in Turkey," in *Political Parties and Political Development*, ed. Joseph LaPalombara and Myron Weiner (Princeton, 1966), p. 120.

[34] Arif T. Payaslioglu, "Turkey," in *Political Modernization in Japan and Turkey*, ed. Robert E. Ward and Dankwart A. Rustow (Princeton, 1954), p. 421.

[35] These comments on the level of Turkish developments are based on Peter F. Sugar's article, "Economic and Political Modernization in Turkey," in *ibid.*

1908,[36] and the military provided a source of leadership and technical cadres. This fairly advanced resource level gave Ataturk a good base for a national party, but it also meant that he had to contend with several well-defined accountability groups, including the bureaucracy, the urban elite, and the military, all of whom were well represented in the Republican People's Party.

The Ottoman Empire had been an independent power, although one effectively constrained by the Great Powers of Europe in the domestic and international spheres. Following the World War, conditions were appropriate for the appearance of a national movement led by the military and designed to restore the integrity of the Ottoman Empire's core through political redefinition.

Ghana

The leadership of the Convention People's Party was not composed of professional revolutionaries, nor of deployable agents or military men, politicized or otherwise, but rather of *déclassé* nationalists. Their ideology has been described by one student of Ghanaian politics as "a search for perspective in the African revolution," and although "it leaves much to be desired as an ideology [this] is perhaps its greatest advantage, for pragmatism thus remains a feature of the new ideological look."[37] The C.P.P.'s ideology was basically nationalist and was made up of heterogeneous elements from Marxism, Leninism, and Christianity. The "pragmatic" nature of this ideology might be described as diffuse, contradictory, and vacillating. The stable aspects of Nkrumaism included: "(1) a vanguardist conception of party organization as a way to move masses towards socialism and (2) [Nkrumah's] conviction of the need for the proper economic organization of society through the ownership of the means of production by the state."[38]

---

[36] See Dankwart A. Rustow, "The Development of Parties in Turkey," in *ibid.* p. 126.

[37] David E. Apter, "Ghana," in *Political Parties and National Integration in Tropical Africa*, ed. James S. Coleman and Carl G. Rosberg, Jr. (Berkeley and Los Angeles, 1964), p. 304.

[38] See Colin Legum's excellent article, "Socialism in Ghana: A Political

Contradictory elements were combined with these Leninist and Marxist elements, such as the Christian and biblical idiom of Nkrumahism. Nkrumah's ideology was notably lacking in coherence. This is not to suggest that there were no inner contradictions in Lenin's ideology or that it was not modified in response to changing environments, but Lenin's fundamental assumptions were more explicitly defined, and Lenin, unlike Nkrumah, worked them out before he gained power. As an ideology Nkrumahism was revolutionary in intention and reformist in action, largely because of its combination of contradictory elements and its lack of fundamental and related assumptions about what to do and what to avoid. The party structure of the C.P.P. demonstrates the conflict between what was formally prescribed and intended and what actually occurred. In fact, the party was heterogeneous; despite its rhetoric, at no time was it close to being an "organizational weapon." Zolberg, for example, has pointed out that "far from transforming Ghana into its own image [the C.P.P. had] come to reflect all cleavages, components, norms, and structures that prevail in an underdeveloped country." [39] In other words, the "revolutionary armor" of the C.P.P. — the NASSO-ists, the P.V.A.'s and the "Spark" — did not define the C.P.P.'s distinctive identity. According to one observer, these elements represented no more than "one or two cells in the honeycomb of the power structure; and even they [did] not always support the President's ideas." [40]

At the time it assumed independence, Ghana was a colonial dependency of Great Britain, and little disorganization-disintegration existed. The process whereby Nkrumah and the C.P.P. came to power might be termed an "accepted revolution," in the process of which the colonial power itself played an interesting role. As Post has noted, "in Ghana the CPP found it more difficult to subordinate traditional authority to its own, for whereas the French had tried wherever possible to appoint 'chiefs' who in

Interpretation," in *African Socialism*, ed. William H. Friedland and Carl G. Rosberg, Jr. (Stanford, 1964), p. 134.

[39] Aristide Zolberg, *Creating Political Order*, p. 98.

[40] Legum, p. 135.

fact possessed no traditional authority, the British has confirmed [them] . . . and used them as their agents." [41] In consequence, the social status, economic wealth, and political power of traditional elites were not decisively altered. As for the colonial power's intransigence, one must consider what Post calls the "remarkably amicable relationship [which] in fact developed between [Nkrumah] and the Governor." [42]

In considering the strategy and outcome of the nation-building process under Nkrumah, one must view his statements on "imperialism" against the colonial rather than neocolonial situation which Ghana experienced; one must contrast the revolutionary ideology with the peaceful transfer of power, and one must contrast Nkrumah's demand and desire for a decisive breakthrough with a social system left basically intact.

Until the mid-1950s, the level of development in Ghana remained limited to the production of such goods as cocoa. No major structural change had occurred in the economy.

Finally, Ghana's resource level at the time of independence was considerably better than that of the rest of West Africa. A larger proportion of children were attending school there than anywhere else in West Africa during the colonial period. Nevertheless, the defining characteristics of Ghana's resource level were an inadequate number of trained personnel, and training only for subordinate positions. In 1951, manpower output in Ghana was made up of six people with university degrees (148 in 1961), 719 with technical school certificates (858 in 1961), 413 with Secondary School certificates (3,430 in 1961) and 6,400 with Middle School certificates (26,500 in 1961). [43]

Egypt

The leadership of the Egyptian revolution consisted of the military — but of a particular sort. Finer's description of the Egyptian

---

[41] Ken Post, *The New States of West Africa* (Baltimore, 1964), p. 58.

[42] *Ibid.*, p. 22.

[43] See *ibid.*, pp. 113, 131, 138, 142, 143 for data and conclusions on the Ghanaian resource level.

army and leadership is relevant: "The Egyptian army of 1952 affords sharp contrasts. It had never been esteemed. It had fought but once and ignominiously. Its officers were of humble social origin. By 1952, the 'Free Officers' who made the coup were rabid with nationalism, furious with what they deemed to be corruption and nepotism in the matter of commands and equipment, seething with political and class resentment at the effendis who lorded it over their families in the villages."[44]

This particular elite was thus substantially different from any ideal typical model of military professionalism.[45] Its ideology was on the whole nationalist, as it is still, and its goals included the destruction of the "monarchy, the power of the landlords, foreign influence and the corruption of political life."[46] In the last eighteen years the ideology of the Egyptian leadership has assumed more and more of a consensual-breakthrough quality. Initially, the Egyptian elites ideology was rather diffuse, based on the demand for national regeneration. In the social-economic sphere the Egyptian elite lacked any comprehensive or coherent program. It was only ten years after the army coup d'état that the President expressed the doctrine of Arab Socialism "which emphasizes rapid economic development and evisions the country as one great organization."[47] Here was a variation on the process of muddling

---

[44] S. E. Finer, *The Man On Horseback* (New York, 1962), 59.

[45] One major obstacle to fruitful analyses of how military organizations behave politically is the assumption that their formal definition as professional armed organizations is sufficient for understanding the behavior of different military organizations-elites in different contexts — the same sort of assumption as the uncritical postulating of a range of shared characteristics for nation-states because they exist in a delimited geographical area, i.e. Latin America. It may well be that certain Latin American nations may best be understood by comparing them with certain East European national experiences during the interwar period rather than with other Latin American nations. Similarly, the Cuban military might be more profitably compared with the Chinese Communist Party than with the British military.

For a sophisticated analysis of military organizations see Robert Price, "Theoretical Approaches to Military Rule in the New States: Reference Group Theory and the Ghanaian Case" (forthcoming 1971 in *World Politics*).

[46] Peter Mansfield, *Nasser's Egypt* (Baltimore, 1965), p. 43.

[47] See James Heaphey, "The Organization of Egypt: Inadequacies of a

through. In Nasser's case ten years of dealing with "immediate practical problems" such as the Suez conflict in 1956 and the issue of industrial investment led to the realization of the need for change that was comprehensive and integrated rather than incremental and uncoordinated.

To conclude, however, that originally the "Free Officers" had no ideology is as incorrect as to conclude that Castro had no ideology before coming to power, or to say that Nkrumah had a "pragmatic" ideology.[48] It would be more correct to say that each of these individuals had diffuse ideologies with specific biases. Their biases were clarified and made more explicit once they were in power and had to confront a series of very concrete constraints — as in Castro *vs.* his own political movement, the July 26th organization, and in the heterogeneous nature of the comprehensive nationalist movement that existed in Ghana. In Egypt, Nasser was confronted at one time or another by the landed bourgeoisie, the Moslem Brotherhood, the industrial and financial bourgeoisie, and elements within the army associated with these social-economic-political elements. In the context of specific issues that arose he attempted to reduce the political relevence of these various strata and organizations.[49] In one respect, however, this increasingly consensual-breakthrough development has not been consistent — that is, in the realm of ideology, demonstrating again the importance of ideology in shaping political outcomes. Nasser's most explicit ideological statement was contained in the Charter of National Action which was proposed to the National Congress of Popular Forces on May 21, 1962. In this defining statement Nasser rejected a breakthrough posture in favor of a reconciliatory one. In his words: "It is impossible to achieve political democracy where one class dominates all the others. . . . It is impossible to either

---

Non-political Model for Nation-Building," *World Politics* 18 (January 1966): 178.

[48] Examples of the "no ideology" theses are Mansfield, *Nasser's Egypt*, p. 44; Theodore Draper, *Castro's Revolution: Myths and Realities* (New York, 1962); and Apter, "Ghana."

[49] See Anouar Abdel-Malek, *Egypt: Military Society*, trans. Charles Lam Markmann (New York, 1968), pp. vii–xxxvii, 49–189.

ignore or deny the necessary and natural conflict between classes, but it is essential that this struggle end in a peaceful solution within the framework of national unity and through the elimination of class distinctions."[50] In a similar vein, Heykal in *We and Communism* argued that whereas communism offers the solution of the "dictatorship of the proletariat," which means "the suppression of other classes by one class in a complete and definitive fashion," Arab socialism calls for "a process of dissolving the contradictions of class in the framework of a national union."[51] The partial and contradictory nature of the breakthrough process in Egypt can be symbolically captured by the image of an ideology that remains basically cooperative and by a set of policies oriented to a breakthrough. The indecisive aspect and distinctive quality of the Egyptian revolution were vividly demonstrated in the debate surrounding Nasser's presentation of the Charter of National Action. According to Abdel-Malek, the nationalizations in 1961–1962 had decisively altered the political-economic environment. Yet, according to the same author, Nasser's proposed Charter elicited a political attack from right-wing religious forces that was supported by "the former rich, who had progressively recaptured full use of their political rights once the main sources of economic power were safely in the hands of the state."[52] It is my thesis that the continual reappearance of hostile social forces capable of presenting their views politically has been a consequence of Nasser's specifically nationalist ideology with its emphasis on reconciliation. This ideology has been the major constraint and confining condition facing the regime in its attempts at wide-scale mobilization of the population (namely, Nasser's Liberation Rally, National Union, Arab Socialist Union) and industrialization. It has acted to thwart, redirect, and dilute the impact of policies that are consensual and breakthrough-like and to rule out other policies that are necessary if those in existence are to be effective.

---

[50] Quoted in *ibid.*, p. 327.

[51] Quoted in *ibid.*, p. 292. Abdel-Malek notes that Heykal's argument "most certainly reflected Nasser's thinking."

[52] *Ibid.*, p. 338. See p. 167 for Abdel-Malek's statement on the decisiveness of the nationalization measures in 1961–1962.

Both the resource level and the developmental level in Egypt at the time of the revolution were low. Before the revolution, the Egyptian elite received its education at foreign-run schools; the "boys and girls who went there frequently could neither read nor write Arabic and prided themselves on not being able to do so. They felt no sympathy for the great mass of their fellow country-men."[53] Education has now been designed to produce cadres that are technically proficient and nationally oriented, but in 1951 there were very few cadres and the level of development was rather low. Egyptian industrialization had begun in the 1930s, and "between 1938 and 1951 production rose by 138 per cent," but "the heavily protected industrial sector was limited to a very small range of industries."[54] In 1964, Dr. Aziz Sidqi, Deputy Prime Minister for Industry and Mineral Wealth, stated: "In 1952 industries were limited in number and variety—a few spinning mills, some oil pressing mills, flour mills, cement factories, etc."[55] Financially, when the Free Officers took power, Egypt in Peter Mansfield's words "was tottering into bankruptcy as a result of the irresponsible actions of the last Wafd government; there were heavy deficits in the budget and the balance of payments in both 1951 and 1952."[56]

[53] Mansfield, *Nasser's Egypt*, p. 43.
[54] *Ibid.*, p. 146.
[55] Quoted in *ibid.*, p. 146.
[56] *Ibid.*, p. 133.

3

Comparative Analysis

WE ARE NOW in a position to engage in a number of comparisons drawing on the information introduced through the "national profiles." Specifically, the comparisons will have to do with nation building, the strategies of reformism and revolution, and the concept of commitment.

The Soviet Union and India may be conceived as "polar types." The Bolshevik Party possessed the organizational characteristics conducive to a "breakthrough" strategy and came to power in a situation of social disintegration. It compromised with its environment as a tactical not a strategic measure (N.E.P. period) and in 1928 it started the Second Revolution, breaking its earlier commitments by the use of force and violence and engaging in a "ruthless attempt, at all costs, to destroy the existing way of life."[1] In India, by contrast, the commitments made during

---

[1] Zbigniew Brzezinski, *Ideology and Power in Soviet Politics* (New York, 1962), pp. 23–24.

the forging of a comparative nationalist movement still persist, making it difficult for the Congress to provide national leadership. The policy of shifting alliances continues, and its self-defeating logic is evident in the current difficulties the Congress faces politically and economically.[2] Neither the ideology nor the structure of the Congress Party can be characterized as radical. Moreover, the situation in which Congress came to power helped to prevent any qualitative change either in its ideology or in its leadership structure. The costs associated with avoiding a revolution are currently experienced through the relative ineffectiveness of economic policies (as measured by the self-proclaimed goals of the elite), as well as limited political leadership and community building at the national level.

The Soviet and Indian cases represent complete opposites in terms of organizational and situational factors. The Soviets possessed a breakthrough ideology and structure as well as a favorable situation to work with; the Indians had none of these. But important as the situational factors were, organizational factors seem perhaps even more important. The Soviets, as soon as possible, gave evidence of their ideological set by engaging in "a deliberate activity aim[ed] at a substantial change of the social, economic, cultural, and political features of society, a change whose pace [was] so rapid and uncompromising toward the past as to justify calling it a radical departure from the previous patterns."[3]

To understand Soviet behavior, it is necessary though not sufficient to examine the specific content of the Party's ideology.

---

[2] See the chapter on India in Barrington Moore, *Social Origins of Dictatorship and Democracy*, and also Reinhard Bendix, *Nation-Building and Citizenship* (New York, 1964), chapter titled, "Public Authority in a Developing Political Community: The Case of India," pp. 215–299. The recent struggle within the Congress Party between Mrs. Ghandi and the "Syndicate" is the most visible and dramatic illustration of the costs to leadership associated with a policy of shifting alliances.

[3] See George Lenczowski's definition of radical regimes in his "Radical Régimes in Egypt, Syria, and Iraq: Some Comparative Observations on Ideologies and Practices," Reprint No. 31, Department of Political Science, University of California, Berkeley, p. 32. (This article originally appeared in the *Journal of Politics* 28 [February 1966], 29–57.)

All regimes that come to power confront a "recalcitrant reality" —
but the definition of this reality is to some extent a function of
the goals and policies of the regime. Thus, the resistance of the
peasants in the Soviet Union was related to the extensive and intensive controls imposed by the regime beginning in the late 1920s,
and these controls were in turn related to the regime's goals and
perceived constituency. One long-run goal of the regime was the
transformation of the peasant into a "new Soviet man." The regime
believed its major constituency to be the working class, and this
belief had a great deal to do with its refusal to compromise with
the reality of a less than monolithic Leninist party in control of
an overwhelmingly peasant country, exhausted after an international and civil war. Given its declared "constituency," a sector of
the regime under Stalin successfully defined the control and transformation of the peasant and the creation of a legitimating and
supportive social base as vital to the regime's survival. Especially
within the international context, control of the peasant and industrialization were thought necessary, because the major powers
of the world were capitalist and therefore by definition hostile.[4]

In short, the goals and perceived constituency of the Soviet
regime were completely compatible with — and in a sense even
demanded — a policy of rapid industrialization as well as transformation and control of the peasantry. Rapid industrialization
was not viewed as an end in itself (though such a displacement
of goals has undoubtedly occurred in the Soviet Union) but as a
necessary means to secure the regime's internal and international
survival. The goal of "transforming man" and the universal constituency — the working class — presented the Soviet elite with a
specific ideological content, one which contributed to the elite's
acting on its ideological sense of urgency.

There is an additional element involved in the ideological-
organizational nature of the Bolsheviks which reinforced and in
part created their "breakthrough" orientation and behavior. Leninist ideology possesses a unique feature which, when combined

---

[4] On these points see Joseph Stalin, "Industrialization of the Country
and the Right Deviation," in Nicolas Spulber (ed.), *Foundations of Soviet
Strategy for Economic Growth* (Bloomington, Ind., 1964), pp. 266–281.

with the goals and constituency of Marxism, increased the probability that the Party's "sense of urgency" would be acted upon rather than compromised. This feature, which has been termed the "Leninist reversal,"[5] refers to the "sense of urgency," which Leninism has in a much greater degree than Marxism, the "reversal" being the Leninist innovation of forcing a situation which in Marxist terms would not be considered sufficiently mature. It was this tendency to force a given situation that critically heightened the Soviets' concern with time, and even more so their fear of "backsliding." In turn, this fear resulted in a hyperconsciousness of the costs attached to binding commitments. More specifically, viewed as political and ideological imperatives, Stalin's actions, although not always appropriately timed in Marxist terms, had to be legitimated in such terms. Thus, one "premature" act created the setting for additional acts. Under Stalin the combination of Marxist views with a Leninist operating code produced and reinforced a marked "sense of urgency" which was matched by a set of appropriate policies. An analogy might be useful here: I have in mind the person who steals from the till to make a bet, collects his winnings, and legitimates his original departure from the rules of the organization "all in time," that is to say, before the auditor arrives. Such a person may be compared with the Leninist who departs from the "Marxist rules," and who then rushes to create a situation which will justify the original departure, thereby satisfying the pre-existing (Marxist) rule. But one departure from the rules increases the probability of other departures to compensate for the first, and the time element becomes more and more pressing, as the Party's increased need and demand for control demonstrates.

This situation can be contrasted with that of the Indian Congress Party. By definition, most nationalist regimes have a more limited constituency and scope of goals than do communist regimes. For several reasons they may not feel that comprehensive industrialization is immediately necessary. To begin with, nation-

---

[5] The term is used by Robert A. Feldmesser in an excellent article, "Social Classes and Political Structures," in *The Transformation of Russian Society,* ed. Cyril Black (Cambridge, Mass., 1960), p. 223–253.

alist elites do not rely ideologically upon a specific social class base
for their survival or legitimation. Industrialization may also be
viewed in less urgent terms than in the Soviet Union because of
the greater conflict over goals which often characterizes nationalist
elites. Rapid industrialization involving a significant degree of
coercion and destruction may well be viewed ambivalently by an
elite concerned with preserving as well as changing the components that make up the nation. Such a posture leads to the "traditional" being not only suspected but also valued in a concrete as
well as symbolic fashion. The Indian regime's policy toward cows
is one striking example of such a posture. National identity may
be defined politically in terms of citizenship and not identified
with the immediate and rapid social-economic transformation of
the nation.[6] In turn, this orientation may be at least partly due
to the lack of any type of "Leninist reversal" in nationalist ideologies and thus the absence within the leadership of an urgent
need to reassure itself of the correctness of its power, beliefs, and
policies.

For all these reasons a nationalist regime, such as the Indian,
may intentionally or unintentionally "compromise with reality"
more readily and completely than a Leninist regime with its "two
steps forward" orientation.[7]

---

[6] This statement should not be taken as implying that elites with specifically nationalist ideologies are not oriented to social change. Rather, the
thrust of such an ideology, the organizational form which tends to be adopted
by elites with such an ideology, and the corresponding interaction pattern between established social-economic elites and members of the nationalist party
tend to result in a less urgent and definitive program for social-economic
transformation.

[7] The difference between a reformist and a revolutionary approach to
society might be compared to the differences Weber noted between Roman
Catholicism's and Calvinism's approach to man. As Weber points out, Catholics and Calvinists have similar goals. Both, for example, are concerned with
the transformation or salvation of man; however, either because they operate
on different assumptions concerning the reality they must deal with ("sinful
man") or because they arrive at different conclusions concerning that reality,
they employ different strategies and create different institutions to achieve
their goals. Similarly, though both reform nationalists and revolutionary elites
are concerned with transforming their societies, they differ in the strategies and

The Soviet and Indian cases also highlight the interaction of organizational and situational factors. The absence of widespread disintegration in India strengthened the posture of certain elements within the elite and of certain strategies over others. The dominant sector of the Indian elite adopted a "working through" rather than "against" strategy and this was related to the elite's major goal, political independence. The receptivity of the British (a situational factor) reinforced the strategy of "working through,"

---

institutions they employ because of their different assumptions and conclusions about the reality they must deal with ("unreconstructed society").

In the same way that Roman Catholicism has the sacrament of absolution, reform nationalists place the greatest value on its secular counterpart, political-social reconciliation; just as Roman Catholicism allows for the structural expression of this sacrament in the institution of the confessional, reform nationalists create comprehensive (national) coalitions. The result in both cases is the same. The Roman Catholic Church working in principle for the transformation of man's life "weakened just this [outcome] by one of its most important means of power and education, the sacrament of absolution [and the institution of the confessional]." The reform-oriented elite, standing in principle for the transformation of society, defeats its own goal by the premature emphasis on reconciliation and coalition. Both Roman Catholicism and reform nationalism allow for what Kirchheimer calls the maintenance of the "old data." Just as the outcomes are similar, so are the reasons behind these outcomes. The reform nationalist realizes that in many cases social reality is indivisible and that consequently the valued aspects cannot always be clearly or noncoercively separated from the devalued ones and he ends in allowing for the maintenance of that reality, basically intact.

Recognizing that "man was not an absolutely clearly defined unity to be judged one way or the other," the Roman Catholic Church "weakened its requirement that man change his life" through the sacrament of absolution. If reform nationalism is the political equivalent of Roman Catholicism, then revolutionary socialism is the political equivalent of Calvinism. If reform nationalists and Catholics stress absolution-reconciliation and penance-coalition, revolutionary socialists and Calvinists stress intransigence toward that part of their environment which does not conform to their vision of a reconstructed reality. Similarly, they devote their efforts to the construction of an elite or elect which asserts its identity in contrast and opposition to the rest of "unreconstructed man or society" and offers itself as a model to be emulated and not to be bargained with.

For Weber's comments on Roman Catholicism and Calvinism see *The Protestant Ethic*, pp. 116–126.

the priority of independence as a goal, and the leadership (Gandhi–
Nehru) chosen by the Congress. In short, the situation faced by
Congress facilitated a reformist or participative strategy; moreover, the Congress ideology, as defined by the most influential
Party leaders, reinforced the adoption of a "participative" strategy
toward the British, and made it increasingly difficult to adopt alternative strategies after independence had been secured.

The Soviet case was just the opposite. Though it was working
in a disintegrated environment, the regime still faced a number
of constraints defined by its political "allies," by internal factions,
and by a hostile peasantry. In this case, however, ideological precepts favored the minimization of commitments. Thus, previous
to the 1921–1928 period of "working with" its environment, the
Soviet leadership avoided significant commitments to its allies
and to its membership by suppressing the opposition and factions.
In 1928, the Party embarked upon a massive transformation of its
environment by launching industrialization and collectivization
policies — in part because of its concern over the existence of real,
potential, or imagined constraints on its ability to initiate change.

A comparison of the Turkish and Mexican strategies with
those of the Chinese and Yugoslavs should help to elucidate the
role of organizational as opposed to situational factors. All four
of these elites came to power through revolutionary means, after
a prolonged period of struggle during which significant elements
and areas were mobilized in the Deutschian sense of being made
available for recommitment.[8] But the strategies employed in the
first two cases differed markedly from those employed by the Chinese and Yugoslavs. The latter took advantage of an open situation
to attempt a comprehensive redefinition of community and a comprehensive program of industrialization. They attempted to make
a decisive breakthrough. This does not suggest that the Yugoslavs
and Chinese elites employed the same means and/or achieved the
same type or degree of success. In fact, all four elites may have
failed to achieve a decisive breakthrough: in Yugoslavia and China
because of the extent to which certain modes of behavior, percep-

---

[8] Karl W. Deutsch, "Social Mobilization and Political Development,"
American Political Science Review, LV (September, 1961), 494.

tion, and identification were — and are — internalized in the population; in Turkey and Mexico because of the failure to attempt a decisive breakthrough.

There are several reasons why these sets of elites opted for different strategies. The first involves the nature of elite ideology. Turkey is instructive as an example of a non-Leninist case. Under Ataturk, social and economic problems were not considered unimportant, but until 1931 the Republican Peoples Party "had no systematic social-economic program" and even after 1931 the program that did exist was vague and inconsistent.[9] The ideology of the Turkish elite was more than anything else simply diffuse. By contrast, the ideology of the Chinese elite was a model of clarity. In his book *Political Participation in Communist China* Townsend argues that the Chinese elite's ideology was shaped into a coherent set of principles during the period of struggle so that "by 1949 . . . the Party had unified its ranks under Mao Tsetung's leadership, had developed its theory of what government under CCP control ought to be, and had shown that this theory could be successfully translated into practice." This does not mean that the ideology did not "retain its share of myths, unrealized ideals, and unresolved contradictions,"[10] but it was certainly far more carefully worked out than the Turkish (or Mexican) ideology. For Turkey, the lack of coherent policies has been attributed to the fact that "the parties and their leaders . . . concentrated their attention on ending a despotic rule and capturing power rather than on constructive future programs,"[11] but this argument does not help to explain why the C.C.P., which concentrated on similar issues, was able to draft a more consistent set of policies. The answer lies only partly in the C.C.P.'s formative period of isolation and struggle. An additional segment lies in the more specific orientation toward social-economic and political problems, provided by Leninism and Stalinist experience. Within this

---

[9] Arif T. Payaslioglu, "Turkey," in *Political Modernization in Japan and Turkey*, ed. Robert E. Ward and Dankwart A. Rustow, p. 430.

[10] James R. Townsend, *Political Participation in Communist China* (Berkeley and Los Angeles, 1967), p. 36.

[11] Payaslioglu, p. 430.

framework, the particular policies implemented by the C.C.P. were also the result of its own environment and experience.

In addition to the diffuseness-coherence dimension of ideology, a second aspect of ideology, one affecting the nation-building strategy that an elite adopts once in power, involves the difference between specifically nationalist and transnationalist ideologies.

Elites specifically concerned with national values have often created polities that succumb to "second revolutions." This has been true of Chiang's China, of Egypt under the Wafd, and of the United States under the Federalists. In part, this development occurs because after coming to power specifically nationalist elites do not complete the breakthrough that they initiate:[12] the question is why not? Juan Linz has suggested one answer:

> . . . the leaders of such regimes may opt between regarding political mobilization as desirable or preferring to rule without it. The option may reflect ideological predispositions and influences toward social change or arresting such change, *but we shouldn't consider this the only or decisive factor*. In fact, we could argue that the choice will depend more on the opportunities offered by the social structure, the political context and the international situation for a mobilization in support of those in power than on the outlook of the rulers.[13]

In terms that accord with our analytic framework, Linz is arguing that situational determinants are more important than organizational (i.e., ideological) ones. However, an argument can be made that organizational factors, though not sufficient in and of themselves, are more important than situational factors in shaping the type of breakthrough that an elite attempts and accomplishes.

A limited test of this hypothesis can be made by examining the same four elites, Turkish, Mexican, Yugoslav, and Chinese.

---

[12] In Johnson's terms, "a simple revolution intended to resolve certain dyssynchronized conditions may produce new conditions of disequilibrium which the elite is unable or unwilling to relieve through policies of change, thereby setting the stage for a later revolution." Chalmers A. Johnson, *Revolutionary Change* (Boston, 1966), p. 139.

[13] See Juan Linz, "An Authoritarian Regime: Spain," in Erik Allardt and Yrjo Littunen (eds.), *Cleavages, Ideologies, and Party Systems* (Helsinki, 1964), p. 306.

In Turkey, despite certain international pressures, Ataturk attacked the invading Greeks and carried on a successful war of independence: the international "situational constraint" was not accepted. After participation in a world war and a war of independence, Turkey's social and political situation (as at a later date in Yugoslavia and China) presented the elite not only with constraints but also with a number of opportunities, such as the existence of socially mobilized elements ready to support its policies. Yet in both the Turkish and Mexican cases the nature and scope of these "opportunities" were narrowly defined and not simply limited by unfavorable, objective, situational circumstances. Perhaps the best example of this difference can be seen in the sort of co-opting carried out by the various elites. Whereas in Turkey and Mexico the pattern was one of informal co-opting marked by the actual sharing of power (if not always authority), in China and Yugoslavia the pattern was one of formal co-opting in which responsibility for policy implementation alone was shared with existing elites; the established, "traditional" elites were not permitted to affect critical policy decisions in any substantive way.

At a later point Linz comes much closer to identifying the operative constraints in the Turkish and Mexican contexts when he argues that "Undoubtedly such social and structural factors may be overcome if the leadership is really committed to the ideal of a mobilized society."[14] Here Linz significantly changes his position; as it stands it is as unacceptable as his first statement, but it is more compatible with the position presented here: namely, that in both Turkey and Mexico the diffuseness of the ideology combined with a specifically nationalist content resulted in indecisive breakthrough. In both instances, the "old data" was often able to retain its institutional definition and base in certain politically relevant areas. Thus, in desiring to establish a labor organization, the Mexican elite had a monolithic ideal, but it "was never hammered into the operating institutional form of a single great all-encompassing confederation, because men like Calles and Cardenas were unwilling to suppress fully dissident groups . . . the leaders decided it was a lesser good to crush all obstacles if

---

[14] *Ibid.*, p. 309.

this meant total intervention on the part of the government." [15]
Similarly, the Turkish elite "unlike its Soviet neighbours . . .
was unwilling to force the needed amounts out of the peasantry,
and the methods adopted . . . never yielded enough." [16]

The interaction of ideology and party structure provides an
additional perspective on the process of "spiraling commitments."
In Mexico and Turkey, the priority of national independence and
the vagueness of other goals resulted in "comprehensive nationalist movements" acting as the main instrument of change. Such
movements were the concrete expressions of the self-imposed constraints surrounding these nationalist elites. Thus, both the Turkish and Mexican elites prematurely created a "party of representation" before achieving a decisive breakthrough. [17] These elites,
because of their ideological diffuseness and specific national values,
made commitments that the Chinese and Yugoslav elites were able
to avoid because their ideologies were more coherent and more
transnational in character, and therefore permitted a greater de-

---

[15] L. Vincent Padgett, *The Mexican Political System*, p. 96.

[16] Peter F. Sugar, "Economic and Political Modernization in Turkey," in
Political Modernization, ed. Ward and Rustow, p. 165.

[17] There are of course very real differences between the Mexican and
Turkish revolutions. The Mexican revolution, at first, was one in which peasants and workers were an active element, but this was not so in Turkey, as
Ergun Ozbudun has pointed out in his article, "Established Revolution vs.
Unfinished Revolution: Contrasting Patterns of Democratization in Mexico
and Turkey," in *Authoritarian Politics in Modern Society*, ed. Samuel P. Huntington and Clement H. Moore (New York, 1970), pp. 380–406. In addition to
having specifically nationalist ideologies and being overwhelmingly concerned
with national unity and reconciliation, the Mexican and Turkish elites were
both interested in stability, and they were faced with similar problems in political integration. The current status of the Mexican polity and the costs associated with a strategy of national development based on a specifically national ideology are dealt with in several places. See, for example, John Womack, Jr., "The Spoils of the Mexican Revolution," *Foreign Affairs* 48 (July
1970): 677–688; Vincent Padgett's comments on political integration in Mexico
quoted above; Robert I. Rhodes, "Mexico — A Model for Development?" *Science & Society* 34 (Spring 1970): 61–77; Moises Gonzalez Navarro, "Mexico:
The Lop-Sided Revolution," in *Obstacles to Change in Latin America*, ed.
Claudio Veliz (New York, 1965), pp. 206–230; Pablo Gonzalez-Casanova, "Internal Colonialism and National Development," in *Latin American Radicalism*, ed. Irving Louis Horowitz et al. (New York, 1969), pp. 133–137.

gree of violence toward whatever aspects of the environment were seen as obstacles.

Coming full circle to the phenomenon of "second revolutions," the following hypothesis can be offered: Where elites with diffuse and specifically nationalist ideologies prematurely create parties of representation, decisive breakthroughs do not occur, and second revolutions tend to occur. Decisive breakthroughs are more usual where elites possess coherent and transnational ideologies which minimize value and structural commitments to elements within their environment.

The final set of comparisons will continue to focus on the interaction between organizational and situational determinants of nation-building strategies. In particular, the character and extent of political autonomy experienced by a given political system will be considered in terms of the effect it has on the appearance or nonappearance of ideologies demanding "decisive breakthroughs" and political elites concerned with implementing such ideologies. Neocolonialism seems to play a very important role in the appearance of this sort of ideology, yet it has not been investigated in anything approaching a satisfactory fashion.[18] However, unless we are willing to write off Mao, Marti, Castro, Nkrumah, and others as victims of anxiety with a low capacity for tolerating complexity and ambiguity, the phenomenon of neocolonialism seems to warrant a more serious consideration.

Four major aspects of a neocolonial situation may be identified. First, there is the credible threat of political, military, and/or economic intervention by a powerful nation-state in the affairs of a less powerful one.[19] Second, there is the diffuse nature of control that is exercised by the superordinate power. Such control is neither "direct" nor "indirect" in that the dominant power is not usually physically present in a formally controlling role. Nevertheless, the

---

[18] One article that is relevant to the study of this phenomenon is that by Merle Kling, "Towards a Theory of Power and Political Instability in Latin America," in *Political Change in Underdeveloped Countries*, ed. John Kautsky (New York, 1962), pp. 123–140.

[19] As used here, intervention differs from influence in that it implies the use of coercive measures to obtain outcomes that are seen as necessary or desirable by the more powerful unit in the relationship.

controlling power provides the premises for the major political and economic decisions made within the dependent country. It is able to do so as a result of the very "latitude" inherent in a neocolonial arrangement. "Latitude" (the third aspect) refers to the political and economic sphere within which political actors of the dependent country are able to act independently of the controlling power and enjoy the perquisites of power.

The latitude experienced within a neocolonial situation might be viewed in terms of a "zone of indifference" which an indigenous elite enjoys under the neocolonial power. Such a zone suggests the existence of a real if fragile area of political authority enjoyed by the indigenous elite in relation to the neocolonial power. The latitude associated with such a zone allows for and stimulates competition between political groups for the limited perquisites of power, but at the same time the competition tends in a number of ways to maintain the neocolonial relationship. Since status, power, and economic perquisites are available within the system, "appropriation politics"[20] can be rewarded, and there is thus a positive incentive to maintain the system as it is. There is also a negative incentive working in the same direction — namely, a faction that makes excessive demands, such as calling for an end to the neocolonial situation risks the neocolonial power's intervention on the side of its political rival. Finally, the system of sinecures makes it possible for a neocolonial system to assimilate significant numbers of mobilized individuals. To complete the picture, we must realize that the latitude inherent in a neocolonial situation is also a source and index of the system's fragility. It is, after all, latitude and not autonomy that is experienced, and within that latitude only one type of conflict can be accommodated: appropriation politics.

The fourth defining aspect of a neocolonial situation — and it is in some ways the most important — is the emulative posture adopted by the less powerful partner toward the culture, the social

---

[20] The notion of appropriation politics refers to a political arena where the major concern is with the securing of perquisites of various kinds. It is an elaboration of Weber's notion of "appropriation parties." See Max Weber, *Economy and Society*, ed. Guenther Roth (New York, 1968), 1:286.

norms, and the political institutions of the dominant nation. This emulative posture cannot be explained simply in terms of the greater power of the dominant nation but must be related to the lack of a strong political community in the subordinate nation. This argument will be distasteful to certain types of nationalists, but one of the major bases for a neocolonial relationship is the tendency of the elite stratum of the dependent nation to identify with what is perceived to be a higher-status referent.

It may be hypothesized that a neocolonial situation affects the perceptions and responses of certain elite segments in two important ways. First, the ideological responses to the situation will tend to be more virulent and extensive than the responses to direct or indirect colonial rule. The diffuse nature of the neocolonial "threat" stimulates the creation of a comprehensive ideology which can explain the nature of this threat. Marxism–Leninism, particularly its theory of imperialism, is one such ideology, and to a significant extent this may explain why both Mao and Castro adopted it.

Second, the neocolonial political system is sufficiently fragile that it is often unable to maintain enough support and coherence to deal with politico-military opposition. This is not to say that revolutions cannot also succeed in a completely colonial context (the Algerian example is all too clear), nor that revolutions are bound to succeed in neocolonial systems (recall the fate of the Huks). Still, to the extent that a given political system is neocolonial, its capacity to handle intense and comprehensive demands is severely circumscribed.[21]

The comparsions concerning the experience of the Chinese, Egyptian, Cuban, and Ghanaian elites are designed to demonstrate the ways in which organizational, situational, and historical factors

---

[21] One final point: locating certain structural conditions (such as neo-colonialism) which are conducive to the adoption of radical and not moderate (nationalist) ideologies enables one to differentiate among nationalist responses. Tucker has certain problems in differentiating radical nationalist regimes from communist or fascist ones; they would be helped by specifying certain structural (situational-historical) conditions as independent variables. See Robert Tucker, "Toward a Comparative Politics of Movement Regimes," *American Political Science Review* 55 (June 1961): 281–289.

combine to facilitate the appearance (or nonappearance) of a coherent ideology and of an elite that is seriously concerned with
achieving a "decisive breakthrough." We are concerned then with
the configuration of factors leading to the appearance of an ideology and an elite which stress the minimization of commitments to
elements within the environment as well as to the organization
members who uphold the ideology and translate it into action.
We are equally concerned with the conditions that shape the extent and character of success that an elite with such an ideology
may experience.

In terms of our sample, the following considerations seem to
be relevant. The Chinese, Cuban, and Egyptian elites developed
out of a neocolonial situation; the Ghanaian elite did not. It might
therefore be argued that the neocolonial situations were more
conducive to the selection of a virulent and comprehensive ideology than the Ghanaian situation. Further differentiation reveals
that the Chinese and Cuban elites chose a "consensual" rather than
a "cooperative" ideology much sooner than the Egyptian and
Ghanaian elites. Finally, the Chinese elite embraced a well-defined
ideology during its period of revolutionary struggle, whereas the
Cuban elite did so only after it was in power. One last consideration: the first three elites (the Ghanaian again being the exception)
came to power because they possessed a military force, and once in
power they maintained their control over this force.

A number of conclusions can be drawn on the basis of these
considerations. The Chinese and Ghanaian elites appear to be
polar types; the Cuban and Egyptian elites seem to be intermediary
types. The Chinese elite soon perceived that it was existing in a
neocolonial situation, and defined it as such. The negative historical experience of organizational commitment to the Kuomin-
tang (K.M.T.), the possibility offered by a large country free from
direct colonial control, together with Lenin's warnings against
close collaboration with non-Party elements contributed to the
Chinese elite's decision to isolate itself physically and in certain
respects politically also. They did this by creating a situation which
circumvented constraining commitments, and stimulated the
development of a political institution with a distinctive identity

and a body of trained, deployable cadres. With such an institution, the Chinese elite gained power with a minimum of commitments and had the necessary force to break those at will.

The Ghanaian elite lacked everything the Chinese elite possessed, except the desire to liquidate its commitments. The Ghanaian case may justifiably be viewed as one in which situational factors played a relatively greater role than organizational factors in shaping the nation-building process. The Ghanaian elite did not exist in a neocolonial situation that would facilitate choice of and adherence to a breakthrough ideology at a fairly early point in its drive for political autonomy; moreover, there was no disintegrating social system to facilitate a period of political isolation and the establishment of a distinctive political identity from the heterogeneous elements within the Convention People's Party. Rather, the receptiveness of the British, their direct presence, the diffuse character of Nkrumah's ideology, and the presence of competing Ghanaian elites contributed to Nkrumah's failure to clarify his ideology and to establish a coherent institutional core for the C.P.P. Moreover, Nkrumah could not prevent the proliferation of commitments which made it impossible for him to do anything but exacerbate his difficulties with each succeeding policy. In a very critical appraisal of Nkrumah, Fitch and Oppenheimer castigate him and the "socialist experiment in Ghana" for having failed "because the attempt to break with Ghana's colonial past was not made soon enough, and because when it was made, it was not complete enough."[22] But in arguing that Nkrumah should have adopted a revolutionary nation-building strategy at the outset, they do not seem to appreciate the significance of situational factors. Rather they perceive such factors as favorable for such a strategy and more significantly as thoroughly malleable to the will of the Ghanaian nation-building elite.

The fate of Nkrumah and the C.P.P. was controlled by a process of "spiraling commitments," commitments not always consciously made, not always desired, and certainly not always controlled. To the extent that Nkrumah's guide during the pre-

---

[22] Bob Fitch and Mary Oppenheimer, *Ghana: End of an Illusion* (New York, 1966), pp. 83–84.

independence and immediate post-independence era was a rather diffuse ideology comprised of contradictory elements, Nkrumah made a number of constraining "side bets" by "working with" rather than against the colonial power. His future alternatives were thus highly circumscribed. True, if Nkrumah had possessed a greater degree of ideological vision he might have been a better judge of the commitments he was making, and of their possible consequences, but what matters here are the consequences of his opting for a "Maoist" strategy.

Chalmers Johnson in his discussion of the Chinese revolution makes a fundamental point when he argues that "Communist 'organizational weapons' are important, but they scarcely account for the entire dynamic of a Communist society, or for that matter any other totalitarian society." He continues: "It was not totalitarian instruments of mass manipulation that originally led the Chinese masses into their pact with the Communist elite; it was, rather, the effects of the war and the national awakening that the war induced." [23]

This statement emphasizes how important the configuration of certain factors is to the success of a given strategy. Fitch and Oppenheimer fail to realize the role of certain situational factors in preventing political isolation from becoming political oblivion. Ghana did not experience the widespread social mobilization appropriate to a Maoist guerrilla response. Even if Nkrumah had formulated his ideology sooner and in a more specific fashion, the number of alternatives open to him would have been greatly circumscribed by his environment.

If Ghana and China are "polar types," then as I have suggested, Egypt and Cuba may be viewed as "intermediary types." Two sets of comparisons can be made using the polar and intermediary cases, one with Cuba and China, the other with Egypt and Ghana. The Cuban case demonstrates a number of points, among them the importance of historical accident. Batista's second coup in 1952 acted as the catalyst for Castro's decision to "isolate" his movement, to break all his commitments to the existing political system, and to confront it directly. Prior to the coup, Castro's ideol-

---

[23] *Peasant Nationalism and Communist Power,* p. 11.

ogy was "consensual" in intention and aspiration; after 1952 it became "consensual" in fact because of the guerrilla war. In Castro's case one might argue that the period of isolation and the nature of his ideology, when combined with his possession of military force, were sufficient to enable him to avoid binding domestic commitments. However, in analyzing the future development of Cuba, we should realize that neither the specificity of the ideology nor the period of isolation were as great or as formative as in China.

In comparing the second set of cases, the history of the Egyptian regime under Nasser provides an interesting contrast to the fate of the Ghanaian regime. The main point of difference rests with the organization that gained power: the army in Egypt, the C.P.P. in Ghana. The decisive difference lies in the nature of the army as an organization and in its distinctive competence. Although the Egyptian elite did not come to power after a prolonged period of struggle and "formative" isolation, it nevertheless came to power controlling the organization with the most distinctive identity in the entire system. To quote Gamal Abdel Nasser: ". . . the situation demanded a force concentrated within a framework that separates its members to a certain extent from the continual conflict between individuals and classes, a force drawn from the very heart of the people whose members can trust one another and have full confidence in themselves, a force so equipped as to be capable of a swift and decisive action, and these conditions only prevailed in the Army." [24] Thus, although both Nasser and Nkrumah assumed power with ill-defined objectives and eventually "muddled through" to a radical position, Nasser, unlike Nkrumah, controlled an institution which minimized its external commitments and also provided him with the means to break the commitments he made during his first ten years in power.

Finally, a comparison of Egypt and Cuba (both radical nationalist regimes, one with a Leninist ideology, the other without) demonstrates the difficulty that revolutionary elites of whatever ideological orientation experience when they attempt to create a political party *after* they have gained power.

---

[24] Gamal Abdel Nasser, *Philosophy of the Revolution* (n.p., n.d.), p. 24.

4

Conclusions

THE CONCLUSIONS to be drawn here relate to the organizational and situational conditions that shape the various nation-building strategies characterizing different political elites. Specifically, they have to do with the consequences of particular strategies and combinations or sequences thereof on an elite's ability and success in achieving a "decisive breakthrough" once it was gained power. In addition, they are related to the success of certain nation-building elites in attempting to create a coherent, national, political community.

The first conclusion to be drawn from our analysis is that a period of struggle and formative isolation is an indispensable condition which facilitates the appearance of a political organization with a distinctive and coherent identity. The importance of a Yenan-like experience can be explained through the notions of elite autonomy, precarious values, and indoctrination. In contexts where traditional political institutions can maintain their posi-

tion as the "'primary source of continuity and legitimacy'" during periods of social mobilization, the role of political parties is
secondary in that they "help make the traditional institutions legitimate in terms of popular sovereignty, but they are not themselves a source of legitimacy."[1] However, none of the cases we
have examined, not even the Ghanaian, fits this model. In each
of these a prior condition for the creation of a national political
community was, and in some cases still is, the creation of an effectively institutionalized political party, one capable of becoming
a primary source of authority. Yet it is precisely in communities
where there are competing principles of legitimacy, along with
disorganized or rigid traditional political institutions, that the
creation of a new political institution is most difficult.[2] Within
such communities, a period of struggle and isolation is critical in
that it gives a nation-building elite the opportunity to define its
goals more clearly, to test its ideological formulations in the context of political-military conflict, and to concern itself with learning as well as with organizational survival. Such a period of struggle also gives an elite the opportunity to create an "institutional
core," a body of cadres whose primary and overriding commitment is to the party.

In short, such a setting allows for an intensive indoctrination of potential cadres. Revolutionary parties are not the first
institutions to create and take advantage of a certain form of isolation in order to build an institutional core. In their attempt to
create cadres with few commitments to the external environment,

---

[1] Samuel P. Huntington, "Political Development and Political Decay,"
in *Political Modernization*, ed. Claude E. Welch Jr. (Belmont, Calif., 1967),
p. 240.

[2] According to Selznick, "Although every effective policy requires sus-
taining social conditions, the urgency of this need varies greatly. It is more
important when aims are not well defined, when external direction is not
easily imposed or easily maintained, when fluid situations require constant
adaptation, and when goals or values are vulnerable to corruption. This
openendedness generates the key problems of institutional leadership. Among
these is the defense of institutional integrity — the persistence of an organization's distinctive values, competence and role." Philip Selznick, *Leadership in
Administration*, p. 118.

monasteries became equally concerned with indoctrination, a process that Erickson has perceptively defined as

> charged with the task of separating the individual from the world long enough so that his former values become thoroughly disengaged from his intentions and aspirations; the process must create in him new convictions deep enough to replace much of what he has learned in childhood and practiced in his youth. Obviously then the training must be a kind of shock treatment, for it is expected to replace in a short time what has grown over many formative years; therefore indoctrination must be incisive in its deprivations, and exact in its generous supply of encouragement. *It must separate the individual from the world he knows* and aggravate his introspective and self-critical powers to the point of identity-diffusion, but short of psychotic dissociation. *At the same time it must endeavor to send the individual back into the world with his new convictions* so strongly anchored in his unconscious that he almost hallucinates them as being the will of a godhead or the course of all history.[3] [my italics]

The second conclusion deals with ideology. Although a period of struggle and isolation often helps an elite to clarify its ideology, there are certain ideologies that more or less demand periods of struggle and isolation. Ideologies of this sort are often transnational in some critical feature and contain what Inkeles has termed a "mystique" or commitment to a higher purpose, such as the dialectical laws of history,[4] which ultimately negates commitments to any lesser values or objects.

Once in control, an elite that has such an ideology, defined early in its struggle for power, is more likely to achieve a "decisive breakthrough" than an elite that has not formulated such an ideology at an early stage or has no such ideology at all. Without such an ideology, a nation-building elite in power is likely to find itself making a significant number of unscrutinized, uncontrolled, and costly commitments.

The third conclusion concerns the environment in which a

---

[3] Erik Erikson, *Young Man Luther* (New York, 1958), p. 134.

[4] Alex Inkeles, "The Totalitarian Mystique: Some Impressions of the Dynamics of Totalitarian Society," in *Comparative Politics: A Reader*, ed. Harry Eckstein and David E. Apter (New York, 1963), p. 476.

revolutionary elite operates. It appears that the probability of a "decisive breakthrough" is increased by widespread disintegration within a given social system. More specifically, systemic disintegration occurring through direct and intense foreign pressure and producing large-scale social mobilization is particularly conducive to the effective institutionalization of a revolutionary political party and to the achievement of a "decisive breakthrough." This does not imply that revolutionary elites cannot come to power and achieve a decisive breakthrough without this kind of disintegration, but it does suggest that other forms of disintegration are less apt to produce a political institution capable of protecting its integrity as well as its existence and of achieving a "decisive breakthrough" with little organized opposition at the outset.

The fourth conclusion, unlike the first three, relates to the period after the elite has achieved power — that is, the stance that an elite will adopt toward its environment after it has been successful in its revolution. We have come to the conclusion that reformist elites with a "specifically nationalist" ideology are likely to engage in a policy of premature national reconciliation. Reformist elites are defined by a common tendency to co-opt established elements within their environment and to bargain with them over critical as well as routine issues. They often engage in this behavior before the established elements have been effectively constrained or transformed by the new regime. Owing to such tendencies, reformist elites can usually achieve no more than a "partial breakthrough," since they critically reduce the influence of some traditional institutions but not all, at certain levels but not at others, and the reduction is more often formal than real.[5]

---

[5] One can differentiate revolutionary and reformist regimes on this issue — the willingness to bargain, compromise with, and incorporate traditional elements before their social, cultural, and political role has been decisively transformed. Reformist regimes tend to allow for the structural integrity of such elements whereas revolutionary regimes attempt to deny them their structural integrity while allowing them their individual assimilation; see in this connection Barry Richman's discussion of the Chinese Communist Party's treatment of national-capitalists in his *Industrial Society in Communist China* (New York, 1969), pp. 895–913. Too often a simple distinction is made that revolutionary regimes totally reject tradition whereas reform-

It is important to realize that the failure to achieve a decisive breakthrough is frequently not dependent on situational constraints alone, but on organizational and, ultimately, value constraints. Both radical and moderate nationalist elites value as well as reject numerous aspects of their environment. Because of the obvious impossibility of always discriminating between the valued and rejected aspects of their environment, the actual situational constraints they often face, and their lack of a transnational "mystique," nationalist elites run the risk of losing their "revolutionary dynamism" before they have created a new national paradigm: a new political formula which is accepted by a number of strategic publics, a new distribution of political power, a new set of social and political institutions, and in some essential respects a new political culture.

---

oriented regimes arrive at "mixes" of tradition and modernity; see Rajni Kothari, "Tradition and Modernity Revisited," *Government and Opposition* 3 (Summer 1968): 288–293. In fact, revolutionary regimes may also attempt to blend aspects of tradition and modernity. One student of contemporary China (Richman, p. 226) argues that "the contemporary sociological-cultural environment in . . . China is the product of some traditional and historical human values that the regime has capitalized on and put into widespread application, a reshaping or modification of various other earlier values, and a molding of some entirely new values."

The critical question is often not whether tradtion is in some way accommodated but rather under what auspices the meeting of tradition and modernity occurs. If it occurs through what Kothari in analyzing the Indian case describes as political integration through incorporation of the traditional (see Rajni Kothari, *India*, pp. 420–422), the outcome will be quite different from what it is when traditional elements are first transformed and then selectively re-integrated. The outcomes will be different according to whether a political elite selectively incorporates aspects of modernity into the traditional (*ibid.*, p. 3) or makes a decision to define society in terms which approximate modernity and within that setting allows for the selective integration of traditional elements. The economic consequences of following the first course have been noted by Richman in his comparative statements on India and China. Richman notes how in India "high caste Indians trained in engineering and the physical sciences often greatly prefer to work in offices . . . rather than a factory" (*Industrial Society*, p. 217), and how "even in the larger privately owned Indian firms — except for a relatively small number of progressive ones — there is a strong tendency for the head of the family to maintain virtually complete authority and responsibility on all major issues where there

The dynamic character of the conclusions I have drawn here can be brought out more clearly when they are considered together. For example, a revolutionary elite will be subject to a process of spiraling commitments if it lacks a period of struggle and isolation, exists in a situation relatively free from disintegration, and lacks a coherent ideology (let alone a coherent transnational ideology with a universalistic mystique). These commitments will in turn act as constraints on the elite's ability to institutionalize its organization effectively and to achieve a decisive breakthrough. In such a case this sequence might occur: ideological incoherence leading an elite to undesirable commitments, thus creating a political organization lacking coherence, discipline, and integrity. Moreover, such an organization would be susceptible to control from its environment, and it would therefore be unable

---

are other well-educated and potentially effective family or non-family members in the managerial hierarchy" (p. 263). Indeed, he says (p. 290), "it appears that traditional religious and cultural values still play a more pervasive and important — though declining role — in the behavior and working lives of Indians, including industrial personnel. . . . India lacks a practical ideology of the Chinese type which transmits in standardized language concern with achievement on a continual basis to the working population."

Nor are the consequences of the Indian-reformist approach to tradition limited to the economy; indirectly they extend to the cultural and political sphere. Richman notes (p. 136) that Indian workers are more apathetic, pessimistic, insecure, and uncertain than Chinese workers, and he relates this to the fact that "in China, the social structure is such that numerous illiterate workers who become literate can obtain better jobs and/or proceed further with their education. This is generally not the case in India." Richman also stresses the greater feeling of efficacy and achievement orientations among Chinese workers, the greater emphasis on egalitarian considerations (i.e., in terms of wage scales and participation in factory affairs), and the community dimensions of economic life (pp. 816–817).

Although it would seem that with some verbal magic, such as talk of an incremental revolution (see Kothari, *India*, p. 430), one can present a scenario of gradually and noncoercively incorporating modernity into a traditional setting, at the level of social reality and political choice the task of relating tradition and modernity is more difficult. In fact, it appears that where traditional values and institutions are fundamentally antithetical to secular-achieve-ment-egalitarian orientations, nation building cannot occur consistently and coherently unless there is a revolutionary breakthrough in which the old values and institutions lose their power to decisively shape social outcomes.

to make use of the disintegration that existed in the social system and it would tend to arrive at a premature policy of national reconciliation. An alternative sequence might include an elite which experiences a period of struggle and isolation, possesses an ideology characterized by a universalistic mystique, and inhabits a social system marked by widespread disintegration and social mobilization. An elite of this character is likely to avoid making commitments that will result in either the attenuation of its organizational identity or in a policy of premature national reconciliation.

The second set of conclusions that can be drawn from our analysis relates to the consequences associated with distinct (i.e., reformist or revolutionary) nation-building strategies. We are concerned with negative and unintended consequences, those directly related to an elite's ideology and political strategy, and those having a significant impact on the type of success and problems an elite encounters in its attempts at nation building.

Perhaps one of the most significant negative consequences of a reformist approach to nation building is the reduction of what Frey has termed the over-all level of power within the system.[6] This often occurs because of the reformist policy of premature national reconciliation which involves significant compromises with local elites, the possible construction of a multiparty system, and electoral mobilization before the accomplishment of a decisive breakthrough. Although the concentration of power may be a necessary condition for policy and structural innovation, for a number of material and ideal reasons, the typical behavior of reformist elites is inimical to the appearance of this concentration. In fact, when reform-oriented nationalist elites intentionally or unintentionally allow for the maintenance of the "old data" in the system, they add to the problems, obstacles, and costs associated with party institutionalization, industrialization, and the redefinition of political life.

A second consequence of reformism, one which confronts those nationalist elites who pursue such a strategy because of commitment

---

[6] Frederick Frey, "Political Development, Power, and Communications in Turkey," in *Communications and Political Development*, ed. Lucian Pye.

or necessity, involves an elaboration of the first consequence in terms of leadership. Reform-oriented nationalist elites that follow a course of premature reconciliation exercise very limited control over the process and definition of party institutionalization because of their restricted autonomy with respect to social forces. They also exercise limited control over the policy-making process, a case in point being the actual as opposed to the intended character of industrialization in contexts such as the Indian and Ghanaian.[7]

A third and extremely important consequence of national-reformist strategy is the lack, or very low level of administrative, economic, and political integration. In Mexico this situation is exemplified by the existence of what Padgett has termed a second or "marginal world," one in which "the quantity of the rural population which falls within this . . . category seems to have increased over the past decades." Within this marginal world, there is "a sense of conformity, of withdrawal from any conflict, of the acceptance of paternalism, of skepticism," and the people know little or nothing of the revolutionary heritage . . . as the basis of legitimacy for the present system."[8] In other countries, the lack of integration is exemplified by the existence of two fairly distinct communities with their own elites, values, and constituencies — the sort of situation which, according to Karpat, exists in Turkey.[9]

It should be pointed out, however, that nationalist regimes which settle for a reformist strategy are not the only ones confronted with a set of negative, unintended consequences which obstruct, defeat, or interfere with their attempts at nation building. Leninist elites and regimes opting for a revolutionary strategy face similar obstacles, though not necessarily from the same quar-

---

[7] See the chapter on India in Barrington Moore's *Social Origins of Dictatorship and Democracy*, Reinhard Bendix's comment on rural development and landownership patterns in *Nation-Building and Citizenship*, and Legum's article on Ghana in Friedland and Rosberg's *African Socialism*.

[8] L. Vincent Padgett, *The Mexican Political System*, pp. 229–231.

[9] Kemal Karpat, "Society, Economics, and Politics in Contemporary Turkey," *World Politics* 17 (October 1964): 51, 54; see also Dominique Van Neste, "La Turquie et le problème d'intégration," *Civilisations* 15 no. 2 (1965): 188–205.

ters, in their attempts to create new political communities. The sources of the obstacles can be grouped into five categories.

First although the success of a revolutionary elite's breaking-through policy is dependent on the avoidance of certain commitments, such a policy necessarily entails making certain others. At the level of values, there is a commitment to the domination and manipulation of one's constituency. Such a commitment obstructs a future reconciliation between elite and public on the basis of mutual acceptance even when a decisive breakthrough has been effected. This kind of obstacle contributes significantly to the difficulty Leninist elites experience in their attempts to legitimate themselves.

Second, a value and political commitment to manipulation is reinforced by a commitment to the social and political stratum that is created, somewhat unintentionally, to carry out the "decisive breakthrough"; this stratum is what Djilas has termed the New Class. Such a stratum is usually overtly and explicitly antagonistic to any sort of national reconciliation not defined in terms of domination. This political stance is paralleled by the New Class's ideological defense of the "dictatorship of the proletariat."

Third, the existence of such a New Class obstructs the continuing process of nation building in revolutionary systems in yet another fashion. Often, the New Class has at best a limited appreciation of the complex economic nature of industrialization, but because it has held a strategic role during the breakthrough period it has acquired sufficient power and status to resist any attempts to redefine the policy of industrialization.

Once the destructive aspects of breaking through are accomplished, a fourth negative consequence that Leninist elites must contend with involves party institutionalization. There are two dimensions to this particular point. First, the process of breaking through threatens the process of party institutionalization because breaking through involves the creation of a structure inimical to the interests, power, and autonomy of the party: that structure is the security police (or revolutionary army). A second consideration is the type of institutionalization that Leninist parties undergo when they concentrate mainly on breaking through. In Weberian terms this type could be called patrimonial; it involves the power and identity of an institution being defined in terms of the leader's political identity and power. Such a structure has negative implications for the party's ability to consider a wide range of alternative solutions to salient or potential problems, to devote time to policy as opposed to power considerations, and to establish an institutional value for its members.

Finally, when a revolutionary elite achieves a decisive breakthrough in the face of an opposition that holds qualitatively different ideological and political premises, it often does so at the cost of losing some flexibility, regarding its ability to formulate new ways of dealing with problems that arise or reappear after the initial breakthrough has been completed.[10]

It thus becomes apparent that the breaking-through process which Leninist revolutionary elites initiate and experience provides mixed blessings regarding their goal of creating new political communities. Indeed, such a process presents these elites with a more or less circumscribed legacy of problems relating to each of the other major areas of the nation-building process: party institutionalization, industrialization, and community building.

---

[10] Point 5 is obviously closely related to point 1, and in a real sense the two statements delineate two aspects of a single phenomenon.

PART II

Nation Building in Romania: Priorities and Strategies, 1944-1955

5

Argument and Areas of Analysis

ONE CATEGORY of political systems that has not yet been examined is "derivative regimes" such as those which appeared in the East European context following the Second World War. An analysis of one such regime in terms of the argument thus far presented might help us not only to understand the political character of the regime but also to evaluate the utility and appropriateness of our argument.

Our argument has suggested that nation building depends on an elite's effecting a decisive breakthrough, with the use of an instrument capable of directing such a process, initiating policies designed substantively to support and shape that process, and enjoying significant autonomy within its environment.

With reference to Romania, I shall argue that the Romanian elite sector headed by Gheorghe Gheorghiu-Dej was aware of and concerned with effecting a decisive breakthrough and that such a breakthrough was perceived as *the* necessary condition for the eventual creation of a socialist political community. During this period, Gheorghiu-Dej and his political subordinates were primarily concerned with system building rather than community building,[1] and felt that the latter process was dependent on a decisive breakthrough (in Leninist terms the "dictatorship of the proletariat") effected by a political party based on democratic centralism (with the latter element emphasized), and implementing a policy of industrialization.

The analysis in Part II will focus on (a) the organizational and situational characteristics of the Romanian elite during the period 1944–1955, (b) the strategies it pursued and the premises that shaped them, (c) the importance attributed to achieving a decisive breakthrough, (d) the objectives of the breakthrough, (e) the means used to effect it, (f) the success of the breakthrough process, and (g) the Romanian elite's perception of the relationship between the process of breaking through and the other processes which we have noted as necessary aspects of the nation-building process.[2]

---

[1] I shall use the concept of *system building* to refer to attempts at creating a new political structure: new patterns of elite-public interactions possessing a formal, organizational, and instrumental character. *Community building* will refer to attempts at creating new political meanings which are shared by elites and publics and which possess an informal, institutional, and expressive character. These are analytic constructs and coexist to varying extents in any given political reality. For similar distinctions of this order see Philip Selznick's discussion of organizations and institutions in his *Leadership in Administration, passim*; Franz Schurmann, *Ideology and Organization in Communist China*, pp. 4–6, on the difference between organization-roles and social systems-status; and particularly Alfred Meyer, "Authority in Communist Political Systems," in *Political Leadership in Industrialized Societies*, ed. Lewis J. Edinger (New York, 1967), p. 93.

[2] These aspects include industrialization, community building, and party institutionalization.

6

Organizational and Situational Factors

FOLLOWING THE OUTLINE in Part I, the organizational and situational factors in the Romanian context are ideology, leadership, party structure, extent of social disintegration, resource level, mode of coming to power, and level of development.

Ideology

Modern political thought has largely surrendered the conception of society informed by a natural structure . . . the conviction has grown that society is an artifact, a pragmatic creation that men can design to meet their needs or wishes; there is no inherent structural principle in society standing in the way of what men want. Once men ceased to think in terms of the "nature of society" it become increasingly easy to justify the use of violence to "create" a new society.[1]

[1] Sheldon S. Wolin, "Violence and the Western Political Tradition," *American Journal of Orthopsychiatry* 33 (January 1963): 27.

Two aspects of the Romanian elite's ideology are relevant here. In terms of our categories Leninism is a consensual ideology, and it quite explicitly emphasizes the characteristics of modern political thought which Wolin has enumerated. The general significance of such an ideology to the task of breaking through should be obvious. Of equal importance, however, is the rather formal, dogmatic, and even superficial way in which the sector headed by Gheorghiu-Dej approached and appreciated its ideology. On coming to power, the Romanian elite possessed and was committed to a Leninist-consensual ideology, but it did not have a set of politically and situationally relevant definitions derived from that ideology. In short, it lacked a "practical ideology." [2]

Leadership

In 1944 the leadership of the Romanian elite was far from clear. Ştefan Foriş had been deposed from his position as Secretary-General,[3] and the Romanian Communist Party had four leadership nuclei: the faction around Gheorghiu-Dej, Pătrăşcanu, the Pauker–Luca faction, and Party members such as Bodnaraş who occupied boundary roles between the Communist Party of the Soviet Union and the Romanian Communist Party as well as (it would appear) among the various factions within the R.C.P. Some

---

[2] A "practical ideology" is not synonymous with a pragmatic orientation. Rather, it refers to a set of action-oriented beliefs that are defined in terms which in significant respects reflect and are congruent with a given social reality and political situation. The term itself is taken from Franz Schurmann's *Ideology and Orientation in Communist China* (see esp. pp. 17–44).

[3] Too little is known about the Foriş episode to draw any sound conclusions. In particular, Foriş's position in the Pauker–Dej conflict and his actual role in the 1930s need clarification. For statements on Foriş see Ghita Ionescu, *Communism in Rumania* (New York, 1964), pp. 79–81; and Nicolae Ceauşescu, "Cuvîntare la adunarea activului de partid al municipiului Bucureşti (aprilie 26, 1968)," in *România pe drumul desăvîrşirii construcţiei socialiste* 3 (Bucureşti, 1969), 188, where he says: "Similarly, the commission, analyzing [Gheorghiu-Dej's] accusation against Foriş that he was an enemy agent, have established that he was not guilty, that he was executed without any legal basis and even without a trial, so that in this case also an assassination occurred."

have even argued that as early as "the eve of World War II, the leaderless Romanian Communist Party . . . had virtually disintegrated."[4] Importantly, however, in the midst of this chaos there existed a more or less homogeneous group composed of "former industrial workers of Romanian ethnic origin and Eastern Orthodox religious background, known within the party as the 'workers group'" committed to or aligned with Gheorghiu-Dej. This group had been brought up in the Party underground and "steeled in struggle and prison . . . forged into true professional revolutionaries, untainted by nationalism or even patriotism and absolutely devoted to Moscow."[5] This group had its own elite nucleus split up according to prison location rather than partisan base, accepting for the most part Gheorghiu-Dej's leadership, communicating with one another, engaging in ideological-political debate,[6] and attempting to formulate political and policy positions. In the Party's own words:

> Under the leadership of Comrade Gh. Gheorghiu-Dej, the basic cadres found in the Tîrgu-Jiu camp — comrades Chivu Stoica, Gh. Apostol, N. Ceaușescu, Al. Drăghici and others — restored the organizational unity of the party, undermined by opportunist elements . . . Communists, collectives of imprisoned antifascists in all prisons — Caransebes, Lugoj, Văcărești, Mislea, the antifascist collective led by comrade Alexandru Moghioroș in the Tîrgu-Ocna prison, the collectives in Rîbnița, in the Tîrgu-Jiu, Vapniarca, Grosulovo jails — constituted a combative force, powerful and united based on Party-minded positions.[7]

This description is of course idealized, but the essential point is no doubt true: that there existed several more or less ideologically cohesive groups, in communication with one another, aware of

---

[4] Stephen Fischer-Galati, ed., "The Party and Political Organizations," in *Romania* (New York, 1957), p. 69.

[5] D. A. Tomasic, "The Romanian Communist Leadership," *Slavic Review* 20 (October 1961): 481.

[6] See D. Nistor and V. Piucă: ". . . prisons and camps in which communists were imprisoned were transformed into genuine marxist-leninist universities." "Munca ideologică a Partidului," in *Statutul Partidului Comunist Român* (București, 1966).

[7] *20 de ani de la eliberarea Romániei* (București, 1964), pp. 14–15.

their political-ideological distinctiveness, and capable of acting together against elites with different backgrounds, experiences, and loyalties.

Party Structure

Western students all seem to agree that the Romanian Communist Party in late 1944 had approximately one thousand members. This lack of numerical strength, combined with the elite factionalism and the rather indiscriminate and uncoordinated recruitment which occurred between 1944 and 1947, hardly made a good basis for a viable political institution. In fact, depending on how indiscriminate the recruitment actually was, Gheorghiu-Dej's description (at the Party Congress in 1955) of the recruitment policy during this period as "liquidationist" appears to be justified.[8] Two points relating to the issue of structure should be added. First, if Ceaușescu is to be believed, the actual Party membership as late as March, 1945, was 35,800.[9] This is quite different from saying that the party grew to a few hundred thousand in a few weeks.[10] If the party was capable of differentiating forms of commitment to the new regime (i.e., full Party member, members of defense units, and members of socio-political organizations linked to the Party), then although it was by no means highly coherent or definitively controlled, the elaboration of the party as an organization was not as chaotic as many have held. This is particularly true in light of the situation that prevailed in the country and the priority certain members of the elite assigned to gaining visible and intense support (i.e., from young members of the Iron Guard) before dealing with the question of party institutionalization.

------

[8] Gheorghe Gheorghiu-Dej, *Rapport d'activité du Comité Central du Parti Ouvrier Roumain présenté au II Congrès du Parti* (Bucureşti, 1956), p. 162; hereafter cited as *Rapport d'activité*.

[9] See *Scînteia*, March 7, 1970.

[10] See Stephen Fischer-Galati, *20th Century Rumania* (New York, 1970), p. 83. According to Gheorghe Tuţui in his article, "Dezvoltarea Partidului Comunist Român in anii 1944–1948," *Anale de istorie* 6 (1970), 6, the Party's strength in February 1945 was 16,000, in March 35,000, in April 42,633, in July 101,810 and in October at the time of the National Party Conference 256,863.

Second, and more indirectly related to the issue of structure, is the question of Party support. This is an important but neglected topic. In dealing with issues involving the availability of potential members, and the motivations behind applications for membership, one may draw very misleading conclusions unless one is aware of the fact that actual membership is not always an adequate index of a movement's strength.[11] On the basis of information now available, it would appear that the R.C.P. could draw on more social support than its membership indicated.[12] This does

[11] This same question of membership and support can be applied to the current position of the Black Panther Party in the United States. Statements to the effect that this organization possesses no more than 4,000–5,000 members are incomplete and misleading if they are read as comments on the party's influence and membership base. It would appear that the party's influence is a good deal broader, particularly among young blacks. But even if that is true, one must be careful in drawing conclusions. Simply showing that the R.C.P.'s influence in 1944 or the Black Panther's influence in 1970 extended beyond its membership does not mean that one can go on to assume that (*a*) this influence extended over most or all major issues; (*b*) this support base would act with the organization; or (*c*) would maintain its positive orientation toward that organization. This kind of investigation into support areas can, however, give the analyst a more sophisticated appreciation of the character, role, and political potential of the organization he studies, and it can also perhaps make it more difficult for him to reach conclusions that favor his own political values.

[12] In *20th Century Rumania*, Fischer-Galati does focus on the support the Party received in the interwar period. It is his belief that during these years the membership may have reached a few thousand while the Party was able to get 75,000 votes "[or 2 percent of the total ballots cast] in all parliamentary elections antedating the Party's Fifth Congress of 1932" (p. 75). He also suggests in the same work that while opportunism and pressure were responsible for many memberships in the year 1944, "the causes of the opportunism and the nature of the pressure have not been determined." Though he goes on to say that "investigation does lead to slightly different answers from those previously supplied," he does not mention the new information or evidence that warrants new conclusions either in this work or in the one to which he refers the reader to discover the new information, namely, his earlier book, *The New Rumania*, pp. 26 ff.

In any case, the question of support can be dealt with in terms other than membership. For example, one would want to know how strong competing parties were and whether or not there were organizations associated with or controlled by the Communist Party that did have substantial and/or growing support. According to the O.S.S. survey carried out in Romania after its

not suggest, however, that the R.C.P. was by any means the popular choice in the 1940s nor that it could very effectively control the support that it did enjoy. This situation of ineffective control may be taken as an index of the lack of a well-developed, socially and politically embedded party organization.

Social Disorganization

In 1944 the Romanian elite faced an environment characterized by extensive disorganization rather than extensive disintegration. Gheorghiu-Dej stated that "Romania found itself in a disastrous economic situation,"[13] and in a fairly recent speech, Nicolae Ceaușescu noted that "industrial output in a number of branches in 1944 had dropped to about 50% in comparison with the pre-war level; only 10% of the machine tools existing in 1943 were still in operation; the transport capacity of the railways decreased to 30% in comparison with 1943."[14] Ceaușescu also pointed to the drought

---

liberation, most of the nation was uncommitted to any party; see Gabriel Kolko, *The Politics of War* (New York, 1968), p. 406. Only the Peasant Party demonstrated significant support: in Kolko's words (p. 156), "The OSS acknowledged that most Rumanians were cynical toward all the political groups." Concerning our second question — were there organizations attached or aligned with the R.C.P. that did have support — Kolko notes that the "Ploughman's Front . . . was the fastest-growing political organization during this period," and the Ploughman's Front was closely connected with the Romanian Communist Party. (For more on the Ploughman's Front see Henry Roberts, *Rumania: Political Problems of an Agrarian State* [New Haven, 1951], pp. 260–261).

[13] Gh. Gheorghiu-Dej, "Raportul politic al Comitetului Central la Conferinţa Naţională a Partidului Comunist Român, Octombrie 1945," in Gh. Gheorghiu-Dej, *Articole şi Cuvîntări* (Bucureşti, 1951), p. 32.

[14] Nicolae Ceaușescu, *The Romanian Communist Party — Continuer of the Romanian People's Revolutionary and Democratic Struggle, of the Traditions of the Working Class and Socialist Movement in Romania* (Agerpress: May 6, 1966), pp. 64–65. This "data" is, as John Michael Montias has put it, "both methodologically suspect and factually tenuous; they can at best afford a general notion of the extent of a country's losses" (*Economic Development in Communist Rumania* [Cambridge, Mass., 1967], p. 16). For our analysis, however, the data at least serve to indicate the general dimensions of the economic disorganization in Romania after the Second World War.

in 1945–1946, the burden of reparations, and the "freezing of Romania's foreign currency and bonds in the Western capitalist countries." At the same time, however, such critical institutions as the army (or sectors thereof), the Uniate, Orthodox, and Catholic churches, the "historic" parties, and the monarchy continued to give evidence of their organizational integrity and/or political relevance. From the Party's point of view, the situation was far from completely open and malleable.

Resource Level

In the area of resources, too, there were more constraints than opportunities. As noted, the Party had few members and few adequately socialized and experienced cadres, far less than were needed to carry out its ambitious goals. In 1949, the first Plan was drawn up for only one year. Among the reasons given for this were the lack of "statistical and documentary material elaborated on scientific lines, especially prepared with a view to planning," and the fact that "our experience, both of the technical apparatus and the economic staffs, did not admit of drafting a plan for a longer period." [15] The question of resources is not simply (or even primarily) technical, however; rather, it relates to the character and goals of a specific regime.

This was revealed by the Romanian elite's reaction to the existing administrative structure. The abundance of bureaucrats was not looked upon as a valuable resource, for not only was the bureaucracy accustomed to autonomy from political control and hopeful of continued and significant political influence, but also it poorly approximated a performance-oriented model. [16]

---

[15] Gh. Gheorghiu-Dej, *The Plan of the Rumanian People's Republic for 1949* [Report to the Grand National Assembly by Gh. Gheorghiu-Dej] (Bucureşti, 1949), p. 7.

[16] For an analysis of the type of bureaucracy that characterized interwar Romania see Fred Riggs, *Administration in Developing Countries*, pp. 15–21, 105, 182–184, 303; also see pp. 206, 221–237, 263, 407. For an analysis of the Romanian interwar bureaucracy in Riggsian terms see Ilie J. Smultea, "Political Development and Bureaucracy in Romania Prior to World War II," Ph.D. dissertation, University of California, Berkeley, 1968.

Level of Development

I have already noted the effect of the Second World War on the performance and viability of the Romanian economy. At least three points are worth making. (*a*) The level of development in Romania was dependent not only on economic and technical considerations but also on political ones — in particular, the fact that a good deal of the economy was not directly subject to the control of the Romanian Workers Party until 1948, together with the necessity of paying reparations to the Soviets and the existence of joint companies (Soviet–Romanian). (*b*) It is possible to specify, thanks largely to Montias' work in this field, the ways in which and the extent to which the Romanian economy was disrupted by the war. In 1938 Romania was producing 6.6 million tons of crude oil, 133,000 tons of pig iron, 284,000 tons of crude steel, 510,000 tons of cement, and 289,000 tons of rolled steel; in 1947 only cement had returned to its prewar output.[17] Montias has also analyzed the considerations that help to explain the slow recovery of the Romanian economy between 1944 and 1947: Romania's contribution to the anti-German war effort after its liberation in August, 1944, the destruction of Romanian property by both the Germans and Soviets as well as the confiscation of Romanian property by the Soviets, the low output of the agricultural sector, and the foreign exchange crisis. (*c*) Despite the widespread disorganization and economic stagnation, in terms of natural resources, technical cadres, and existing plant, the potential still existed for a significant elaboration of economic performance, something the Romanians began to demonstrate in 1949 with the appearance of the first Plan.

Mode of Coming to Power: Constraints and Opportunities

In the Romanian case as in others, the mode of coming to power had a great impact on the character of the breakthrough. Machiavelli's notions are often borne out — that for innovators the major question is "whether they depend upon others . . . whether

---

[17] Montias, *Economic Development*, pp. 21–22.

in order to carry out their designs they have to entreat or are able to compel," and that "all armed prophets have conquered and unarmed ones failed"[18] — but in the position of the Romanian elite there were contradictions. It possessed a force adequate to minimize its "entreating" gestures toward domestic opposition, but at the same time it was almost totally constrained because the armed force at its disposal was not under its control. In 1945 it was explicitly recognized that the Party's political power was dependent on the "decisive aid [*ajutorul hotărîtor*] of the Red Army."[19] Perhaps the best example of the constraints and opportunities present in the situation was the Tudor Vladimirescu division, nominally a Romanian army unit subject to the Party's control but at the same time a unit that had been created in the Soviet Union and was staffed with a considerable number of Soviet political, military, and police cadres. Most of the constraints attached to the Romanian Party's dependent mode of coming to power are fairly obvious: essentially, the Soviet Union was in the position of providing the major premises for the Romanian elite's choice of strategies and thus determined which of the Romanian Party's specific priorities could be acted on. But the opportunities involved in this relationship should also be specified.

To begin with, the presence of the Soviet Union allowed for a political revolution in a context that was disorganized but not disintegrating. Soviet presence both contributed to the "revolutionary situation" and compensated for its weakly defined character.[20] In at least one other important way, the Romanians benefited from their essentially colonial dependence on the Soviet Union during the late 1940s. It has been argued that "the sacri-

---

[18] Niccolo Machiavelli, *The Prince and The Discourses* (New York, 1950), p. 22.

[19] Gh. Gheorghiu-Dej, "Raportul . . . Octombrie 1945," p. 21.

[20] Lenin says that a revolutionary situation exists when "the lower classes do not want the old way and when the upper classes cannot carry on in the old way . . . revolution is impossible without a nationwide crisis." *Left-Wing Communism, An Infantile Disorder* (New York, 1940), p. 65. The presence of the Soviet army enabled the R.W.P. to prevent the "upper classes" from carrying on in the old way, and to articulate, manipulate, and direct the dissatisfaction among the lower classes with the "old ways of running things."

fice of cultural or national political values, which is normally bound up with the acceptance of foreign colonial rule, usually finds no compensating economic reward"; [21] but in the Romanian–Soviet case, aside from the fact that the majority of the Romanian Party elite did not, at this point, see the sacrifice of cultural and national political values as inconsistent with its immediate goals, the Romanians were encouraged in their desire to industrialize. Although Soviet political support of such a program was not an automatic response, and the Romanian elite had very little control over such a decision, it is nevertheless significant that, unlike other colonial powers, the Soviet Union was ideologically predisposed toward supporting a policy of comprehensive industrialization. [22]

The distinctive quality of the Romanian–Soviet colonial relationship can be illuminated by comparing it with the case of Ghana. The Romanian and Ghanian elites were alike in neither having enjoyed a period of "creative isolation" conducive to party institutionalization, nor in having operated in an environment of substantial disintegration. Given the rather extensive constraints on their autonomous choice of strategies, both elites had "to look over their shoulder all the time instead of looking only to their goal." [23] On its own, neither elite had much chance to secure and concentrate political power or effect a revolutionary breakthrough. The critical difference lies in the contrasting ideological-political character of their respective colonial powers.

A good deal can be said on the question of whether or not the Romanian Party elite's basic commitment to the Soviet Union

---

[21] Karl Deutsch, "The Price of Integration," in *The Integration of Political Communities,* ed. Philip E. Jacob and James V. Toscano (New York, 1964), p. 158.

[22] This argument is not meant to imply that the Soviets did not simultaneously exploit the Romanian economy in an extremely rapacious fashion, particularly in the immediate postwar years. As an example, however, of how the Soviets contributed to the Romanian Party's economic program even in those years see Montias' discussion of the role which the joint companies played at this time, i.e., prior to the Nationalization of Industry in June, 1948; *Economic Development,* pp. 20–21.

[23] Richard Lowenthal, *World Communism: The Disintegration of a Secular Faith,* p. 246.

beginning in the 1920s was "correct." One could argue as follows: given the lack of widespread disintegration in Romania, the small working class base, the limited extent of social mobilization, and the radical goals of the Party elite, the commitment to the Soviet Union, though a definite risk to the Romanian Party's power and identity, was no greater than the risk involved in a policy of political independence during the interwar period. The link with the Soviet Union was, indeed, a very real threat to the party's identity and power, and Ceauşescu himself, in a speech in May, 1966, criticized the Comintern for neglecting certain concrete conditions which should have played a greater role in determining Party policy in Romania during the interwar years and for undermining the autocephalous status of the Romanian Party. He argued quite correctly that the neglect of national conditions jeopardized the party's power potential, while the practice of imposing Soviet-chosen individuals as the leaders of the party distorted its political and national identity.[24]

Ideally, the Party would have formulated its own program, mobilized the population behind it, and selectively drawn on the Soviet Union and the C.P.S.U. In reality the situation was much more restrictive, and the Party's choice of commitments can only be evaluated in terms of this less than ideal situation. The defining aspects of the real situation were these: (*a*) a Soviet party increasingly concerned with gaining full control over non-Soviet communist parties, particularly those located in strategic areas; (*b*) a domestic political and social system that was disorganized but still viable; and (*c*) a political system that was committed to the elimination of communism nationally and internationally. The only elaboration the first point needs is that the prestige of the C.P.S.U. and increasingly of Stalin, at a time when there was no other Leninist regime in the world, was bound to cause problems of reference and loyalty for national communist parties. It is with respect to the second and third points that one must analyze the

---

[24] See Ceauşescu, *The Romanian Communist Party*, pp. 23, 28, 37–38; also Max Weber, *The Theory of Social and Economic Organization*, trans. Talcott Parsons (New York, 1947), p. 148, for a discussion of the concepts autonomous, autocephalous, heteronomous, and heterocephalous.

"correctness" of the Romanian Party's adherence to the Comintern. One might argue that if the Romanian Party was to maintain its political integrity and organizational autonomy as well as add to its power, it should have either "gone to the mountains" and based itself on the discontented peasantry or attempted to integrate itself into the existing political order. However, given the anti-communist orientation of the existing regime, the small working class base, and the power of the National Peasant and (increasingly through the '30s) Iron Guard organizations among the peasantry, it is probable that if the leaders of the Communist Party, lacking major areas of support, had pursued an integration strategy, they would have been individually co-opted and deprived of any significant role.

Nor does it appear that a guerrilla strategy would have been very successful if it had been attempted. It can be argued that a Communist party free of Soviet control might well have taken advantage of the discontent among the peasants in the same manner as the Iron Guard did; the growth of the Iron Guard demonstrated that there was a sizable portion of the young and the peasantry available for political recommitment. But there are several reasons to suggest that the Communists would not have been able to draw successfully on this same base. As Eugen Weber has pointed out in his article on the Iron Guard, there were indeed sections of the young and peasantry that were either unattended to by existing political organizations or mobilized, that is, definitively uprooted from their social-political settings.[25] But one must be careful to *distinguish between elements in a social system that are neglected and elements that are mobilized.* In general, one can hypothesize that neglected elements are available to a more radical set of political-ideological appeals than are elements that, in Deutschian terms, are assimilated; but there are real limits to the range of

---

[25] See Eugen Weber, "The Men of the Archangel," *Journal of Contemporary History* 1, no. 1 (1966): 101–127. This article and Weber's "Romania" in Hans Rogger and Eugen Weber, eds., *The European Right* (Berkeley and Los Angeles, 1966) are excellent examples of analysis that integrates historical, political, sociological, and comparative perspectives.

appeals that such neglected elements are susceptible to, because, although they may possess a wide range of intensely felt grievances, they have not been uprooted or decisively alienated from their social-cultural-economic settings. These settings may be disorganized, but they maintain a level of coherence that favors a positive response to radical programs of within-system change over revolutionary appeals, such as those of the R.C.P., which call for at least a temporary denial of national values as well as established cultural definitions and ways of life.[26]

The Party was successful to some extent among certain mobilized sectors such as the Jewish and Hungarian minorities, but it was quite unsuccessful with the mobilized Romanian youth. This may well have had something to do with the desire of individuals engaged in significant redefinitions of their personal and political character to minimize the costs to their existing identity. For the distrusted and mobilized member of a minority group or the politically aware and excluded unskilled worker the costs of identifying as a Communist were probably less than those of identifying as a member of the Iron Guard. For most members of the mobilized Romanian youth stratum, however, the opposite was likely the case. For them, fewer elements of their existing middle class–nationalist identity had to be discarded or decisively altered in order to become a Guardist than to become a Communist.

A final deterrent to those who might have considered joining a guerrilla group was the opposition of the existing regime, which

---

[26] In this connection see the success of the Ploughmen's Front in Transylvania in the 1930s. According to Roberts, at this time it "seems to have been a straightforward radical peasant movement" (*Rumania: Political Problems of an Agrarian State*, pp. 260–261). Roberts says (p. 250): "The Communists, unlike the Social Democrats, tried hard to penetrate the countryside but the land reforms had weakened its revolutionary potentialities." The land reform, as Roberts shows, by no means refutes the contention that the peasantry as a whole was neglected by the regime and the leading parties. But his point about the impact of the reform on the availability of peasants to revolutionary appeals does demonstrate the need to be sensitive to the differences among an assimilated (if partly dissatisfied) sector of the population, an unattended to (and seriously dissatisfied) sector, and a mobilized sector available for revolutionary changes.

was committed to enforcing a sustained policy of repression and persecution of Communist cadres and had all the power to do so.[27]

As for the period 1944–1955, in many ways the risk to the Romanian Party's power and identity was a "non-issue."[28] Friction did exist between the Soviet and Romanian elites (and within the Romanian elite, that is, over issues such as collectivization and recruitment), and as of 1953 there was a fairly long list of issues and areas in which there was some form of conflict (and, it may be assumed, some degree of antagonism): reparations payments, contributions to the Korean conflict, the joint companies, and at least some partial payment for the upkeep of Soviet troops in Romania.[29] But material considerations such as the perceived dependence on the Soviet Union and ideal considerations such as the commitment to a dichotomous world view and the belief in the Soviet Union as the guarantor of the world socialist system (as in the Korean conflict) provided short-run rationales for the subordination of Romanian interests. Finally, historical accident in the form of Stalin's death, at a time when such rationales appear to have been wearing thin in certain sectors of the Romanian elite, may be assumed to have forestalled the raising of any existing antagonisms to the level of political principle. This general argument seems to be particularly valid in relation to Gheorghiu-Dej, whose orthodoxy and political struggle for preeminence during this period contributed to a position that defined Romanian interests as dependent upon and in accord with Soviet presence and policy.

Thus the Romanian Party's commitment to the Soviet Union during the period 1944–55 was beneficial as a result of at least three factors, only one of which was subject to Romanian control:

---

[27] See *ibid.*, p. 188–189, where Roberts notes the "earnest and efficient manner in which the government pursued the Communist party," and contrasts it with the "obvious indulgence with which the Iron Guard and other fascist formations were treated."

[28] For a discussion of "non-issues," of problems which may be identified by an "outside observer" but are not perceived by actors in a given situation, or if perceived are for various reasons not translated or defined in issue terms, see Peter Bachrach and Morton Baratz, "Two Faces of Power," *American Political Science Review* 57 (September 1963): 632–642.

[29] See Ionescu, *Communism in Rumania*, pp. 94–218, and Fischer-Galati, *20th Century Rumania*, pp. 70–127.

(*a*) the changing definitions of Soviet self-interest, which by 1948 resulted in a demand for and support of industrialization in Romania, the point being that the Soviets' redefinition of interest cannot be simply and directly related to the shared ideological-policy preferences which existed between the Soviet and Romanian elites as to the value of breaking through and industrialization; (*b*) the historical accident of Stalin's death in early 1953; (*c*) the maneuvering of the elite sector headed by Gheorghiu-Dej, which within the given context did contribute to the Romanian Party's ability to enhance its power and to act on its major goals.

Historical Legacy

To complete the discussion of organizational and situational factors that defined the Romanian Party's position upon coming to power and shaped the definition of its strategy and goals, one must have some appreciation of the type of political community that preceded the period beginning in 1944.

I would argue that to the extent that nation-states existed in Eastern Europe during the interwar period, these units were limited and fragile in that they did not politically include or integrate the majority of individuals formally included within their territorial boundaries. This lack of integration, of *de facto* political exclusion, possessed two dimensions: instrumental and expressive. Instrumentally, these political systems were not successful in penetrating their respective societies in other than a sporadic and for the most part coercive fashion.[30] In addition, the level of economic and technical interdependence among the various sectors and regions of these countries varied noticeably. Perhaps of greater

---

[30] One can differentiate the penetration from the breaking-through process by noting that the former does not necessarily aim at the decisive alteration of political power relationships. Particularly, so far as the penetration problem is defined as one of "establishing confidence and rapport between rulers and subjects," the breaking-through process is not coterminous with the penetration process. On the other hand, both are defined in terms of increased effectiveness of formal governmental institutions. The relation between the two may perhaps be best expressed by viewing the process of breaking through as the revolutionary solution to the penetration problem. (The quotation is from Lucian Pye, *Aspects of Political Development* (Boston, 1966), pp. 64–65.

consequence, the elites and major sectors of the population lacked meaningful, shared sentiments of community and a relatively consistent, jointly shaped set of commitments to the nation-state itself.[31] In particular, in most of these countries the absence of a set of national publics in possession of politically relevant resources, articulating their interests and aspirations, and capable of offering sustained support for political programs led to the development of political systems — as in Romania — whose intense nationalism may in part be viewed as an index of their fragile political-social identity.[32] In Romania, as Weber, Roberts, and others have shown, the rise and success of the Iron Guard with its emphasis on national regeneration and on the upgrading of the peasant was in many ways a response to this situation of fragile integration.

It is also possible to characterize Romania during the decade preceding the Second World War as a neocolonial nation.[33] As a small nation, Romania was always restricted in terms of its available options in the international arena. Its behavior was — and still is — greatly shaped by the intentions, concerns, and behavior of more powerful political-military units (be they empires or nation-states) such as France, Russia, and Germany. This alone is not sufficient to warrant the label neocolonial; there must be a configuration of related and interacting dependencies — military, political, cultural, and economic.[34] If neocolonialism refers to a political unit that is threatened with intervention by one or several more powerful states, whose economic life is shaped by premises pro-

---

[31] See Hugh Seton-Watson, *Eastern Europe Between the Wars, 1918–1941*, pp. 122–156. The majority of peasants and workers were in effect not members of the national-political community.

[32] On the structure and definition of political life in the Balkans during this period see Traian Stoianovich, "The Social Foundations of Balkan Politics, 1750–1941," in *The Balkans in Transition*, ed. Charles and Barbara Jelavich (Berkeley and Los Angeles, 1963), pp. 330–340.

[33] For a definition of neocolonialism the reader is referred to Part I, pp. 53–55.

[34] For one of the most sophisticated analyses from the dual perspective of comparative politics and international relations see Henry L. Roberts, "Politics in a Small State: The Balkan Example," in *The Balkans in Transition*, pp. 376–396. For those interested in the current effort at "linkage theory" this article is excellent.

vided from outside the national community, whose elite — lacking an effectively integrated political system based on a differentiated and politically involved set of publics — defines itself by emulating the culture and institutions of other nations, then during the 1930s Romania was a neocolonial nation.

Increasingly throughout the '30's, Germany posed a threat of intervention. During the same period of time Romania's economy was externally controlled: "Between five- and six-sevenths of industrial capital investment was owned or made available by foreigners. Foreign capital owned two-thirds of the oil industry, dominated the insurance business, controlled the banks."[35] As Stoianovich comments in his analysis of the Balkans, "The capitalist class was dependent upon the state, the state was dependent upon foreign capital."[36] In addition, the majority of peasants and workers were not effectively represented, let alone involved, in political life. Effective political action was the monopoly of notables and clusters of socially, culturally, and/or administratively established individuals rather than public and institutionalized party organizations. This syndrome was completed by, helped produce, and in return was sustained by a political-social elite that defined itself in terms of emulating non-Romanian references, one that looked not internally to the nation but externally for its status, esteem, and support.[37]

At this point I suggest no conclusion as to how successful the Romanian Party has been in redefining Romania's status and character as a political system and community. I do suggest, however, that in 1944 the elite of the Romanian Communist Party was acutely aware of Romania's defining characteristics as a political unit during the interwar period, and that one can understand the behavior of Gheorghiu-Dej and Ceauşescu only in the context of the legacy I have just outlined.

---

[35] Eugen Weber, "Romania," p. 529.

[36] Stoianovich, "The Social Foundations," p. 336.

[37] Descriptions of the way in which the Romanian elite aped the style of Western European life are as numerous as they are amusing and sad. Vivid descriptions of the cultural emulation may be found in Leigh White's journalistic survey, *The Long Balkan Night* (New York, 1944), pp. 48–158.

7

The Breaking-Through Process

BOTH THE INITIAL TIMING and the character of the breaking-through process in Romania were directly related to the set of organizational and situational factors I have just defined.

The period 1944–1947 was primarily one of reformism — of the partial though significant restructuring of the political system. In one of the most authoritative statements on this period, Jozsef Revai, a former leading member of the Hungarian Communist Party, commented that, if anything, reformism was being carried too far. Within the Hungarian party, he said, there were ideological arguments that socialism could be achieved peacefully through a coalition of peasants and workers without the dictatorship of the proletariat, and some comrades failed to recognize that the task of social-political transformation required that "power [be] undivided in the hands of the proletariat and the working class does not share the power with other classes."[1] Revai was

---

[1] Jozsef Revai, "On the Character of Our People's Democracy," in *Readings on Contemporary Eastern Europe*, ed. C. E. Black (New York, 1953), p. 85.

speaking only of the Hungarian case, but it appears that at the autumn, 1947, session of the Cominform the Soviets applied this critique to most of their East European dependents.[2]

It is possible to distinguish three major characteristics of this general area, and specifically Romania, during this period. (1) It is reasonable to assume that the Romanian, like the Hungarian and other parties, lacked "a unified, clarified, elaborated attitude in respect to the character of the People's Democracy and its future development."[3] Lacking specific Soviet guidance and any "practical" ideology of their own, some cadres may have increasingly elevated reformism as a tactic to the level of a strategy. (2) During this period the Romanian Party, from the perspective provided by its ideology and goals, did effect very significant reforms. These included the installation of a regime in March, 1945, that was considered responsive to the Party's demands, the publication of the agrarian reform bill (the same month), the establishment of joint Soviet–Romanian economic units (Sovroms), the trial of Antonescu, the political elimination of the National Peasant and National Liberal parties, the trial of the Peasant leaders Maniu and Mihalache, and the elimination of the monarchy.[4] (3) Prior to 1948 the Romanian Party did *not* undertake systematic, comprehensive, and coordinated moves to redefine the social and cultural as well as the whole of the economic and political sectors of the country. This type of decisive action characterized its behavior beginning in 1948.

The period of reformism was shaped by three factors: (*a*) the already mentioned organizational weakness of the Romanian Party, (*b*) the endogenous situational constraints in the form of semi-viable institutions and a low level of disintegration, and (*c*), most important of all, the existence of exogenous situational constraints in the form of Soviet policy decisions. By the middle of 1947, however, the Soviet elite had revised its policy stand in favor of a revolutionary orientation which called for a policy of breaking through and rapid and comprehensive industrialization.[5] This

---

[2] See *ibid.*, p. 83.

[3] *Ibid.*

[4] See Ghita Ionescu, *Communism in Rumania*, pp. 106–143.

[5] See Revai, p. 83, where he specifies the autumn, 1947, meeting of the

new orientation and policy was in accord with the expectations and aspirations of most East European elites, including the Romanian.

As the Romanian elite became concerned with implementing a decisive breakthrough and a policy of industrialization, the Soviets, for their own reasons, supported their aspirations, but the Romanian elite tended, I believe, to perceive this relationship between Soviet demands and Romanian aspirations in terms of a necessary rather than possible congruence of interests. In other words, the Romanians assumed that given their shared ideological and organizational premises with the Soviets, Soviet support would be more or less automatic and free from major conflicts of interest, and there would be an identity, rather than a congruence, of interests.[6] This assumption may well explain why the Romanian reaction was so strong when, later on, they met an intransigent Soviet reply to their industrial aspirations. Indeed, when the Romanians realized that their development was dependent upon a possible but not necessary congruence of interests with their "principal," the Soviet Union, a major political and ideological crisis occurred.

Breaking Through as the Core Problem

The major emphasis of the Romanian Workers Party[7] during the period 1948–1955 was on effecting a "decisive breakthrough," but it was not the only one. The isolation of core problems is a continual concern of Leninist elites, and in organizational-theoretical terms the R.W.P. saw the breakthrough as the core problem of this specific period or developmental stage.[8] As a member of the

Cominform as the time when the Soviets initiated the revolutionary line, which was elaborated upon at the Cominform meeting the following summer.

[6] If there is such a thing as an organization psychology, one might hypothesize that to the extent a given organization is dependent on another (i.e., as a child is on his father) and generally perceives this organization as a positive force, the combination of dependence, fear, and appreciation (or as in the child-parent relationship, love) will generate assumptions about the identity of interests that exists between the two.

[7] The R.C.P. became the Romanian Workers Party in early 1948 after its fusion with the left-wing segment of the Social Democratic Party.

[8] See Robert L. Kahn et al., *Organizational Stress: Studies in Role Con-*

present Romanian elite has explained it: "the assurance of a competent leadership depends in the first place, on the understanding and capacity of the party organization to organize its work in such a way as to draw from the multitude of problems, the principle-essential one(s), on whose resolution the raising of the entire work of the party to a higher level depends."[9]

On a substantive as opposed to theoretical level, the Romanian elite's emphasis on breaking through as the core problem was related to its concern with the maintenance and enhancement of its revolutionary political character as well as to the way in which it related its various goals. As for the concern with its political character, Haas has argued that "bureaucracies that ignore the precariousness of their initial position, that hold out for a dynamic program immediately although they have few reliable clients, run a desperate survival risk," while "survival depends on satisfying both clients and staff in a perpetually adaptive manner."[10] The Romanian elite after three years of relative restraint now had a reliable "client," thanks to the new Soviet posture, and it oriented itself toward a "dynamic program" of breaking through and industrialization in order to satisfy its client — the Soviet elite — and its own staff of leading cadres, who, given their revolutionary goals and ideology, perceived a policy of continued reformism or limited change as their major survival risk.

As suggested, the elite's emphasis on breaking through was also linked to the way in which it related its several goals. Specifically, the completion of a decisive breakthrough was seen as essential for the success of the socialist revolution and the creation of a socialist political community. Both theoretical and substantive considerations reinforced the tendency of the Romanian Leninist elite to take existing situational constraints and "encourage head-on confrontation with them."[11]

---

flict and Ambiguity (New York, 1964), p. 338, for a discussion of the notion of "core problem."

[9] Gheorghe Călin, "Conducerea competentă — trăsatură esenţială a muncii de partid," in *Stilul de Muncă al Organelor de Partid* (Bucureşti, 1966), p. 52.

[10] Ernst Haas, *Beyond the Nation-State* (Stanford, 1964), p. 116.

[11] J. P. Nettl, *Political Mobilization* (New York, 1967), p. 306.

The Breaking-Through Process: Objects and Means

At best, an analysis of the distinctive character of the Romanian breakthrough should help to elaborate the concepts of breaking through and clarify the elements that shaped the Romanian elite's attempt to redefine its social, political, economic, and cultural environment.

There is no doubt that the range of objects considered as appropriate targets was comprehensive. Institutions directly related to political life, such as the army, political parties, and the monarchy, were given immediate priority, but other institutions — economic, religious, educational, and informational — with a more indirect impact on political life and/or with a more diffuse character were also considered critical. But the character of a breakthrough depends on the means employed as well as on the objects affected — on the forms, combinations, timing, and character of violence that are used. Indeed, the extent to which the violence is rational or irrational not only has a direct and significant impact on the character of the breaking-through process but also has a lot to say about the elite itself. Any act of violence, of course, will have elements of rationality and irrationality, but in the Romanian case one can single out areas in which one element was more or less dominant. In its attitude toward the Press, where the Communists controlled the supply of newsprint, the elite used rational and indirect forms of violence.[12] As for the peasants, Gheorghiu-Dej's statement in 1949 about "limiting and eliminating the kulak gradually, [by] forbidding the sale, buying, and leasing of land,"[13] may be taken as at least formal recognition that indirect violence was thought to be an effective instrument for breaking through in this area — especially, one can add, if more direct forms of coercion were also used, such as the imprisonment of political opponents and their organizational elimination. The Nationalization decree

---

[12] See Romulus Boila, "Press and Radio," in *Captive Romania*, ed. Alexander Cretzianu (New York, 1956), pp. 259–261. This volume is not noteworthy for its analysis, but it is useful for details of the Romanian breakthrough.

[13] Gh. Gheorghiu-Dej, "Lupta de clasă în România în etapa actuală," in *Articole şi Cuvîntări*, p. 396.

of June, 1948, was an example of the direct and rational use of coercion in industry and the Romanian elite's approach to the country's religious institutions provides an illustration of the combination of methods used to destroy or at times decisively circumscribe the autonomy and influence of politically relevant structures. Purges of the clergy were accompanied by legislative decrees manipulating the age limits for religious officials and the minimum limits of eparchies and dioceses, as well as abolishing certain theological institutions.[14] Furthermore, the campaigns against the various religious institutions were apparently part of a deliberate policy of sequential rather than simultaneous breaking through.

The relation of the breaking-through process to the ideological character of the Romanian elite becomes apparent when one looks at its financial policy. Discussing the currency reform of 1947, one non-communist observer has noted that the associated income tax rise was "far from uniform, [striking] far harder at those whom the communists are particularly anxious to do away with."[15] In particular, rates on agricultural incomes were more than five times greater than on wages, and on commercial incomes more than eight times greater.

The Romanian elite's educational policies provide a final example of the rational use of a mixed set of coercive policies. To begin with, there was the direct removal of personnel. According to one observer a particularly vivid demonstration of this took place in the School of Letters and Philosophy at the University of Bucharest where "no less than 80 per cent of the old staff of professors and instructors were eliminated."[16] Along with purges of this sort, there were attempts at resocializing Romanian teach-

---

[14] See Emil Ciurea, "Religious Life," in *Captive Romania*, ed. Cretzianu, p. 168.

[15] Radu Plessia, "Financial Policy," in *ibid.*, p. 123.

[16] Emil Ciurea, "Education," in *ibid.*, p. 207. See also Ionescu, *Communism in Rumania*, pp. 175–176. Rationality, it can be said, is a function of one's goals as well as the relationship between the means employed and the goals that are specified. Given the Romanian Party's goal of completely redefining the Romanian social system, widespread purges were rational. The timing of the purges, the manner in which they were carried out, and the treatment of those purged in many instances were undoubtedly irrational.

ing personnel, partly by substituting Soviet models for Western ones. Finally, to supply the larger number of administrative personnel needed and to ensure the proper political socialization, the Law on Education provided for the creation of special schools designed to produce cadres that were politically and ideologically committed to the Party.

Despite these examples, it is an open question as to how much of the Romanian elite's breaking-through behavior involved the rational as opposed to the irrational use of violence. How much was systematically related to the goal of transforming and/or constraining established elements within its environment, to enhancing the Party's institutional strengths, to recommitting strategic elements within the population to the Party, and laying the foundation for the appearance of a new political community based on an unmanipulated and uncoerced reciprocity between elite and public is difficult to say. The significant incidence of irrationality has been recognized by the present leader of the Romanian Party and State, Nicolae Ceauşescu. Speaking to the cadres of the Ministry of Internal Affairs in July, 1967, Ceauşescu made this comment:

> In their speeches some comrades justly referred to the fact that in the course of years, especially at the beginning, there was sometimes a lack of political discernment in the activity of the security organs, no distinction being made between hostile activity, directed against the revolutionary gains of the people, and some manifestations linked to the natural process of transforming the people's consciousness and mode of thinking. Therefore, some abuses and transgressions of socialist legality were committed, measures were taken against some citizens that were not justified by their acts and manifestations.[17]

The Romanian elite may have been given formal recognition to the need for persuasion and the judicious use of coercion, but in many critical instances it failed to uphold this ideological tenet. One such instance was the process of collectivization. Gheorghiu-Dej expressed a formal awareness of the role of persuasion in his

---

[17] Nicolae Ceauşescu, "Cuvîntarea . . . la consfătuirea cu activul de bază al Ministerului Afacerilor Interne," *Scînteia*, July 19, 1967.

speech of 1951 on "The Tasks of the Romanian Workers Party in the Struggle for the Strengthening of the Alliance of the Working Class with the Working Peasantry and for the Socialist Transformation of Agriculture.[18] Nonetheless, the incidence of "administrative measures" was enough to warrant comments on at least two different occasions. In criticizing the Pauker faction at the 1955 Congress, Gheorghiu-Dej accused it of "trampling on the principle of free consent by the peasant-workers in the socialist transformation of agriculture," of instigating provocative measures, and striking a blow at the alliance of the working class and working peasantry.[19] Whether or not Pauker and/or Luca were directly at fault, the first attempts at collectivization were highly irrational. In 1961 Gheorghiu-Dej noted that "in the name of the struggle against the Kulaks, more than 80,000 peasants, most of them working peasants, were sent for trial; more than 300,000 . . . were tried in public which provoked great concern among the peasant masses brought to attend these infamous frame-ups."[20]

A second and very remarkable instance of the irrational use of violence involved the Danube Black Sea Canal project. This project, initiated, it appears, by Comecon in 1949, was intended to produce a positive symbolic and expressive reaction and involved the large-scale mobilization of scarce human and material resources. According to Bossy, between one- and two-thirds of the labor force was made up of various categories of political prisoners,[21] persons who were "members of the former democratic parties . . . middle classes, recalcitrant members of the intelligentsia, 'kulaks,' . . . 'saboteurs,' or 'idle workers'."[22] The economic outcome of this project has been described as follows:

---

[18] Gh. Gheorghiu-Dej, "Sarcinile P.M.R. în lupta pentru întărirea alianţei clasei muncitoare cu ţărănimea muncitoare şi pentru transformarea socialistă a agriculturii," in *Articole şi Cuvîntări*, p. 285; see also pp. 227–287.

[19] Gh. Gheorghiu-Dej, *Rapport d'activité*, p. 164.

[20] Ionescu, *Communism in Rumania*, p. 201, quoting from *Scînteia*, December 7, 1961.

[21] George H. Bossy, "Transportation and Communications," in Fischer-Galati, ed., *Romania*, p. 340; see also Ionescu, *Communism in Rumania*, pp. 194–195.

[22] Ionescu, *Communism in Rumania*, p. 195.

By 1952 only 3 kilometers (of a projected 75) of the canal were completed, and by 1953 when work on the canal was stopped only 7
kilometers had been fully excavated. The whole project, the major
project of the regime during its first decade in power — ended in utter
failure. The lives of thousands of Romanian workers, enormous investments, and millions of hours of back-breaking labor had been
wasted on 7 kilometers of canal, some swamp drainage and irriga-
tion, one cement factory, two thermoelectric plants, and 78 kilometers of new roads.[23]

Politically, also, the project was a failure. In the first place the
regime made very little if any attempt to resocialize the political
prisoners; it was a strictly coercive undertaking. And as a symbolic
endeavor it brought only scorn from the people: it hardly fulfilled the elite's promises of achievement, and it was too obviously
associated with Soviet demands expressed through Comecon.

The obvious question is, why was there such a high incidence
of irrationality accompanying the breaking-through process in
Romania during the period 1948–1953? An answer to this question involves the highly emulative nature of the Romanian attempt
to break through, and the noticeably uncritical manner of emulation. Given the significant connection between unthinking or non-
selective emulation and the irrational use of violence, the obvious
question to pursue is why the Romanian elite demonstrated a
marked propensity to emulate so uncritically.

Here again one must go back to the distinctive quality of the
Romanian elite's formative experience and context. Most members of the elite nucleus of the Party had had prison experiences.
One point has already been made with regard to this prison experience: namely, that in so far as it allowed for some degree of
political-ideological socialization, for the formation of cohesive ties
among at least certain elite elements, and for the partial formulation of general policy orientations, it was analogous to the partisan
experience of the Chinese communists. Importantly, however, the
differences between the (Chinese) partisan and (Romanian) prison
experiences are far more consequential than the similarities. To
begin with, important sections of the Romanian elite did not

---

[23] Bossy, pp. 340–341.

"enjoy" this experience. Furthermore, those who did not often underwent quite different formative experiences. But the most critical difference in the formative experience of the two elites has to do with the character of the isolation imposed by prison experience in contrast to that associated with a partisan experience. Here we can view "prison existence" as a general experience which may assume a number of forms; its distinguishing characteristic is the inability of an elite in such a context to test as well as formulate its political principles. A partisan experience allows for precisely such testing, feedback, error correction, and reinforcement. Thus, the Chinese elite came to power with "a set of political principles that it had tested for several years in . . . areas . . . under Communist control." [24] Unlike the Chinese, the Romanians who had had a "prison experience" did not acquire a "practical ideology" directly related to its specific national environment. [25]

In addition, its dependent mode of coming to power critically undermined the Romanian elite's capacity to control fundamental aspects of its organization and leadership. Consequently, even in power this elite was highly circumscribed in terms of its ability to focus on, learn from, or act on its environment. [26]

---

[24] James Townsend, *Political Participation in Communist China*, p. 36.

[25] "In the post-liberation period, a period of intensive economic and cultural upbuilding, of the radical reorganization of society, our Party was faced with a multitude of completely new problems and tasks. Although as is known, we have scored big successes in all spheres, we must say that sometimes we were lacking the necessary experience and knowledge to find and adopt the most adequate solutions. This is also due to the fact that in the years of underground activity our Party did not always pay due attention to the thorough studying of the problems and social development of Romania, to the concrete particularities and balance of forces within the Romanian society. . . . The consequences became more evident when, after taking over, our Party was confronted by some problems for which it was not yet adequately prepared." Nicolae Ceaușescu, *The Leading Role of the Party in the Period of Completing Socialist Construction* (pamphlet issued by Agerpress: May 8, 1967; published in *Scînteia*, May 7, 1967), pp. 7–8.

[26] One major stumbling block to the development of political competence once the elite had gained power was the ever present factionalism — notwithstanding Gheorghiu-Dej's assertion in 1946 that "In the leadership of our party dissension is unable to exist because the leaders of the party do

The high incidence of uncritical emulation by the Romanian elite is to be explained then not simply in terms of Soviet demands for detailed emulation but also in terms of the elite's uncertainty as to how to achieve an ideologically and politically correct breakthrough. This uncertainty was related not only to the magnitude of the endeavor, but also to the Romanian elite's lack of politically and situationally relevant experiences and principles. It is within this context that the mechanistic adoption of the Soviet model and the high incidence of irrationality associated with the process of breaking through can be understood.

How to Define Success

The tasks of defining, relating, and understanding the rational and irrational components of the Romanian breaking-through process raise a more general question. Within the Romanian context we must ask to what extent the process of breaking through was successful. But in order to do this we must first of all be clear about our definition of "successful." In a recent work Reinhard Bendix points out that although all development is partial in that it involves "various amalgams of tradition and modernity," it is necessary to "distinguish between types of partial development."[27] An obvious implication of Bendix's argument is that one learns very little from statements that merely point out the partial nature of any breakthrough. He is also implying, quite rightly, that success is not so much a matter of degree as a matter of quality. To talk about a lack of thorough penetration by a communist party, or of "thorough subordination," as some writers do, means very little and if anything is misleading. We are still left with the task of establishing the definition of a successful breakthrough. A look at the relationship that existed between the Romanian Party and certain strategic social strata such as the peasantry and the intelligentsia may provide us with the elements of an answer.

It is known that as of December, 1955, "the whole socialist

---

not represent individual or factional interests" (*Articole şi Cuvîntări*, p. 80). This factional conflict was of course sustained and to some extent provoked by the Romanian Party's dependent relationship vis-à-vis the Soviet Union.

[27] Reinhard Bendix, *Nation-Building and Citizenship*, p. 9.

sector (state farms, state land, collective farms, and agricultural associations) covered only 26.5 per cent of the country's arable land."[28] If one defines success in terms of degree, it would appear that the Romanian breakthrough in this critical area was not a success. The elite's policy toward at least one sector of the intelligentsia also seems to exemplify partial (i.e., unsuccessful) breaking through. For example, Ionescu has pointed out that although at first the Party treated the intelligentsia "as class and party enemies rather than as specially equipped elements useful to society,"[29] with the post-1948 stress on industrialization the regime began to differentiate between the technical and creative intelligentsia: "After 1949 . . . a partial truce was called in the persecution of the former bourgeois architects, agronomists, engineers, scientists . . . and all kinds of technicians. Some of them were released from prison, quickly rehabilitated, and quickly given jobs of responsibility."[30] Ionescu discusses the implication of this "truce" in terms that are directly related to the question of breaking through. He suggests that after a period of time the intelligentsia in both the Soviet Union and Romania received special positions. In the Soviet Union, this intelligentsia "was often yesterday's workers and peasants (or sons of) whereas in Rumania this stratum was of hired middle-class specialists . . . the social crystallization which thus took place in a much shorter time caught in it quite different layers, men and mentalities. These men were differently moulded, above all, in their attitude towards the state."[31]

Here the Soviet experience is taken as the norm. Moreover, the assumption is made that in gauging the success of the break-through process, the chief question is degree (how much change) rather than quality (what kind of change). There is even in the final statement a certain assumption which, intentionally or unconsciously, subsumes the question of quality under degree.

But despite all this, there are several significant aspects of the

---

[28] Ghita Ionescu, "Social Structure: Rumania Under Communism," *Annals of the American Academy of Political and Social Science* 317 (May 1958): 54.

[29] *Communism in Rumania*, p. 238.

[30] *Ibid.*, p. 176.

[31] "Social Structure," p. 62.

Romanian elite's relationship with the technical intelligentsia which lead one to conclude that although the process of breaking through in this area was partial, it was rather successful. As Ionescu himself notes,[32] many technical personnel were replaced by rapidly trained workers and peasants. Also, it is fair to suggest that the high degree of coercion applied to significant members of the technical intelligentsia between 1948 and 1950 deterred any overtly hostile acts when some of them were reinstated and made them anxious to demonstrate their usefulness and even trustworthiness. Indeed, comparative data relating to the behavior of restored technical personnel would suggest that the reinstatement of such individuals does not in itself threaten the decisiveness of the breaking-through process. Azrael, for example, in his analysis of the Soviet co-optation of old regime technical specialists, points out that "resistance [by the specialists] appears to have given way not to passive compliance with orders but to conscientious collaboration and active cooperation." In explaining this phenomenon, Azrael correctly singles out the critical role that professionalism played among many of these specialists who "subscribed to ideologies that radically denigrated the utility of all political activity and elevated intense participation in professional activity either to a transcendant value in its own right or to a paramount obligation within the framework of a broader ethic of nonpartisan public service or supra-political, developmental nationalism." Azrael isolates another factor which operated to remove the potential threat posed by widespread reinstatement when he explains why "bourgeois specialists often became convinced of the validity of Bolshevik goals and procedures." He argues that this conviction was largely due to the "consensus generating effects of access to executive privileges and perquisites" as well as to the "impact of involvement in responsible work."[33] At a higher level of analysis, Azrael's point indicates the probability of a change in attitude as a function of a changing social-political context and set of reference groups.

These points cannot, of course, be mechanically transferred

---

[32] *Communism in Rumania*, p. 176.

[33] See Jeremy Azrael, *Managerial Power and Soviet Politics*, pp. 29, 35, 50.

to the Romanian case, but they do appear to be essentially valid in that context as well as in the Soviet. It seems plausible to conclude that the Romanian elite could count on the professionalism of its reinstated technical personnel and could also expect to see significant changes in attitude related to the redefined political context within which such personnel operated. In May, 1967, Ceauşescu remarked: ". . . if our Party has managed to successfully solve the big tasks incumbent on it, this has been due as well to the fact that concomitant with the advance of cadres from the ranks of workers and peasants, it paid outstanding heed to the old specialists. . . . We can state with satisfaction that the old cadres of specialists . . . made a valuable contribution to the achievements of the Romanian people in building up socialism."[34]

Also as in the Soviet case, the monopoly the R.W.P. possessed over employment worked to suppress any conflict that might have appeared within the ranks of the technical intelligentsia between loyalty to profession and loyalty to the organization. Since all organizations were run by the same elite, there was very little room for conflict between what Gouldner has termed cosmopolitan and local orientations.[35] Finally, one must take into account the special kind of support the Romanian elite wanted to elicit from its technical personnel. Given its emphasis on breaking through, the Romanian elite was primarily concerned with effective technical performance. At that point the Romanian elite was probably more interested in getting the technical intelligentsia to recognize the Party's power than in ensuring the loyalty of reinstated bourgeois personnel. Because of the Party's instrumental orientation toward the technical intelligentsia, the Party elite did not fear that the

[34] *The Leading Role of the Party in the Period of Completing Socialist Construction.* Ceauşescu made similar remarks in his speech to the Union of Communist Youth (*utecişti*) on February 11, 1968 (*Scînteia*), where he noted the Party's success in uniting the efforts of the older (bourgeois) intelligentsia with those of the new socialist intelligentsia.

[35] On the question of loyalty to organization *vs.* loyalty to profession, see Peter M. Blau and W. Richard Scott, *Formal Organizations* (San Francisco, 1962), p. 71; and Alvin W. Gouldner, "Cosmopolitans and Locals: Toward an Analysis of Latent Social Roles — I, II," *Administrative Science Quarterly* 2 (1957–1958): 281–306 and 444–480.

use of coercion would bring a reversal of support from them. In other words, the type of support it cared about was compatible with a fairly wide use of coercive sanctions.

To turn to the agricultural sphere, it is quite true that after the Party's initially violent and irrational approach to this question encountered strong opposition from the peasants,[36] the Party redefined its posture and began to act more consistently on its commitment to persuasion. By 1955 only one-quarter of the arable land was under "socialist" management. This could be said to bear out Marx's reasoning that "whomever one seeks to persuade, one acknowledges as master of the situation."[37] In order to ascertain who was "master," however, one must place the party-peasant relationship in context. The Party was indeed weak, and this was especially revealed in its experience with collectivization. But one must remember that, owing to the destruction of the established political parties, the monarchy, and the propertied classes, the subordination of the major religious institutions, and the Party's control of the media, police, and army, the peasants had no way of expressing their opposition by political means or through politically relevant institutions. This absence of a political context along with the presence of a Soviet force meant that the peasants could only obstruct. Lacking political organization the peasants were a threat to the regime, but a manageable one.

Within this context Stalin's words, when applied to the Romanian elite's concessions to the peasants in 1951 and 1953, have a good deal of significance. According to Stalin, "it is not a matter of reforms or of compromises and agreements, but of the

---

[36] Peasant opposition was quite evident. According to Ionescu: "In the winter of 1949 and throughout 1950 the peasants opposed the teams of collectivizers . . . The militia and even the army were brought in against the villagers. Long sieges were laid against entire regions, and with the help of some partisan groups, the peasants fought pitched battles against the forces of the government. The regions Dolj, Argeş, Bihor, Bucharest, Timişoara, Vlaşca, Hunedoara and the part of Western Transylvania populated by Moti were the scenes of such events." *Communism in Rumania*, p. 200.

[37] See Karl Marx, *The Eighteenth Brumaire of Louis Bonaparte* (New York, 1963), p. 88. The real question is, of course, what sort of "master"; that is, what kind of power does one's opponent possess?

use people make of reforms and agreements." That is to say, it is the conditions under which reforms occur that determine their meaning and outcome. Of course, within any concrete historical situation, there is no absolute certainty as to the consequences of a given policy, but Stalin's argument is persuasive: with the establishment of the "dictatorship of the proletariat," he said, reformist policies may actually have the effect of "disintegrating" hostile strata, classes, or organizations while simultaneously affording the revolution a respite and giving it an opportunity to "recuperate its forces and prepare the conditions for a new offensive."[38] His scenario was in fact closely approximated in Romania: concessions in 1951 were followed by offensives in 1952, concessions in 1953, and renewed offensives in 1955, leading to the almost total predominance of the socialist sector in agriculture in 1962.[39]

In summary, several points can be made about the Romanian breakthrough and about the process of breaking through in general. First, all political breakthroughs are partial; decisive breakthroughs may be defined as those that make a return to the *status quo ante* impossible.

Second, in order to accomplish a decisive (or successful) breakthrough it is necessary to transform or constrain the institutions at all levels of the polity that allow for the political presentation of counterelite values.

Third, an elite engaged in breaking through must eliminate all alternatives to support — if only in the form of obedience — of

---

[38] J. V. Stalin, *The Foundations of Leninism* (Peking, 1965), pp. 98, 99.

[39] See J. M. Montias, *Economic Development in Communist Rumania*, pp. 88–91. I am in no way implying that an omniscient Romanian revolutionary elite programmed a set of revolutionary-reformist approaches to the question of collectivization, i.e., so controlled its environment that it was always capable of knowing precisely when to stress a "reformist" approach to the peasantry and was always in complete control. Undoubtedly, the situation between 1949 and 1955 was more open than this. But I do think that the Romanian elite's emphasis on breaking through made it more likely that occasional switches to a reformist stance would not jeopardize its ability to undertake a systematic redefinition. By denying oppositional elements any political outlet for their grievances, the Romanian elite increased its chances of relating reformist measures to revolutionary goals.

its policies. Such an effort can be based on an elite's own strength and/or the support rendered to such an elite by an external power.

Finally, in order to achieve a successful or decisive break-through the elite must show substantial commitment to a policy, or policies, designed to bring about the socio-economic transformation of the system and to produce added increments of support from strategically located social strata.

Leninist elites, it seems to me, face fewer organizational-ideological constraints than other elites in achieving a decisive breakthrough and are in fact positively aided by their ideology in their attempts at breaking through. A useful context for the elaboration of these points is a comparison of fascist and Leninist elites.

Eugen Weber, one of the foremost students of fascism and of Romanian history, has convincingly argued that facists are concerned with destroying the settled order, and that fascists are not the same as reactionaries.[40] Nevertheless, it is evident that fascists have not achieved any great success in the quest for social transformation, at least in comparison with Leninist regimes. In any intensive, specific comparison of the two, the relative weight of organizational and situational constraints would have to be ascertained, but it appears that organizational and particularly ideological factors play a critical and independent role in the failure of fascist regimes to achieve a successful breakthrough.

In the first place, fascism stresses class cooperation whereas Leninism stresses class antagonism. Secondly, fascists (particularly the Romanian Iron Guard) stressed the priority of men over programs, whereas Leninists,[41] and specifically Romanian Leninists,

---

[40] See Eugen Weber, *Varieties of Fascism* (New York, 1964), p. 14.

[41] On the point of class antagonism *vs.* class cooperation see *ibid.*, p. 46; and A. James Gregor, "African Socialisms, Socialism and Fascism: An Appraisal," *Review of Politics*, 29 (July 1967): 345. On "Men over programs," see Weber, *Varieties of Fascism*, p. 105. A. F. K. Organski's "Fascism and Modernization," in *The Nature of Fascism*, ed. S. J. Woolf (New York, 1969), is one of the best general analyses of fascism, although it does have two major shortcomings: it does not adequately recognize the relative autonomy enjoyed by fascist political parties in relation to their social-economic basis of support, and in addition, although Organski appears to be correct in his conclusion that fascist elites act to preserve the socio-political status quo, he does not

stress programs and men. Finally, Leninists in general and particularly the Romanian Leninists have stressed one specific program — industrialization. It is this combination of an instrumental orientation, a view of class struggle as necessary and beneficial, and an intense commitment to the specific program of industrialization that makes the Leninist breakthrough distinctive and contributes to the elite's chances for a decisive breakthrough.

---

sufficiently analyze the interplay between those aspects of fascist ideology that are change-oriented and those that are maintenance-oriented. Such an analysis would allow for a better understanding of the complexity of fascism and of why its revolutionary orientations fail and conservative-reactionary elements succeed in providing its basic thrust. I should note that in my view Nazism is something quite different from Fascism.

8

The Breaking-Through Process
and Industrialization

IN DISCUSSING the founding of a new republic, Machiavelli suggested that "he is to be reprehended who commits violence for the purpose of destroying, and not he who employs it for beneficient purposes."[1] Leninist elites such as the Romanian elite perceive a dual nature in the process of breaking through — a negative or destructive aspect and a positive or constructive aspect. In the Party's words: "Social-historical practice has revealed the weakness of the theses of bourgeois propaganda which attempts in a slanderous fashion to reduce the socialist revolution to a work of destruction and the role of the socialist state to that of violence. The creative, constructive aspect represents, as pointed out repeatedly by Lenin, the fundamental aspect of the dictatorship of the proletariat."[2] The constructive aspect is defined as industrialization; more important, the negative and positive aspects of breaking through are

---

[1] Niccolo Machiavelli, *The Prince and The Discourses*, p. 139.
[2] *The Plan of the Romanian People's Republic for 1949*, pp. 8, 29.

seen as interdependent, Thus, the use of coercion to transform or constrain established elements within the society creates the social space within which the process of industrialization can take place. Simultaneously, that process makes a critical contribution to the goal of a decisive breakthrough. In this sense, Party-directed industrialization was not simply an economic process but also a coercive-political endeavor,[3] which contributed to the process of breaking through to the extent that it contributed to widespread social mobilization. In Brzezinski's words, "the masses flocking to the cities and industrial work sites were hoping for something they did not clearly grasp but by coming they were helping to weaken the existing social bonds, to undermine the social institutions of the past which the Communists felt had to fall."[4] Gheorghiu-Dej formulated the relationship of industrialization and breaking through as follows: "To the existence of a developed industry is connected the existence of the working class which represents a guarantee of the democratization of our public life, a guarantee of the liquidation of feudalism and landlords."[5] In short, the Romanian elite perceived rapid and comprehensive industrialization as an essential component of a decisive breakthrough.

Type of Industrialization and Commitment to Industrialization

Beginning in 1949 a radical change occurred in Romania in the conditions under which choices affecting industrialization were made, in the criteria for decisions, and in the vision behind such decisions. During the interwar period "industrial progress . . . was mainly of the import substituting kind, typical of developing countries in the world today. As late as 1938 finished industrial

---

[3] The process of industrialization in the context of a revolutionary breakthrough approximates very closely Weber's notion of "economically oriented action," i.e., action which though "primarily oriented to economic ends, [makes] use of physical force as a means." Max Weber, *The Theory of Social and Economic Organization*, p. 159.

[4] Zbigniew Brzezinski, *The Soviet Bloc* (Cambridge, Mass., 1967), p. 102.

[5] Gh. Gheorghiu-Dej, "Raportul . . . Octombrie 1945," in *Articole și Cuvîntări*, p. 54.

products still represented only 2 per cent of total exports, while exports of machinery and equipment were negligible up to World War II."[6] But with the definition and direction of industrialization in the hands of the Romanian Workers (Communist) Party, there was a rather significant shift in the character of that process: "Under Communist leadership . . . industrialization has not been limited to import substitution; the transformation of the economy has also had a remarkable impact on exports. In 1948 finished industrial products made up 7.2 per cent of exports, in 1956, 19.6 per cent."[7]

The attempts at industrialization were in many respects as inefficient as those of the interwar period, but were not piecemeal, and certainly the more recent considerations attached to industrialization were quite different from those of the pre-communist period. From 1948 on, industrialization was aimed at increasing the size of the working class and breaking through the "middle classes" — just the opposite of what it had been in the interwar period.[8]

One general point can be made here. Industrialization is not a neutral-technical process. What is significant in terms of its "place" in the nation-building process is its character: the conditions under which it occurs, and the political-ideological orientations that shape it, particularly the value that is attached to it. To understand the nation-building process in Romania since 1945, one must have some appreciation and understanding of the relationship that has existed between the breaking-through process and the type of industrialization that was effected, and to do this one must consider the type of commitment the Romanian elite made to its industrialization program. Leninist elites demon-

---

[6] J. M. Montias, *Economic Development in Communist Rumania*, p. 10.

[7] *Ibid.*

[8] As Stoianovich points out in his article on the "Social Foundations of Balkan Politics," although the government of interwar Romania (like those of Greece, Bulgaria, and Yugoslavia), "tried to solve the economic crisis by fostering industrial development . . . the governments were afraid that an overly rapid increase in the number of industrial workers might lead to their overthrow and the establishment of a new social regime." See *The Balkans in Transition*, ed. Charles and Barbara Jelavich, pp. 339–340.

strate a propensity to elevate instrumental values "to the level of consummatory values with the result that the goals of the state, *particularly those of modernization and industrialization, become sacrosanct*," [9] and the Romanian elite has been no exception.

Commitment and Consequences

Such an ideological commitment significantly affected the Romanian Party's desire and capacity to achieve a decisive revolutionary breakthrough and also affected its ordering of policy priorities. The absolute commitment to the process of industrialization provided the regime with the "resolve, faith, and enthusiasm" that Gheorghiu-Dej deemed necessary in the removing of obstacles to the elite's goals and increased the regime's capacity to accept and rationalize the various costs involved in large-scale social change. The critical role assigned to industrialization in the process of social transformation served to justify the Party's impersonal and coercive attitude toward its national constituency and thereby facilitated a breakthrough. The absolute commitment to industrialization also implied that this policy was not negotiable, that its priority for the Romanians was unquestionable. The Soviet decision in 1948 to make such a policy incumbent on all East European elites had the effect of reinforcing the absolute nature of the R.W.P.'s commitment to industrialization, its desire to translate that commitment into policy, and its confidence in its ability to do so successfully. [10]

---

[9] David Apter, *The Politics of Modernization*, p. 359; (italics added).

[10] For an excellent discussion of the relation between the Soviet "command" to East European elites to industrialize and the confidence of these elites that they could do so, see Paul Shoup, "Communism, Nationalism, and the Growth of the Communist Community of Nations after World War II," *American Political Science Review* 56 (December 1962): 890. On the whole, this article is the finest to date on the relation of nationalism and communism in Eastern Europe.

9

The Breaking-Through Process
and Community Building

BETWEEN 1945 AND 1955 the lowest item on the Romanian elite's scale of priorities was the direct concern with creating a new political community. In saying this I do not mean to suggest that the Party was uninterested in the question of political integration, but I do mean that it was extremely reluctant to base this integration on any form of authority that would involve normative and structural commitments to its national public. The position is not, I think, strange, if one realizes that in order for the Party to become legitimate so early in its history it would have had to refrain from the purposive use of violence and coercion to attain a decisive breakthrough and would have had to compromise its commitment to rapid and comprehensive industrialization.

Because of the reluctance of Leninist elites to make compromises and commitments to individuals, publics, and environments perceived as unreconstructed, their approach to social, political, and cultural development is quite different from that held by prominent Western theorists of national development. Pye, for example, argues thus: "The problems of development, viewed in terms of political culture, involve less the gross elimination of old patterns and values and more the successful discovery of how traditions can contribute to, and not hamper, the realization of current national goals." [1] In particular, so-called civic cultures differ significantly from Leninist systems in that the former are supposedly characterized by "gradual political development . . . [relatively] unforced . . . developed by fusion, new patterns of attitudes did not replace old ones, but merged with them." [2] Leninist political systems, at least in their initial stages, are not "cultures of moderation" and are interested in the selective reintegration of tradition only *after* the political relevance of tradition has been decisively altered. In fact, Leninist elites maintain that only in this way can tradition contribute to the realization of national goals. Although there is much in the Leninist argument that deserves consideration, I am especially interested here in showing that, in identifying and acting as a Leninist elite, the Romanian elite was not primarily concerned with coming to terms with tradition or with authority building at this particular stage. Rather, it was concerned with breaking through, industrialization, and party institutionalization. Its endeavors were system and state oriented, not community and nation oriented precisely because it was the nation *as it existed* that was to be transformed. This is not to suggest, however, that the Romanian elite's intentions, priorities, and policies have not had important consequences for the appearance of a new national political community.

On Authority Building

Given our interpretation, it is necessary to deal with a hypothesis that is much at variance with it. In an excellent article Alfred Meyer argues that shortly after coming to power, communist elites experience a dramatic loss of authority. Consequently, "the task

---

[1] Lucian Pye, "Introduction: Political Culture and Political Development," in *Political Culture and Political Development*, ed. Lucian Pye and Sidney Verba (Princeton, 1965), p. 19.

[2] Gabriel Almond and Sidney Verba, *The Civic Culture* (Princeton, 1963), p. 506.

of re-establishing authority must also impress itself on the communist leadership with the utmost urgency. In fact, one of the processes that has characterized communist systems in relatively early phases of their development is one that I have called the 'primitive accumulation of authority.' The primitive accumulation of authority is a desperate attempt which must be made by many revolutionary regimes."[3]

Undoubtedly, all regimes do need some support for certain policies at given times, but Meyer's argument is inadequate in certain respects, and also misleading. To begin with, the argument that "authority . . . is essential for maintaining a political system, at least in the long run" is irrelevant to the major contention that in the short run ("relatively early phases of their development") Leninist elites make a desperate attempt to accumulate authority. The point should be made that a regime with sufficient strength of its own or with "compensating" sources of strength (such as the Soviet "presence") might be capable of "maintaining [its] dominant position for a period of time with authority playing a minor role"[4] and might even be *anxious* to maintain its immediate position through power rather than authority.[5] The second point is that there are different types of authority. Presthus, for example, notes at least four types: authority through formal role, expertise, generalized deference, and rapport.[6] Undoubtedly, the

---

[3] Alfred Meyer, "Authority in Communist Political Systems," in *Political Leadership in Industrialized Societies*, ed. Lewis J. Edinger, p. 91.

[4] David Easton, *A Systems Analysis of Political Life* (New York, 1965), pp. 278–282.

[5] Jozsef Revai's article ("On the Character of Our People's Democracy," in *Readings on Contemporary Eastern Europe*, ed. C. E. Black) is illuminating on this point. He observes (pp. 88–89) that the dictatorship of the proletariat (i.e., the breaking-through period) "means the exercising of force in oppressing enemies," and that while the dictatorship's essential functions are also constructive, "this does not mean at all that the functions of oppressor and violence . . . should be overlooked as secondary." Revai's entire article is relevant to the point that at the time of breaking through, Leninist elites emphasize power over authority, and also emphasize a very specific type of authority.

[6] Robert V. Presthus, "Authority in Organizations," in *Concepts and Issues in Administrative Behavior*, ed. Sydney Mailick and Edward H. Van Ness (Englewood Cliffs, N.J., 1962), pp. 122–137.

Romanian Party was concerned with gaining recognition of its formal-governmental role, but it was not seeking elite-public rapport except on its own terms—ruling out compromise, commitments, and public constraints. Third, even elites in precarious situations do not have to seek authority from everyone: only certain groups are strategic in terms of elite goals and requirements. The question is whether or not normative incentives are always necessary to elicit the type of performance required from such groups by the regime. For a Leninist elite such as the Romanian, concerned with breaking through and industrialization, the police and skilled technicians might be two strategic groups; and as I suggested earlier, the experience of the Romanian regime would seem to indicate that the use of utilitarian and coercive incentives, together with invidious status comparisons, was more than adequate to bring about the proper performance from strategic groups and the desired type of integration. Fourth, there seems to be a contradiction in Meyer's description of authority building in that for him power, unlike authority, "is founded on coercion and fear rather than legitimacy."[7] If this is so, then the argument that coercion is one of the means Leninist elites employ to gain *authority* is a basic contradiction ("Communist leaders . . . appear to operate on the assumption that coercive methods of accumulating authority are indispensable at least during the period of an initial breakthrough . . .).[8] Finally, it is puzzling that although Meyer carefully distinguishes the period of system building from that of culture (or community building) he assigns the process of "desperate" authority building to the system-building stage rather than to the community-building stage where it logically belongs in terms of his own argument and certainly in terms of ours.

The Locus and Character of Authority Building

It is my contention that to the extent that authority building was a priority in Romania during the stage of breaking through and initial industrialization, its main locus and thrust was within the Party itself. Furthermore, the type of authority that was sought

---

[7] Meyer, p. 91.

[8] *Ibid.*, p. 92.

after and established within the Party as well as within certain elements of society was one based on norms of generalized deference and individual obedience to Party commands rather than on norms of elite-public rapport and reciprocity.

As I pointed out earlier, the Romanian elite was not uninterested in the creation of a new national political community during its first ten years of power, but that task was of less importance than the creation of a body of political cadres. These cadres would serve as prototypes for the new socialist man, and being deeply committed to the Party and its goals, they would help to effect a breakthrough and would be the active agents behind the process of national mobilization. At this point the Party concern for community building at the national level was real but indirect.

There is evidence that the Romanian elite was not the only Leninist elite that adopted this orientation and established such a set of priorities upon assuming power and engaging in a breakthrough. If Bendix is correct, the East German elite's concern with and definition of authority building was in many ways similar to the Romanian's at the same stage of development, that is, when the process of breaking through was considered the "core" problem.

According to Bendix, the demand of the Socialist Unity Party of Germany (S.E.D.) for "contact with the masses" and its attitude toward "activists" were both based on the party's concern with "control over its own apparatus." Thus "contact with the masses" was designed to encourage criticism and self-criticism within the party itself. In consequence, "the distance between functionaries and the 'laboring people' is deliberately enlarged, and . . . the involvement of the functionaries in the activities of the party is rendered still more irrevocable." As for the party's concern with "activists" who were sympathetic or at least not antagonistic toward its goals, Bendix points out that the S.E.D. attempted to "drive a wedge between the 'masses' and all those who are brought by one means or another to cooperate with the party."[9] One might argue that the party's policy toward activists was a case of authority building: (a) that although the S.E.D. (and the R.W.P. in

---

[9] Reinhard Bendix, *Work and Authority in Industry* (New York, 1956), pp. 415, 429–430.

Romania) mistrusted the greater part of the population and was unwilling to establish authority relations with it, (*b*) the party attempted to isolate certain potential support elements, identified them as the nucleus of a new national political community, and established authority relations with them. However, this argument does not hold for either East Germany or Romania. As Bendix has stated, the party created an environment of suspicion and hostility around the activists:

> By so doing the party maximizes its managerial control over its functionaries at the same time that it obtains the cooperation of individual activists under conditions which ensure that they will remain as isolated from each other as they are isolated from their fellow-workers. Activists constitute a collective of individuals, who are all equally dependent upon the party for the satisfaction of their economic interests, but these interests do not result in a common understanding among them.[10]

In Romania as well as in East Germany the low level of party institutionalization, the need for effectively socialized and deployable cadres to implement an ambitious mobilization program of breaking through and industrializaiton, and the ideological strictures against making commitments to an unreconstructed system and population were reflected in a political elite which was primarily interested in control, power, and system transformation rather than in reciprocity, authority, and community definition.[11]

---

[10] *Ibid.*, p. 432.

[11] Powerful though Bendix's argument is, it tends, I think, to be too absolute and too narrow. It does not sufficiently take into account the relationship that exists in Leninist systems between an emphasis on a particular core problem such as breaking through and a particular stance toward the existing community as well as its own political organization. With the accomplishment of a decisive breakthrough there tends to appear within these systems arguments for a different definition of the party and of its relation to the population. Also, the party's concern with control over its cadres even during the breakthrough phase was based on more than power premises. It was intimately related to the concern with mobilization, breaking through, and industrializing. Bendix's use of the "totalitarian model" diminishes his appreciation of the "developmental stage" and policy aspects of the party's behavior during its first years of power.

The paramount concern of both the R.W.P. and the S.E.D. was the party's authority over its own members. Mobilization, the processes of breaking through, and industrialization were defined as the major priorities and essential conditions for the appearance of a new political community. To effect a breakthrough, the party needed a body of cadres primarily and in an ideal sense exclusively committed to the party and its goals. In Gheorghiu-Dej's words, "in the period of socialist construction, the cadres decide all." [12]

Mobilization and Integration

The goal, policy, and process of breaking through were related to community building through the mediating process of mobilization, which by means of party cadres can bring individuals "into networks that involve them directly or indirectly in public affairs." [13] In Romania, cadre-directed mobilization significantly contributed to a more effective integration of elite and mass insofar as the Romanian Party effectively penetrated all areas of social life and either stimulated the appearance of "conscious priorities on a general scale for the first time where none existed previously" [14] or brought about the redefinition of such priorities, goals, and reference groups where they already existed wtihin the non-elite, non-Party sectors of the population. [15] It was to such a process of political penetration and redefinition that Gheorghiu-Dej referred in 1948 in his comment that a "Chinese wall existed between the

---

[12] Gh. Gheorghiu-Dej, *Rapport d'activité*, p. 186.

[13] Samuel Barnes, "Leadership Style and Political Competence," in *Political Leadership in Industrialized Societies*, ed. Lewis J. Edinger, p. 63.

[14] J. P. Nettl, *Political Mobilization*, p. 115.

[15] Too little attention has been paid to the question of how successful Leninist regimes have been in redefining the political cultures of their societies. In the final analysis it is the answer to this question that determines how successful the breakthrough has been. As Leninist regimes turn to the task of political integration, the issue of political culture becomes increasingly significant. This is true both for the political elites in those systems and for those students who wish to delineate the ways in which these countries have been changed after twenty-five years of Marxist–Leninist ideology, organization, and policy.

citizen and the state-apparatus" under the "capitalist-landlord regimes.[16] One result of breaking through was to be the effective political penetration of the population and its incorporation into new, explicitly political forms. In this way the "wall" was to be destroyed (*zidul acesta este surpat*).

It is possible then to argue that the process of breaking through was related to the goal and process of national community building insofar as it brought about the politicization of greater portions of the Romanian population and allowed for a greater degree of integration between the political elite and society. One instance of this process has already been suggested, namely, the migration to the cities and factories which accompanied industrialization. In Romania, "during the first industrialization drive, urbanization proceeded at a rapid pace in conjunction with the rise in employment in industry and other socialized sectors: the urban population increased from 3,747,000 in 1948 (23.5%) to an estimated 4,424,000 in 1953 (26.3% of the population)."[17]

The relationship between breaking through, mobilization, and the goal of creating a new socialist nation is most striking, however, in the R.W.P.'s policy toward the peasants. Somewhat paradoxically, the priority accorded industrialization, together with the perceived social, cultural, political, and economic threat seen as residing in the countryside, resulted in the mobilization, control and integration of the peasant into the socialist system. If the threat "posed" by the peasants reinforced the Romanian elite's commitment to breaking through and industrialization, in turn these commitments brought about an effective penetration by the R.W.P. of Romanian social life, and the mobilization of significant sectors of the Romanian population. The framework as well as the condition for the appearance of a new national political community was thus created.

Several of these points deserve elaboration. To begin with, the Romanian elite's comprehensive definition of the breaking-through and industrialization processes led to the demand that

---

[16] Gh. Gheorghiu-Dej, "Raportul politic al Comitetului Central la Congresul PMR February 21, 1948," in *Articole și Cuvîntări*, p. 125.

[17] J. M. Montias, *Economic Development in Communist Rumania*, p. 29.

agriculture, the rural areas, and the peasantry be major targets. Gheorghiu-Dej stated explicitly in 1949 that "one is not able to construct socialism only in the city. The construction of socialism consists also of the socialist transformation of agriculture."[18] Agricultural transformation was seen as a necessary condition for industrialization, and the latter process was thought to be essential in redefining and breaking through the existing character of peasant life.

The system elevated the working class to the leading position and relegated the peasantry to a secondary and particularly untrusted position, but at the same time it meant that in some respects the effort to integrate the peasantry economically, administratively, and politically was more determined than in systems whose elites claim a basic commitment to the peasants.[19]

This leads to a second point about the character of integration. Integration involves "closing the gap" between elites and their various publics. More precisely, political integration refers to a "shifting relationship between various changing identities within the framework of a variety of possible political arrangements capable of coping with a specifiable range of stresses."[20] Thus, there are different degrees and types of political integration,[21] and it is an open question whether or not a given form of political integration is considered legitimate. In order for a system

---

[18] Gh. Gheorghiu-Dej, "Sarcinile P.M.R. . . . ," in *Articole şi Cuvîntări*, p. 255.

[19] On the low level of political integration between peasants and elite in Mexico and Turkey see L. Vincent Padgett, *The Mexican Political System*, and Kemal Karpat's article on Turkey, *World Politics* 17, no. 1 (1964).

[20] Aristide R. Zolberg, "Patterns of National Integration," *Journal of Modern African Studies* 4 (December 1967): 451–452.

[21] For additional perspectives on political integration the reader is referred to Karl Deutsch et al., "Introduction" to *Political Community and the North Atlantic Area* (Princeton, 1957); Ernst B. Haas, *The Uniting of Europe* (Stanford, 1958), pp. 5–11; Claude Ake, *A Theory of Political Integration* (Homewood, Ill., 1967), esp. pp. 108–110; and Myron Weiner, "Political Integration and Political Development," in *Political Development and Social Change*, ed. Jackson Finkle and Richard W. Gable (New York, 1966), pp. 551–563.

to be integrated, it would appear that as a minimum there must be "passive compliance with the orders of . . . a government." [22]

On this basis then we can say that during this period the Romanian peasantry and the Party were politically integrated but that on the peasants' part compliance was neither active nor spontaneous, given the coercive character of integration.

The phenomenon that best expressed the nature of political integration as it existed during the breakthrough period was the Machine Tractor Station, which as Gheorghiu-Dej pointed out was central to the socialist alliance: "We have the task to develop state machine and tractor stations because they have fulfilled an immensely important role in the consolidation of the alliance of the working-class with the working peasantry, against the kulaks and all of the capitalist elements within the country, and in our policy of convincing and attracting the working-peasantry in the work of constructing socialism." [23] The M.T.S. were basically coercive organizations imposed on the countryside to perform control functions for an elite concerned with concentrating power, minimizing commitments, and transforming its environment. Within this definition, the M.T.S. were supposed to restrict "kulaks" (*chiaburi*), manipulate support from the poor peasants, diffuse technical equipment and information, and, ideally, act as stimuli for the acceptance of cooperative forms of agriculture.

A third and final point concerns the efficacy of this particular "relationship" between Party elite and one critical mass sector: the peasantry.[24] The argument can be made that the leadership style and type of political integration established by the Romanian Party were consistent with its two major goals at the time, breaking through and industrializing, and with its desire to avoid value and structural commitments to what was in its view a threatening, unreconstructed nation.

---

[22] Karl W. Deutsch and William J. Foltz, eds., *Nation-Building* (New York, 1963), p. 7.

[23] Gheorghiu-Dej, "Sarcinile P.M.R. . . . ," p. 274.

[24] I differentiate publics from masses in terms of political awareness, sense of political efficacy, and presence or absence of directive attitudes in regard to presenting demands to regime representatives.

A set of more general considerations about the relationship of political style, political competence, mobilization, and integration tend to support this argument. All nation-building elites must mobilize their populations and provide leadership. As Barnes has said, however, to be effective at mobilization and integration the style of leadership must be related to the level of the public's political competence, the latter consisting of "political skills plus the sense of efficacy necessary for effective political action."[25] In political systems in which a good part of the population consists of parochials[26] — that is, individuals with very little awareness of the political realm: its existence, meaning, or import — the level of political competence is low. And as Barnes has suggested, "there is considerable evidence that people of low political competence cannot be effectively mobilized by democratic styles of leadership. . . . As desirable as the norm of democratic participation is to most of us, in order to achieve effective mobilization, leadership style needs to be fitted to the elevel of political competence of those being led."[27] Moreover, as Frey points out, in settings where the people (i.e., peasants) have low political competence, democratic styles of leadership can obstruct not only effective mobilization but also effective leadership.[28]

It may well be that given its goal of mobilization — breaking through and industrialization — the directive and coercive posture of the Romanian elite was appropriate to the Romanian context.

The Character of the Romanian Political Community, 1945–1955

It is possible to define the Romanian political community during the period of breaking through as a dual compliance system.[29] We

---

[25] Barnes, "Leadership Style," p. 60.

[26] See Almond and Verba, *The Civic Culture*, pp. 3–43, where they discuss parochial, subject, and citizen orientations.

[27] "Leadership Style," pp. 82–83.

[28] See Frederick Frey, "Political Development, Power, and Communications in Turkey," in *Communications and Political Development*, ed. Lucien Pye, p. 325.

[29] The notion of a dual compliance system is taken from Amitai Etzioni, *A Comparative Analysis of Complex Organizations* (New York, 1961), p. 31.

may characterize it as having been a coercive-utilitarian system in which the emphasis on authority relations between community and elite had a low priority. Gheorghiu-Dej indicated how low when in outlining the internal tasks of the Party in 1945 he mentioned "the strengthening of ties with the masses" last.[30] The predominance of commands and messages stressing achievement and performance — that is, instrumental communication — was characteristic of intra-elite as well as elite-public communications, and it was accompanied by a deliberate effort to break up any kind of communication within the society that was perceived as having an expressive or solidary content.[31] Obviously, the Party elite mistrusted the historic, unreconstructed national community and was afraid of making any symbolic or material commitments to it for fear of endangering the tasks of breaking through and industrializing.

One rather direct and important result of the Romanian elite's total commitment to breaking through was its rejection of a traditional nationalist or even a developmental nationalist orientation, which it regarded as clearly inimical to the effective redefinition and transformation of the entire Romanian social system. Neither overtly nor covertly was there during the years 1945–1955 a nationalist slant in the segment of the elite that Gheorghiu-Dej represented.

Not all students agree with this. Fischer-Galati in fact says just the opposite: ". . . few realized that at least as early as 1955 Gheorghe Gheorghiu-Dej and his associates were cautiously pursuing national policies first formulated in 1945 and envisaging a possible eventual assertion of independence from the Kremlin."[32] Much later, it is true, in the early '60s, Gheorghiu-Dej, somewhat unconsciously and with curious results, adopted a distinctly na-

---

[30] Gh. Gheorghiu-Dej, "Raportul . . . Octombrie 1945," in *Articole şi Cuvîntări*, p. 71.

[31] Many writers have termed this situation totalitarianism and "atomization." Whichever concept one uses, however, one cannot in any sense say that there was in Romania at this period a viable political *community*, for such a community depends on norms of reciprocity, on shared sentiments, and mutual recognition, all of which receive some institutional expression.

[32] Stephen Fischer-Galati, *The New Rumania: from People's Democracy to Socialist Republic* (Cambridge, Mass., 1967), p. vii.

tionalist point of view, but between 1945 and 1955, as I shall show, the orientation of the Romanian elite was antinationalist.

Three areas in particular can be used to bring out my thesis: the Pătrășcanu affair, the Tito controversy, and the relationship between the Romanian Workers Party and the Soviet Union.

Lucrețiu Pătrășcanu, who was perhaps the best known and the most accepted of the R.W.P. elite in Romanian noncommunist circles, was both a nationalist and a Leninist, and it appears that he greatly resented the extent and style of Soviet control in Romania after the Second World War. He may also have believed that the Party should make alliances with certain elements within the "historic" parties and exert an effort to build up its authority within the country. Fischer-Galati suggests that Gheorghiu-Dej may actually have harbored certain sympathies with Pătrășcanu, but that if he did he hid them effectively, given his need at that time to demonstrate his "faithfulness to Moscow."[33] Openly, however, Gheorghiu-Dej was hostile, and he and Pătrășcanu were engaged in a struggle for influence (over the Party's orientation) and power that only ended in Pătrășcanu's liquidation in 1954. But beyond simple power, and perhaps a clash in personalities, the hostility between the two was deeper, and directly related to Dej's priority for achieving a decisive breakthrough and to his belief that such a goal could not be achieved if there were a "premature" rapprochement with the population and existing system, that a viable socialist national community could only be possible after a decisive breakthrough. Also, there was a disagreement based on Dej's belief that authority building by a weakly institutionalized revolutionary party such as the R.W.P. would create the very set of constraints that he as a Leninist revolutionary wanted most to avoid. Dej's attitude was informed, then, by at least three considerations: (*a*) considerations relating to personal power, (*b*) material considerations relating to the low level of party institutionalization and the correspondingly fragile capacity of the R.W.P. to deal with the consequences of a reformist strategy in an environment that had not been decisively broken through, and (*c*) ideal considerations relating to Dej's belief

---

[33] *Ibid.*, p. 36.

in the ideological necessity and propriety of a violent breakthrough prior to any emphasis on community building.

Pătrăşcanu's execution in 1954 can also be explained in terms of these same considerations. The execution was not simply a power play by Dej to avoid the possibility that during the "thaw" Pătrăşcanu would be chosen by the Soviets to replace him. In fact, as David Floyd has noted, "it is difficult to believe that Pătrăşcanu represented a real threat to Gheorghiu-Dej in 1954."[34] But in a broader sense, in the context of the immediate post-Stalin period and the Thaw, what Pătrăşcanu stood for could very well have been seen as a personal and programmatic threat by Gheorghiu-Dej and some of his supporters. In the uncertain situation created by Stalin's death, Pătrăşcanu's existence was threatening in that he symbolized a policy orientation which endangered the type of breakthrough that Gheorghiu-Dej deemed necessary and the priority he accorded breaking through. From this point of view, Dej's liquidation of Pătrăşcanu was one way of telling the Romanian Party and the Soviet elite that his commitment to and definition of the breaking-through process were complete, correct, and necessary.

(*b*) Gheorghiu-Dej's attitude toward the Tito phenomenon also casts doubt on the thesis that the Romanian leader was always a nationalist. To understand Gheorghiu-Dej's reaction to Tito's behavior one might do well to remember Machiavelli's words: "It must be considered that there is nothing more difficult to carry out, nor more doubtful of success nor more dangerous to handle, than to initiate a new order of things."[35] Gheorghiu-Dej was concerned with initiating a new order of things in Romania. The difficulty and danger associated with such a task were intensified for the Romanian elite because of their lack of a "practical" ideology and the low level of party institutionalization. More than anything else, Gheorghiu-Dej dreaded a premature national reconciliation.[36] Once he had been assured by the Soviets that in fact

---

[34] David Floyd, *Rumania: Russia's Dissident Ally* (New York, 1965), p. 54.

[35] Niccolo Machiavelli, *The Prince and the Discourses*, p. 21.

[36] Gheorghiu-Dej was explicit in his criticism of the Tito regime: "The nationalist clique of Tito–Rankovich in Yugoslavia follows a policy opposed

Tito was abandoning a policy of revolutionary breakthrough for one of reform before a decisive breakthrough had been effected, his response was predictable.[37] In Dej's words, Tito's Yugoslavia had a "very curious way of constructing socialism: dealing gently [menajînd] in external affairs with Anglo-American imperialists and in internal affairs with kulaks, the mortal enemies of social-ism."[38] For Dej the logical conclusion of a policy which was de-fined (by the Soviets) as one of reconciliation and reform was bour-geois restoration: "Yes, internal and external reaction has suffered serious defeats from us in our country. But it would be ridiculous if we imagine that they will not make attempts to raise their head again, that reactionaries, legionaires, spies, and saboteurs will give up their vile weapons of conflict against the people and its freedoms."[39]

---

to the teachings of Lenin. They follow a policy of reconciliation [împăcare] between the exploiters and the exploited . . . a policy of bourgeois national-ism." Gheorghiu-Dej, "Lenin, geniu al omenirii muncitoare și marele învățător al proletariatului revoluționar," in *Articole și Cuvîntări*, p. 216.

[37] According to a report by Slobodan Stankovic (*Radio Free Europe* [Yugoslavia], May 25, 1969), Vladimir Dedijer, in a new book entitled *J. V. Stalin's Lost Battle*, states that during the Cominform meeting of June 28, 1948, at which Tito was expelled, Gheorghiu-Dej "posed several unpleasant questions" to the Russians concerning the struggle against Yugoslavia. No definitive explanation of this can be offered without more information, but I would suggest that Dej's questions revolved around the issue of orthodoxy. For three years the Yugoslavs had been the most consistent in their attempts at breaking through and in using the Soviet Union as their model. If Gheor-ghiu-Dej identified with the Tito regime he did so to the extent that he thought Tito possessed and acted on a strict and dogmatic interpretation of Marxism–Leninism. Suddenly, this model of orthodoxy was being accused by the Soviets of being just the opposite, i.e., of being a heretic. It may very well be that Dej's "unpleasant questions" were addressed to the discrepancy that lay be-tween the Soviet charges and the stature that the Yugoslav regime had en-joyed because of its revolutionary advances between 1945 and 1948. As to why Gheorghiu-Dej accepted the Soviet argument in 1948, his need of Soviet political support personally and for the policy of breaking through provide adequate explanation.

[38] Gh. Gheorghiu-Dej, "Clica lui Tito — dușman de moarte al socialis-mului," in *Articole și Cuvîntări*, p. 291.

[39] Gheorghiu-Dej, "Raportul . . . February 21, 1948," in *Ibid.*, p. 146.

Thus, although condemnation of Titoism was a stance demanded by the Soviet elite, Gheorghiu-Dej, because of his own rigid interpretation of Marxism–Leninism, could quite honestly condemn Titoism on his own once he was convinced that Tito was deviating from a strictly orthodox orientation in domestic and international affairs. One can probably also assume that the intensity of Dej's condemnation was due in part to his fear that the Romanian Party's emphasis on breaking through, which had only just begun in the summer of 1948, might be threatened if Tito's alleged "reformism" were considered legitimate.

Working with a rigid appreciation of Marxism–Leninism that was not supplemented by indigenously derived modifications, Gheorghiu-Dej probably found it difficult to believe that a Leninist elite such as the Yugoslav could combine revolutionary and reformist policy orientations in the absence of Soviet guidance and definition without losing its revolutionary identity.

Whether or not the Yugoslav elite has been successful in this is beside the point. What matters here is that the Romanian elite, having had no "partisan experience," was formal and dogmatic in its understanding of Leninism, and it would therefore have been difficult for a member of that elite such as Gheorghiu-Dej to look upon ideological-political innovation, as demonstrated by Tito in his defiance of Stalin, as anything other than heresy.

(c) This brings us to the final area in the analysis of nationalism, that of Soviet–Romanian relations. As I have shown, Gheorghiu-Dej viewed the creation of a socialist nation largely as a derivative of success in breaking through and industrializing. Reflecting the lack of a practical ideology, the high degree of uncertainty associated with attempting a breakthrough, and his fear of unintentionally acting on nationalist premises, he identified the Soviet model and Soviet support as the essential elements involved in "initiating a new order." Dej made this quite clear in a speech before the Central Committee in March, 1949, dealing with the state of the Party during the time of the "annihilation [*nimicirea*] of capitalism and the forging of socialism": "Our country has the necessary conditions for success in the work of constructing socialism. 1. The great aid of the Soviet Union, the essential condition for the construction of socialism — ideological aid, political, economic and technical."[40] Quite clearly, if Gheorghiu-Dej and those closest to him felt any nationalism during this early period, it was defined in terms of loyalty to the Soviet Union and a commitment to breaking through the existing Romanian political community in an attempt to transform it in a root-and-branch fashion.

---

[40] Gheorghiu-Dej, "Sarcinile P.M.R. . . . ," in *ibid.*, p. 227.

10

The Breaking-Through Process and Party Institutionalization

IF IT IS TRUE that during the period 1944–1955 the Romanian elite defined the achievement of a decisive breakthrough as its major task, it is no less true that this same elite was equally concerned with the conditions under which this process was to be carried out. The leadership demonstrated a sustained and intense concern with the composition, structure, and character of the Party — and with good reason, for the Party "of a new type," upon which the success or failure of the efforts at breaking through and industrialization depended, was in several important ways an incoherent organization.

I shall attempt to specify and analyze the main features and cause of this incoherence, Gheorghiu-Dej's attempts to increase the Party's coherence (and over-all level of institutionalization), the means he employed, the type of institution he wanted to create, and the considerations which motivated his efforts.

Elite Incoherence

Huntington's point that autonomy and coherence are "often closely linked together"[1] is well taken. Certainly, the R.W.P.'s lack of autonomy in relation to the Soviet Union was one major cause of the elite incoherence which beset the Romanian Party in the late '40s and early '50s. Perhaps the major expression of this incoherence was the structural fragmentation within the regime. Participants within this setting have described both the situation and its consequences. In his speech at the November, 1961, Plenary session of the Central Committee, Alexandru Drăghici, until April, 1968, a member of the Party Presidium, spoke of the factionalism that existed in the Party during the early period. In his words, "the fractionist groups made the ministries which they led veritable fiefs [*adevărate feude*], isolating them from the party and removing them [*scoțîndu-le*] from the Party's control."[2] A similar criticism was made by the present head of the Party and State, Nicolae Ceaușescu, who also pointed out the incapacity of the most critical elite organs to perform their tasks: "Monopolizing in an abusive fashion the leadership of the party, the antiparty group of Pauker and Luca disregarded in fact the operating norms of the Party; during this entire period neither the Secretariat, Politburo, or even the Central Committee functioned."[3]

A particularly important structure (given the emphasis on breaking through) that was, it seems, a "veritable fief" was the Ministry of Internal Affairs. In a speech before that ministry in July, 1967, Ceaușescu recalled that "it was difficult to penetrate into the Ministry of Internal Affairs, this being considered as an interference in the activity of that sector to which no one, no Party section or organ could attend to." It was, he said, a situation that had seriously affected the "authority and leading role of the

---

[1] Samuel P. Huntington, "Political Development and Political Decay," in Claude E. Welch Jr. (ed.), *Political Modernization*, p. 221.

[2] Alexandru Drăghici, speech reported in *Scînteia*, December 15, 1961.

[3] Nicolae Ceaușescu, speech reported in *Scînteia*, December 13, 1961; see also Gh. Gheorghiu-Dej, *Articles and Speeches* (Bucharest, 1963), p. 284.

party." [4] It did so in part because of the decision-making consequences that such a fragmented elite structure entailed.

Thomson and Tuden have suggested four "patterned types of behavior adopted by decision makers in making choices" which they associate with corresponding structures. In combination these are *computation* (decision makers agree on both "beliefs about causation" and "preferred outcomes"), which is associated with a bureaucratic structure; *compromise* (decision makers agree on "beliefs about causation" but not on "preferred outcomes"), which requires bargaining and is associated with a representative structure; *judgment* (decision makers disagree on causation but agree on preferred outcomes), which requires majority vote in a collegial structure; and *inspiration* (decision makers can agree on neither causation or outcomes), which requires an anomic structure and charisma. [5]

In terms of its ideological claims, a Leninist elite such as the Romanian should have been in agreement on questions of causation and on questions of preferred outcomes; thus, they should not have faced any decision-making crises. In fact, however, although the ideology called for such computational decision making, and the formal party structure suggested decision making based on judgment, the Party often found itself in disagreement over issues of causation and preferred outcomes when these issues became a point of specific policy. No one leader existed who could mediate the various factions — a fragmentation not altogether disliked by the Soviet elite — and decision making was uncoordinated and often chaotic. Individual segments of the elite made decisions without considering the criticisms, misgivings, or demands of the other segments. In Ceaușescu's words: "A series of shortcomings have been possible owing to the fact that many measures of high

---

[4] Nicolae Ceaușescu, "Cuvîntarea . . . la consfătuirea cu activul de bază al Ministerului Afacerilor Interne," *Scînteia*, July 19, 1967. (This speech is also found in Nicolae Ceaușescu, *România pe drumul desăvîrșirii construcției socialiste*, II, 393–412.) See also Gheorghiu-Dej, *Articles and Speeches*, p. 204.

[5] James D. Thompson and Arthur Tuden, "Strategies, Structures, and Processes of Organizational Decision," in *Comparative Studies in Administration*, ed. James D. Thompson et al. (Pittsburgh, 1959), pp. 196–204.

importance for our country's life, taken in the past, were not pre-ceded by a thorough analysis and collective debate by the leading bodies of the Party."[6] Indeed, the actual process of decision mak-ing seriously threatened the Party's leadership capacity. Nowhere is this better illustrated than in the case of collectivization. Brze-zinski may well be right that "the internal strength of [a] regime was reflected by its ability to push collectivization forward and overcome internal resistance to it,"[7] especially if by internal strength one means the level and type of institutionalization that characterized a given party. In addition, one might suggest that the *way* in which collectivization was pushed forward reflected the coherence and capacity of a given Leninist elite.

The experience of the Romanian Workers Party with collec-tivization between March, 1949, and 1951 is a striking illustration of the negative effects a low level of institutionalization (as elite incoherence) could have on a policy intended to advance the breaking-through process, provide an essential precondition for industrialization, and contribute to the framework of the future socialist political community.[8] The Party's behavior during this period was marked by the lack of effective control over the Min-istry of Internal Affairs, by the irrational use of violence against the peasants, and by a failure to choose and pursue a consistent policy. Thus, instead of one clear policy toward the peasants there was a series of uncoordinated and often contradictory measures, which of course did nothing to help the breakthrough process.

Chaotic decision making resulted from the lack of political autonomy, the resulting mechanical copying of Soviet experi-ence, and the desire of the various factions to demonstrate their ability and loyalty to the Soviet elite as well as to eliminate their rivals toward whom they felt little reciprocity (again in part due to the lack of political autonomy during the interwar period). Such a pattern of decision making was bound to have a negative effect on the elite's ability to define, and direct, the

---

[6] Ceauşescu in *Scînteia*, July 19, 1967.

[7] Zbigniew Brzezinski, *The Soviet Bloc*, p. 99.

[8] Structural incoherence in the form of elite factions resulted in contra-dictory behavior (i.e., policy) by the Party, which jeopardized what was sup-posedly a shared value (i.e., collectivization of the land).

process of breaking through. It was also bound to make it extremely difficult for the Party to relate the several components of the breaking-through process to their other goals, including self-legitimation.

Membership Incoherence

The marked absence of elite coherence was, as one might expect, matched by a high degree of incoherence in the Party's general membership. Polsby in his discussion of institutionalization has suggested that "as an organization institutionalizes, it stabilizes its membership, entry is more difficult and turnover is less frequent."[9] From 1944 through 1952, the Romanian Workers Party scored very poorly on these indices. From 1944 through 1946, there were instances of mass and indiscriminate admissions; from 1947 through 1952 there was intermittent purging, the consequences of which for the Party rank and file have been well described by Fischer-Galati: "As far as the rank and file was concerned periodical purges directed by one faction or another merely increased the opportunism or fears of the membership with disastrous effects on the party's morale."[10] The purges not only added to the frequency of turnover and membership instability within the Party, but also often failed to achieve their purpose of removing specific individuals. Given the elite's fieflike structure, when a purge affected a specific "fief," an individual holding a responsible position might simply be shifted to a more receptive sector of the regime. Petru Dumitriu sums it up very well in his novel, *Meeting at the Last Judgment*: "Leonas Tanase was thrown out. But one of those other powerful men took him in and made him vice-minister in a department to which Malvolio's authority did not extend."[11]

---

[9] Nelson Polsby, "The Institutionalization of the U.S. House of Representatives," article in draft form made available by author; it has since appeared in the *American Political Science Review* 62 (March 1968): 143–169.

[10] Stephen Fischer-Galati, "Rumania," in *Eastern European Government and Politics*, ed. V. Benes, A. Gyorgy, and G. Stambuk (New York, 1966), p. 227.

[11] Petru Dumitriu, *Meeting at the Last Judgment* (New York, 1962), p. 151.

The Consequences of Incoherence

Perhaps the major consequence of the Party's elite and mass incoherence was its inability as an institution of political leadership to define and protect its boundaries. As I have suggested, Leninist elites place so much emphasis on the priority and urgency of achieving a decisive breakthrough that they create a structure which threatens the integrity and leadership role of the party itself — namely, a security police, or revolutionary army. The period of consciously exacerbated "class conflict" quite naturally emphasizes the importance of the security apparatus. Such a situation may be seen as typical of *all* Leninist regimes during the breaking-through phase. In the Romanian case, this situation was accompanied by Party factionalism, structural fragmentation within the regime, and membership instability — with obvious consequences for the Party's leadership role and general status. Equally obvious are the obstacles that confronted this party in its attempt to increase its level of institutionalization. Some of these points warrant elaboration.

In speaking to the Ministry of Internal Affairs in July, 1967, Ceaușescu accused the security forces "of abuses against some Party and State activists who in certain circumstances had different views concerning some aspects of the political line or made mistakes in their activity." Furthermore, "instead of solving such problems by discussions on a Party line, they were sometimes deferred to the security bodies creating conditions for their interference in Party life, gravely prejudicing the authority and leading role of the Party." [12] Status, authority, and self-confidence all seemed more characteristic of police personnel than of their Party counterparts. These points are vividly illustrated in another of Dumitriu's novels, *Incognito*, where he refers to "the first class citizens, the true Spartans, charged with the security of the State, as opposed to the simple subjects possessed of no political standing; one has only to see the cooperative restaurants where they alone had access." At another point Dumitriu describes the security cadres who "spoke in the overbearing manner of the Securisti, conscious

---

[12] Ceaușescu in *Scînteia*, July 19, 1967.

of being the protectors of the total state . . . members of the ruling class from the moment they put up the shoulder bars of a sub-lieutenant, members of an elite superior in political dignity (even the rank and file) to all other citizens except the top ranking Party workers." [13]

In short, in certain critical respects the Security organization was achieving exactly the institutionalization that Gheorghiu-Dej and a number of his supporters appeared to want the Party to achieve. The situation, however, was far from static in its implications. Obviously the institutionalization of the Security organs — a process facilitated by the incoherent nature of the regime as well as by the designation of breaking through as the major priority — undermined the Party's ability to define its boundaries and in general to assert and defend its autonomy. In particular, the Party found it more and more difficult to secure for its members and for the party role per se the status that it considered legitimate and necessary, to contribute to the confidence of its cadres, and in general to perform the leadership functions which were being threatened by the institutionalization of a rival structure. In many respects, this rival, the security police, was the major element in the breaking-through process, a fact of which it was quite aware, and for a time it was capable of effectively intruding across the frail boundaries of other elite organs.

Attempts to Increase Institutional Coherence

Confronted with this situation, Gheorghiu-Dej undertook three measures in an effort to establish what *in his view* could be considered a coherent party. The first of these measures was the process of "verification." "This verification of the party membership was undertaken as the result of a Central Committee decision of November 1948 aimed at eliminating 'careerist and opportunist' elements which threatened to sabotage the proletarian section of the party as the result of mass admittance." [14] In fact, Gheorghiu-

[13] Petru Dumitriu, *Incognito* (New York, 1964), pp. 19, 35.

[14] Ghita Ionescu, *Communism in Rumania*, p. 204. Altogether this campaign, which lasted until the middle of 1950, resulted in the purging of

Dej's concern with redefining the Party's social-personnel character had been expressed as early as February, 1948, when he noted the necessity of "verifying" the status of each party condidate in terms of his past and his commitment to the Party.[15] Furthermore, it seems that the Central Committee had been sufficiently influenced by Dej and his supporters in 1947 to suspend additional admissions into the Party.[16]

But purging was only one of Gheorghiu-Dej's tactics. In an attempt to create a unified elite sector and a disciplined membership, Dej began to organize a political cadre (which during the "verification" campaign numbered up to 200,000) which would owe its primary allegiance to him rather than to the Party as a corporate entity.[17] The creation of such a patrimonial apparatus within the regime and yet effectively beyond the Party's control is an excellent example of Gheorghiu-Dej's ability: he was able to manipulate the regime's fieflike structure in such a way as to create a cadre that could eventually eliminate that very structure. An added dimension of the relationship between the verification process and the creation of a personal *activ* concerned the quality of membership within the Party. As Gheorghiu-Dej stated: "The verification of the party ranks and the active participation of the

---

192,000 members — more than 20 percent of the membership at the outset. For a statement on the process and the party election of 1951, see *ibid.*, pp. 208–214.

[15] Gh. Gheorghiu-Dej, "Raportul . . . Februarie 21, 1948," in *Articole și Cuvîntări*, p. 138.

[16] Gh. Gheorghiu-Dej, *Rapport d'activité*, p. 163.

[17] For the composition of this political cadre see Ionescu, *Communism in Rumania*, p. 204: ". . . a total of 200,000 investigators had been working, in the strange expression of the resolution, as a 'non-party aktiv' which means that they probably included members of the militia, security police, the Ministry of Justice, and especially the armed forces. At the top . . . the work of these investigators was coordinated . . . by . . . Rangheț . . . Moghioroș [and] Pîrvulescu . . ." As to the loyalty of this trio, Fischer-Galati notes (*The New Rumania*, p. 39) that "Gheorghiu-Dej's men — Rangheț, Moghioroș, and Pîrvulescu — were technically in charge of the investigations." Beginning in 1948, the new recruitment to the Party was supervised by one of Dej's promising protégés, Nicolae Ceaușescu. It appears that Dej was indeed attempting to construct the Party in his own image. For Ceaușescu's position see Fischer-Galati, *ibid.*, p. 39.

mass of members in the debates occasioned by this verification played an immense role in the communist education of the party members, in the growth of their political vigilance and their sense of responsibility toward the party."[18]

Dej's statement is of course exaggerated, but almost certainly the combined verification campaign and the building of a political nucleus did help to increase the level of political and ideological coherence within the Party. Besides removing a significant number of opportunists,[19] it provided the occasion for the appearance of a more cohesive cadre directed by one individual. It did so by creating a situation within which this cadre could be more effectively socialized in certain basic areas such as political loyalty to one individual and greater acceptance of that individual's authority versus simple recognition of his power.

Dej's third measure was the political elimination of elite opponents such as occurred in the 1952 purges of Ana Pauker, Vasile Luca, and Teohari Georgescu, all of whom held sensitive posts in the regime and were involved in the breaking-through process at the highest level.[20]

However, even if these are the measures that enabled Gheorghiu-Dej to impose a certain coherence on the Romanian Party by the early 1950s, the question that still remains is how he was able to put these measures into effect successfully. Five considerations seem most relevant (a) Gheorghiu-Dej's ideological and political preference to have the Party apparatus as his "fief," (b) the Soviet elite's decision to call for a policy of breaking through and industrialization in 1948, (c) the fact that Soviet domination of the various East European regimes did not mean

---

[18] Quoted in *ibid*.

[19] See Ionescu, *Communism in Rumania*, pp. 204–209.

[20] For biographical sketches of Pauker, Luca, and Georgescu see Ionescu, *ibid.*, pp. 355, 353, 352. At the time of the purge Pauker was Minister of Foreign Affairs, Luca Minister of Finance, and Georgescu Minister of Security. All were accused of mismanaging and sabotaging the collectivization drive. The main thrust of the accusations was that they had been guilty of rightist deviations, i.e., of not pursuing collectivization in a properly orthodox fashion. Pauker was also accused of a leftist deviation — of not allowing the peasants to choose for or against membership in a collective.

the complete elimination of domestic political conflict with the possibility of significant outcomes in the form of power shifts and redefinition of policy, (*d*) the purge that Stalin was planning in the early '50s, and (*e*) Gheorghiu-Dej's ability to demonstrate that a native communist was not necessarily the same as a national communist.

With these considerations in mind, one can offer this argument: Given his ideological priorities, the fieflike structure of the Romanian regime in 1948, and the fact that the state and police apparatus were largely controlled by rivals (capable of and willing to devote their not inconsiderable resources to the defense of their "domains"), Gheorghiu-Dej decided to devote his resources to the control and definition of the Party apparatus itself. This, plus the Soviet decision calling for a policy of breaking through and industrialization by its East European "retainer-elites," provided Dej with the position and opportunity to demand a redefinition and strengthening of the Party's role and character. As the Soviet's and Stalin in particular knew, policies of breaking through and industrialization required concentration rather than fragmentation of power at the elite level, as well as the formation of a party cadre characterized ideally by a uniform capacity and propensity to obey commands. The Soviet's appreciation of this contributed to Gheorghiu-Dej's opportunity as General Secretary to initiate and control the verification process. In addition, the fieflike structure of the regime itself allowed Dej a certain latitude of which he took advantage in order to create — within the context of the verification campaign — a political cadre of his own, one with which he could attack and in this case defeat opposing members of the Party elite. But to reach a full explanation of how Gheorghiu-Dej could purge Ana Pauker, one has to add an additional factor: the anti-Semitism involved in what seemed to be the prelude to another major purge within the Soviet Union. As a Jew, Pauker was automatically placed at a disadvantage in her struggle with Gheorghiu-Dej. A related aspect of the situation in 1951–1952 concerns the intended victims and gainers of the purge planned by Stalin. It has been argued that Molotov was one of the intended victims, and according to Gheorghiu-Dej, Molotov was a patron of

Pauker's in the Soviet elite. Furthermore, Khrushchev appears to have been one of those who was to gain from the intended purge.[21] If that is true, Gheorghiu-Dej's rise in 1952 leaves room for some interesting speculation as to who his patron or patrons were in the Soviet elite.[22]

---

[21] See Robert Conquest, *Power and Policy in the U.S.S.R.* (New York, 1961), pp. 190–191; also see Gheorghiu-Dej, *Articles and Speeches*, p. 279, on the Pauker–Molotov connection.

[22] The whole issue of patrons in the 1944–1952 period has received only the slightest attention. It appears plausible that during this time, when Soviet interference in East Europe was at its peak and the East European parties were politically at their weakest, and when many of the elite cadres had spent time in the Soviet Union, there were indeed patronage links of various sorts between notables in the C.P.S.U. and members of the East European parties. For example, Robert Conquest in his fine work *Power and Policy in the U.S.S.R.* (p. 173) speculates on the link between the Doctor's Plot with its anti-Beria thrust and the Slansky affair in Czechoslovakia.

As for Romania in 1952, we have Gheorghiu-Dej's statement linking Pauker with Molotov (see n. 21 above) — but there is much more that we do not know on the subject of possible links between the Soviet and Romanian elites. For example, whom were Lavrentiev, the Soviet ambassador to Romania in 1952, and V. V. Kuznetsov, the Soviet representative to the August (1952) liberation celebration, aligned with within the Soviet elite? Perhaps the most interesting topic for speculation is Gheorghiu-Dej's links with the Soviet elite. Ionescu notes that the Ukranian wing of the C.P.S.U. always had a special interest in the Romanian Party. Referring to the 1952 purge, he says that the "Ukranian wing of the Russian Communist Party, which itself during the last years of Stalin was influenced by Khrushchev, preferred to back the more 'national group' [i.e., Gheorghiu-Dej], of the Rumanian party" (*Communism in Rumania*, p. 214). During this time it was not in fact Khrushchev, however, who was in control of the Ukraine apparatus but L. G. Melnikov, one of Khrushchev's opponents. This would seem to imply that although Khrushchev's links with the R.W.P. may have been through the Ukraine, in 1952 this linkage was fragile at best. But in 1952 a purge was apparently in the offing, in which Beria, Molotov, and perhaps Malenkov were to be removed, leaving Khrushchev in a favorable position. During this time A. A. Epishev, one of Khrushchev's supporters from the Ukraine, became deputy minister of State Security of the U.S.S.R. In Slusser's words, Epishev "was thus a leading official in the Soviet secret police at a time when it was being used as a weapon in the factional intrigue within the CPSU" (Robert Slusser, "Alexei Alexeevich Yepishev," in *Soviet Leaders*, ed. George Simmonds [New York, 1967], p. 142). At approximately the same time Alexandru Drăghici, one of

Finally, Gheorghiu-Dej's ability to control the verification process and to oust the Pauker faction or the major part of it appears to have been related to his effective demonstration that there was no necessary identity between a native communist and a national communist. It has already been argued that at this time Stalin was right in believing that Dej was not overtly or covertly a national communist. There are, of course, more specific factors which could explain Gheorghiu-Dej's success — the support, for example, that he probably received from formally unaligned individuals within the R.W.P. such as Emil Bodnaraş, who held a boundary position between the Soviet and Romanian elites. Nonetheless, the interaction of the five factors I have specified seems sufficient to explain Gheorghiu-Dej's ability to enhance his own power and at the same time to ensure the success of his conception of the character of the Party as an institution of political leadership.

The Character of Party Institutionalization

Since institutionalization always occurs in a specific historical-ideological context, any given institution has a more or less distinctive character reflecting the conditions of its origin and definition.

In the case of the R.W.P., Gheorghiu-Dej was not simply concerned with the abstract process that I have termed institutionalization. Rather, he was intensely concerned with creating a particular type of institution, one that reflected (a) his ideological set, (b) the way in which he defined that ideology, (c) the tasks that he and his Soviet referents identified as demanding action, and (d) the institutional model provided by his major reference point — the Soviet elite. Dej wanted a party that would allow him to "combine the . . . struggle for the carrying out of revolutionary changes with a permanent control over the application of its directives

---

Dej's closest supporters, entered the elite nucleus of the Romanian security apparatus. If Khrushchev, one of the supposed victors in Moscow, was supporting Dej (in his fight with Pauker, Luca, and Georgescu), then the effective link may well have been through the Epishev–Drăghici security net.

For information on Melnikov, Kuznetsov, and Epishev see the works cited here by Conquest and Simmonds.

[*cu un control permanent al aplicarii liniei date de ea*]."[23]   The emphasis on control was perfectly consistent with Dej's Marxist-Leninist ideological commitment and was an expression of it. Viewed from a related perspective, Gheorghiu-Dej's interest was in establishing a higher degree of group (or party) cohesion. The emphasis placed on this goal takes on meaning in the context of the Romanian elite's concern with effecting a decisive break-through, an accomplishment which was correctly perceived as dependent on the creation of an organization whose members would have few external commitments.

In fact, in light of its concern with creating a cadre fairly immune to claims from its environment, the Romanian elite's emphasis on control (or cohesion) was perfectly sound. Studies noted by Blau and Scott have shown that group cohesion does minimize commitments to extra-organizational sources or objects. In their words: "Group cohesion furnishes social support that makes relations with clients less significant for the caseworker and helps him to remain more impersonal toward them."[24] For caseworker read cadre, for welfare client read either friend, family, relative, or "notable," and the importance of group cohesion as an element significantly affecting the decisiveness of a break-through becomes apparent. But the quality of group cohesion that interested Dej and several of his closest supporters must be further defined. Etzioni makes a valuable distinction between what he terms peer cohesion and hierarchical cohesion,[25] the latter meaning the bonds linking actors of different ranks; Gheorghiu-Dej was primarily oriented to this second type of cohesion, both at the elite and mass levels of the party. At the mass level he was concerned with creating a party of sufficiently socialized and de-

---

[23] Gh. Gheorghiu-Dej, "Pentru puritatea rândurilor partidului," in *Articole și Cuvîntări*, p. 404.

[24] Peter Blau and W. Richard Scott, *Formal Organizations*, p. 108.

[25] Amitai Etzioni, *A Comparative Analysis of Complex Organizations*, pp. 187–189. Gheorghiu-Dej was primarily interested in hierarchical-instrumental cohesion, i.e., obedience of lower level cadres to higher level cadres. The only hierarchical-expressive (authority) relations he was interested in creating were those that raised obedience to the level of generalized deference, i.e., made obedience an internalized value.

ployable "agents," cadres who would be responsive to orders emanating only from specific individuals within the party structure. Such an organization approximates what Selznick has termed an organizational weapon or what Ward has termed a command society, and both authors emphasize the effect of these institutions on constraining, limiting, and eliminating the members' commitments to elements outside the organization.[26]

Still, structure is not the only critical factor in shaping the character of an institution, and Dej perceived this. In addition to his concern for the type of structure most congruent with his ideological belief system, the particular way he interpreted this,[27] and the tasks at hand, Dej was concerned with recruitment. He wanted members who would fit into such a command structure and play the role of deployable agent, and he thought they were mostly to be found within the working class or among those whose experience had helped shape a "working class mentality." Such experience could be work within the Party apparatus itself and a corresponding appreciation of that sector's role within the regime.

However, even after the purge of Pauker, Luca, and Georgescu in 1952 Gheorghiu-Dej's view was not the only one within the Romanian elite. In fact, the conflict between Gheorghiu-Dej and Miron Constantinescu[28] may be interpreted as a disagreement over

---

[26] See Philip Selznick, *The Organizational Weapon*; and Benjamin Ward, *The Socialist Economy* (New York, 1967). As Ward has noted (p. 118), one consequence of socializing members of a command society (or organizational weapon) is the "development of attitudes of contempt and distrust for outsiders." All too often these attitudes become defining characteristics of the regime's major institutions, and they may become major obstacles to any future reorientation of the regime toward the population.

[27] I should emphasize that there is a necessary distinction between a set of beliefs and the way in which they are translated into action. To say Gheorghiu-Dej was a Marxist–Leninist is no more precise than to say that Mayor Daley of Chicago is a Democrat. One must take into account the way in which Dej translated his ideological commitments into action, i.e., what types of policy definitions he placed on major components of his ideological set.

[28] Miron Constantinescu deserves a good deal more attention and even conjecture than he has received. He has been variously described as being in some way a Khrushchevite, a nationalist, a Stalinist, a bright young man, and a conceited one. Ionescu provides some information on his background (middle class intelligentsia) and career (see *Communism in Rumania*, pp. 351–352).

what types of individuals and orientations would best achieve the regime's immediate goal of breaking through and its long-range goal of creating a new, socialist, political community. This conflict touched upon ideological considerations involving the definition of membership criteria, policy considerations relating to party admissions, and power considerations concerning the types of individuals who were to occupy responsible positions and define policy.

The criticisms of Constantinescu in the "1957 Resolution of the Plenary Session of the RWP's Central Committee," [29] were primarily a reflection of Gheorghiu-Dej's estimate of the social base and "mentality" necessary for creating an "organizational weapon" and securing a decisive breakthrough. In Dej's opinion, the personality and political beliefs of Constantinescu and those he recruited were antithetical to the requirements of an institution whose personnel were ideally deployable agents. For Dej and those closest to him (including at this point Ceauşescu), obedience was more necessary than questioning, and workers as well as those with a working class "mentality" were more likely to appreciate the need for such a posture and to adopt it.[30] As Gheorghiu-Dej

---

Of particular interest is his relationship with Ceauşescu; both men became associated with the party during the anti-fascist drive in the early 1930s (in the Party Museum in Bucharest there is a picture showing them together under a banner calling for resistance to fascism). In addition to Gheorghiu-Dej's proletarian emphasis, and his commitment to the Party apparatus, Ceauşescu appears to have held a belief in the Party as an organization interacting with the population; Constantinescu, on the other hand, appears to have favored talent-expertise, the commitment to rationalization, and a more aloof-authoritarian posture for the Party. Both, however, appear to place a premium on performance, on national considerations, and on the Party as an institution whose integrity must be preserved and elaborated.

[29] See "Rezoluţia Plenarei Comitetului Central Partidului Muncitoresc Romîn" in *România Liberiă*, July 10, 1957.

[30] In his criticism of Chişinevski, Ceauşescu attacked the practice of recruiting "petty bourgeois elements" (i.e., intellectuals or middle class elements) whom he termed superficial men (*oameni superficiali*); *Scînteia*, December 13, 1961. In his address to the IInd (now VIIth) Party Congress in 1955, Ceauşescu also stated that the Party receives only "working men"; Nicolae Ceauşescu, speech at the *Congresul al II-lea al Partidului Muncitoresc Romîn* (Bucureşti, 1956), p. 760. It would appear then that he chose to support Gheorghiu-Dej's views on personnel recruitment, and to oppose Constantinescu's and Chişinevski's. Ceauşescu's attitude toward Constantinescu was prob-

saw it, the recruitment of individuals with a questioning orientation ("conceit") who were less than willing to accept directives automatically ("petty bourgeois pride") and perhaps too willing to question the value of a patrimonial concentration of power ("arrogance") only prevented ("to be a liquidationist") the development of the kind of political institution upon which a decisive breakthrough depended.

I am not denying the role of personal factors such as Gheorghiu-Dej's probable resentment of the young and possibly conceited Constantinescu, nor the importance of power considerations, but there was certainly more involved. One cannot explain the removal of Constantinescu or the earlier removal of Luca, Pauker, and Georgescu with such a broad statement as, "no matter what the official reasons for Pauker's, Luca's and Georgescu's removal from power in 1952, the real ones are solely connected with the struggle for control of the party."[31] Obviously, one must ask, control for what reasons? Gheorghiu-Dej and a number of his closest supporters wanted control of the Party not merely for power, but in order to assert the primacy of the Party apparatus within the regime, to shape the Party's character in a specific direction, and to give it a content which they saw as properly Leninist and particularly necessary during the breaking-through phase. Gheorghiu-Dej was concerned with the effect of his rivals' orientation and personnel policy on the managerial role of the Party (in Leninist terms, the Party's "leading role"), on the Party's need to recruit personnel whom he viewed as more likely to support the regime, implement its policies, and legitimate its assumption of total responsibility within the context of Romanian society.

In Gheorghiu-Dej's view, individuals from the intelligentsia were politically and ideologically suspect and likely to offer greater resistance to socialization into agent-type roles which stressed obedience to and support of strict superordinate-subordinate command relationships.

But our analysis of the character of the institutionalization

---

ably ambivalent: positive regarding Constantinescu's emphasis of a national perspective and expertise, negative with respect to his less than complete appreciation of the party apparatus and its "working class" base.

[31] Fischer-Galati, *The New Rumania*, p. 39.

process under Gheorghiu-Dej's control is still not complete. We have arrived at some appreciation of Gheorghiu-Dej's emphasis on the central role of the *apparatchik*, on the ideal role of the "deployable agent," and on the importance of the social origin and "mentality" of those selected for "responsible" positions; but we must also look at the particular form the institutionalization process assumed. Beginning in 1952 (one could indeed place its origins in the "verification" campaign), the RWP not only began to approximate an "organizational weapon" but also began to assume a patrimonial character. This was expressed in Gheorghiu-Dej's attempt to establish himself as the primary element in the definition of the Party's character and power. The test of one's loyalty to the regime became loyalty to Gheorghiu-Dej. The criterion for selecting individuals for responsible positions became their relationship to Gheorghiu-Dej, and eventually this pattern was repeated on each lower level. In short, the political elaboration of Gheorghiu-Dej's ideological commitment to the Party as an "organizational weapon" took the form of an institution based on, and reflecting, the power, policy, and personality of its leader — Dej himself.[32] This elaboration of Party character was no "mere accident"; it reflected the need to concentrate power in order to break through, the existence of challenges to Gheorghiu-Dej's power, the model of institutionalization provided by the C.P.S.U. with Stalin at its head, Gheorghiu-Dej's rather rigid appreciation of the ideological belief system to which he was committed, and the political interests of individuals such as Alexandru Drăghici, Dej's security police chief.

Gheorghiu-Dej and the Importance of Party Institutionalization

I have suggested that Dej's efforts to create a specific type of political institution were not based simply on power considerations: it is, I think, rather unlikely that a man who had dedicated his life to a revolutionary political-ideological movement, with all the risks which that implied, should be simply concerned with power. If

---

[32] For a discussion of patrimonialism see Max Weber, *The Theory of Social and Economic Organization*, pp. 346–354.

this is so, what other consideration shaped Gheorghiu-Dej's emphasis on the Party apparatus as the most important organization within the regime (in contrast to and in competition with the State and Security apparatus)? The major reason may well have been Gheorghiu-Dej's formal recognition that the Party was the organization best equipped to perform managerial functions, which were of critical importance in any consciously organized attempt at systemic transformation. Objectively, one can argue that indeed any attempt of this order requires an organization capable of defining, directing, and controlling such a process. Gheorghiu-Dej identified this organization as the "party of a new type." In certain respects, this appreciation of the managerial function was an assertion of the political (the Party apparatus) over the administrative (State apparatus) and coercive (Security apparatus), an assertion that was fully in accord with Lenin's faith in organized political action.[33] For Lenin, and in the Romanian context for Gheorghiu-Dej, only the Party was capable of relating the multiple aspects involved in systemic transformation: destruction, mobilization, coordination, and direction.

At least by demanding that the Party direct the breaking-through process Gheorghiu-Dej formally demonstrated a concern with the character of the process. He appears to have felt that its political aspect must be paramount and that this would only be possible if the Party controlled it — because only the Party had the perspective, the vision, and the distinctive competence to perform and coordinate the many managerial tasks associated with the process of breaking through. In his view, only the Party (with its emphasis on mobilization as well as coercion) could effectively relate to the power of the masses, a task that in practice meant eliciting different types of support within a basically coercive and manipulative framework.

Certainly, at one level Gheorghiu-Dej was correct in his beliefs. Conscious attempts at systemic transformation do depend on an appreciation of the critical role of the political as opposed to the administrative or coercive. This is especially true if that transformation is to be coherent and directed to the eventual appearance

---

[33] See Sheldon Wolin, *Politics and Vision*, p. 422.

of a community based on norms of reciprocity rather than on norms of super and subordination. In another sense, however, it is equally possible and correct to argue that the way in which Gheorghiu-Dej acted on his beliefs concerning the importance of creating a coherent party and giving it the major responsibility for breaking through and industrializing resulted in a significant denial of the values to which he was formally committed.

Patrimonialism, the form of Gheorghiu-Dej's commitment to party supremacy and institutionalization, was antithetical in several respects to the Party's ability to perform a managerial and political role. To the extent that under Gheorghiu-Dej's rule the Romanian regime was patrimonial, it continued to be incoherent in many ways even though the character of the incoherence changed. With the removal of Pauker, Luca, Georgescu, and Pătrășcanu the incoherence was no longer a result mainly of intra-elite fragmentation. Instead, it was an incoherence directly caused by the patrimonial leader's continual attempts to make sure that his retainers did not develop fiefs of their own. Paradoxically, the major instrument available to Gheorghiu-Dej in his attempts to prevent such consolidation was the Security (coercive) apparatus, which quite readily continued to interfere with Party activities. Finally, the patrimonial system was in many ways congruent with traditional (Romanian) ascriptive structures of personal patronage which conflicted with a real appreciation or development of an impersonal, agentlike attachment to the Party. The result was that there were in fact few cadres sufficiently socialized to define and direct a political breakthrough.[34]

---

[34] The Party recognized this shortage of adequate cadres, as is shown by a Party statement issued in August, 1953, to the effect that "In the shortest time possible" there should be set up a "party aktiv of between 80,000–100,000 comrades." As Ionescu points out, "This injunction came as a surprise even to skeptical observers of the party. It seemed hardly credible that a party with a membership of 600,000 could not produce 80,000 satisfactory activists . . ." (*Communism in Rumania*, p. 229). It is not unreasonable to assume that for Gheorghiu-Dej the creation of a capable body of cadres was equivalent to creating a personally loyal body of cadres, i.e., adding to and reinforcing the patrimonial character of the Party and regime. See in this connection Ionescu's comments, *ibid.*, pp. 242–246.

11

The Romanian Party Elite in 1955

THE VIITH CONGRESS of the Romanian Workers Party in 1955 provided the Party elite with an appropriate setting for evaluating
the Party's experience and defining its future tasks. The nature
of the elite's statements leads one to conclude that the political
climate within this stratum was one of increasing confidence combined with continuing anxiety. The increase of confidence was
suggested by Gheorghiu-Dej's remark that "the old state of things
will never return to Romania," and by the Central's Committee's
decision to admit new members into the Party.[1] But the feeling
of confidence was neither complete nor even "defining," for it was
combined with a continued sense of anxiety which reflected the
interests of certain individuals (such as Drăghici), institutions (such
as the Ministry of Internal Affairs), and the very real set of problems confronting the R.W.P. This sense of anxiety was conveyed
by Ceaușescu's remarks that "In the present conditions of passing

---

[1] Gh. Gheorghiu-Dej, *Rapport d'activité*, pp. 23, 167.

from capitalism to socialism the strengthening of political vigilance is necessary."[2] Here the ideological-political concern with (bourgeois) "restoration" and fear of backsliding was legitimated at the Party's major forum—a Party Congress. Even more than Ceaușescu's, Gheorghiu-Dej's statement that "as long as there exist hostile classes in our country, so long as imperialism exists, the enemy will attempt to slip its agents into the party in order to undermine its fighting capacity,"[3] revealed the political anxiety within the regime. Indeed, Gheorghiu-Dej, seemed to be more worried than confident. At one point he noted that "We must not forget that our success does not diminish the enemy's resistance, but on the contrary provokes on his part a desperate resistance."[4] That the Romanian elite and particularly Gheorghiu-Dej were more anxious than confident over their achievements may also be suggested by the position within the elite of Alexandru Drăghici, the head of the Security forces, above Nicolae Ceaușescu, who was in control of Party-organizational affairs.[5]

---

[2] Ceaușescu, speech at the *Congresul al Il-lea al Partidului Muncitoresc Romîn*, p. 164. It is of course difficult, if not impossible, to say how much a statement of this sort was "required" either in the command sense or more likely in the anticipatory sense.

[3] *Rapport d'activité*, p. 166.

[4] *Ibid.*, p. 41. This statement is a classic example of dogmatic emulation of Stalinist precepts.

[5] The relative positions of Drăghici and Ceaușescu in 1955 are of great interest to anyone concerned with elite politics in Romania. In a real sense, these two men summarize two very distinct (and antagonistic) appreciations of what a Leninist regime and socialist community should look like. Drăghici, the head of the security police, and Ceaușescu, the Party secretary, were personal rivals with different political stances, the one Stalinist, the other Khrushchev-like (domestically). In morality-play fashion Drăghici was the embodiment of regime anxiety, while Ceaușescu tended to stand for regime confidence. Throughout 1955 their relative positions in the hierarchy shifted. In April and May Ceaușescu preceded Drăghici; in June the two alternated in terms of precedence; and through the late summer Ceaușescu was conspicuous by his absence and Drăghici was promoted in the ranks of the security forces (*Scînteia*, August 25, 1955). Immediately prior to the Congress, Ceaușescu appeared again before Drăghici, but at the Congress itself Drăghici was listed above Ceaușescu, in the announcement of the Politburo's membership (*Scînteia*, Dec. 29, 1955). The relative balance between the two and the somewhat more

Nevertheless, it does appear that by 1955 the Romanian elite was characterized by a dual orientation of anxiety and confidence. The major process and goal toward which these orientations or postures were directed was of course breaking through.

The Question of Breaking Through

The obvious question to be asked (and answered) concerns the success or failure which the Party had achieved at this point in its history. It seems clear that the Party had been successful in breaking through any and all politically influential structures in the domestic sphere. It had also begun a program of comprehensive industrialization with significant results in terms of the system's economic capacity and performance.[6] In addition, that segment of the elite associated with Gheorghiu-Dej had been successful in creating a higher degree — and distinct type — of coherence within the Party at both the mass and elite levels. Nevertheless, despite these accomplishments the Party was still confronted by a wide range of serious problems. There was the question of Party strength in the rural area, of insufficient ideological training for its cadres, of persistent factionalism, of the neglect of agriculture, and the hostility of its subjects.[7] With this balance sheet, a political climate dominated by an amalgam of anxiety and confidence is certainly understandable. By 1955 the Romanian elite viewed its efforts at achieving a breakthrough as substantial but not decisive.

The question that arises is whether or not the Romanian elite

---

influential position held by Drăghici during this time may be interpreted as a fairly accurate reflection of the political balance and mixture of the regime as a whole.

[6] See J. M. Montias, *Economic Development in Communist Rumania*, pp. 26–53.

[7] The term subjects is used quite deliberately. It is used in the sense that Almond and Verba define the term in *The Civic Culture*. Subjects are individuals who possess a weak orientation toward the presentation of demands on a political system, and rarely perceive themselves as active or effective political participants. Parenthetically, a subject orientation on the part of publics is congruent with *system*-building emphasis by a political elite and both are in significant respects antithetical to a political *community*.

attempted to specify what was needed in order to complete the breaking-through process. It appears that they did, and increased adaptability was the condition they identified as necessary to make a substantial breakthrough a decisive one. But to suggest that the Romanian elite defined adaptability as the major requirement for completing the process of breaking through is not to suggest that all members of the elite shared this perception — nor do I mean to suggest that everyone defined increased adaptability in the same way. Finally, it is not necessary to argue that among those who did share the same definition or appreciation of increased adaptability there was an equal readiness to commit their resources in an attempt to increase the Party's flexibility of response. I do suggest, however, that by the time of the VIIth Congress there was something of a consensus within the Party elite on the need for a greater adaptive capacity by the Party and regime in order to take advantage of what it had already achieved and to increase its capacity to act effectively on its goals. It is in light of this conclusion that one can explain the increased emphasis at the 1955 Congress on interpreting the theory of Marx–Engels–Lenin–Stalin in terms of Romanian conditions. In Gheorghiu-Dej's words: "Our party studies with perseverance this gigantic experience [that of the Soviet Union] and its creative application in a creative manner in the concrete historical conditions of our country."[8]

Such an emphasis was of course related to the uncertainty within the Soviet elite itself at the time which made adaptability something of a necessity for East European elites. Even so, this circumstance should not prevent one from appreciating the concern of certain elements within the Romanian Party about the organization's capacity to deal more flexibly with the problems confronting it.

Finally, and perhaps most importantly, one should be very clear about the nature of what the R.W.P. elite was seeking. Adaptability can be associated with a number of political doctrines and structures. Gheorghiu-Dej sought a greater degree of autonomy for his regime, but a specific kind of autonomy. Kuhn's notion of paradigm and rules is helpful in describing what Gheorghiu-Dej

---

[8] *Rapport d'activité*, p. 159.

was seeking.[9] From 1948 through 1952, the concrete and largely mechanical application of the Stalinist paradigm for breaking through was perceived by Gheorghiu-Dej and those closest to him as necessary and functional. By 1952–1953, however, it appears that a number of important members of the Romanian elite were becoming aware of the need to formulate within the still accepted general framework of the Stalinist paradigm a set of rules which would more adequately reflect the distinct character of the Romanian social environment. In other words, the Romanians were becoming aware of the need for greater operational as opposed to policy autonomy.[10] It would appear that Gheorghiu-Dej, in particular, understood the difference between these two political postures and was concerned with elaborating a domesticist posture and avoiding a national communist one.

In his speech to the VIIth Congress Dej's demand that the "scholastic character" of the Party's propaganda and ideological work be eliminated may be seen as a demand for a more situationally relevant interpretation of the still accepted Stalinist approach to breaking through, as a domesticist position. Similarly, and again with reference to ideology, Dej's statement that "The task of our militants on the level of ideological work consists of combating all forms of reactionary bourgeois ideological influence and particularly the infiltration into our ideology of nationalist and chauvinist conceptions,"[11] may be interpreted as a repudiation of a national communist posture. And if the analysis presented this far has any validity, this repudiation was not simply based on tactical considerations toward the Soviet Union, but on Gheorghiu-Dej's real aversion to being identified or acting as a nationalist.[12]

---

[9] See Thomas Kuhn, *The Structure of Scientific Revolutions* (Chicago, 1962), p. 43.

[10] This stress on rule *vs.* paradigm determination, on within-system *vs.* structural change, on operational *vs.* policy autonomy, is what Brzezinski has attempted to specify in his distinction between domesticism and national communism.

[11] *Rapport d'activité*, pp. 194, 196.

[12] In fact, one could argue that in 1955 Gheorghiu-Dej was still unable to accept the notion of being a national communist without the danger of

In a discussion of Selznick's conception of institutional leadership, Haas says that in an organization "The leadership must learn to use a crisis in the tension between organization and environment as an opportunity for self-assessment and self-definition, to profit from critical experience, to undergo growth in character and understanding." [13] By 1953 a significant segment of the R.W.P. elite was seriously concerned with the condition that would allow the Party to take advantage of the specific problems confronting it so as to increase its own competence and contribute to the successful achievement of its major goals. That condition was believed to be an increased degree of Party autonomy defined as greater flexibility in determining which rules to employ in dealing with given problems.

Given Gheorghiu-Dej's demonstrated loyalty to the Soviet Union, the identity of ideological tenets, the greater coherence and unity of the Party, and Khrushchev's statements, it would not be too difficult to argue that by the end of 1955 Gheorghiu-Dej must have felt there was no reason why the R.W.P. should not, and with permission, exercise greater operating autonomy.

---

backsliding into "bourgeois nationalism," and that to Gheorghiu-Dej the category of national communist was suspect, misleading, and dangerous. In this connection a remark in his December 23, 1955, speech is noteworthy: "The close friendship and fraternal collaboration with the great Soviet Union and with all the countries of the socialist camp are the measure of our national independence and our state security." *Ibid.*, p. 20.

[13] Ernst Haas, *Beyond the Nation-State*, p. 101.

Emulation, Mediation, and Initiation: Romanian National Development, 1955-1965

12

Concerns, Concepts, and Conclusions

BECAUSE THE PERIOD of Romanian history that I shall analyze in
Part III is the most familiar and most frequently studied period,
I want to make the rationale for my analysis explicit. Almost without exception, recent studies of Romania have focused on its contribution to the phenomenon of "polycentrism." Any attention
given to the internal development of Romanian political life has
been in terms of this phenomenon and for the most part has started
and ended with the explanatory notion of nationalism. The perspective of my analysis is rather different: I shall deal with the
events of this time period on a more comparative and conceptual
level. The conclusions I reach are significantly different from those
to be found in the other major analyses of Romania's recent political development. To specify these points more closely: my main
concern is the national development that occurred within Romania during the period 1955–1965. I refer to the Soviet bloc to
the extent that it provided the distinctive context within which

the core problems of Romanian development were perceived, defined, stimulated, and/or resolved.

The question of conceptualization is critical for at least two reasons. The more refined and differentiated the concepts one employs, the more likely it is that one will reach a broader understanding of a phenomenon which is in this case highly complex. On the other hand, to the extent that one uses concepts that are not too closely defined in terms of the phenomena investigated, the subsequent analysis may permit the tracing of hypotheses within a comparative framework. In the following analysis therefore I shall attempt to specify different conceptualizations of the term nation and to relate these to intra-elite perceptions in order to locate the origin, nature, and contradictions in Romanian nationalism during the period under study. In addition, I shall make use of concepts that allow for an appreciation of the Romanian experience in a wider, more general sense. This means working not only with the notion of Romanian sovereignty but also with the concepts of emulation and initiation, as a way of comprehending the conditions under which party institutionalization and autonomy may become major aspirations and possibly major accomplishments of a given Leninist elite.

Perspectives and concepts may be seen as usefully biased restrictions. Ideally, by limiting and specifying an analyst's attention within certain ranges, they contribute to insight and explanation, and in any case they are extremely important in shaping if not determining his conclusions. If my perspectives and concepts differ from those employed in earlier studies of Romanian political life during this period (and particularly the years 1958–1964), my conclusions must also differ. Gheorghe Gheorghiu-Dej, rather than being a determined institutional leader who pursued national autonomy, and flexibly as well as creatively related Leninist and nationalist commitments, is seen to be a rigid national leader, capable of innovating only within very circumscribed limits, and incapable of or unwilling to work out a synthesis of the political and ideological implications of his regime's "independent course" once it was underway. This inability to synthesize, that is, to relate the imperatives of nationalism and socialism under new conditions, is an essential part of the rather intense nationalism Gheorghiu-Dej displayed as he became increasingly independent of Soviet control. A second point is Gheorghiu-Dej's relationship with Khrushchev — at first apparently one of cooperation rather than one of personal and political opposition. With certain variations in tensions and conflict, this cooperative relationship appears to have lasted through the 1950s.

Third, instead of concluding that the Romanian Communist Party was "ruthlessly united," I conclude that the process of party institutionalization was highly conflict-ridden and contradictory. Moreover, expressions of unity were the consequence both of intra-elite agreements on specific issues, often based on different justifying considerations, and of Gheorghiu-Dej's effective patrimonial definition of the Party's structure, leadership, and operation.

A fourth important consideration is that the major phenomenon within the Romanian socio-political system at this time was the appearance of a new social type, a stratum which Dumitriu has called the "new middle class."[1] Only by taking into account this stratum's character and appearance can one adequately understand Romanian national development, including its "independent course," during this period.

---

[1] Petru Dumitriu, "The Two New Classes," *East Europe* 10 (September 1961): 3.

13

A Period of Latent Learning
and Docility, 1953-1957

IT WOULD BE INCORRECT to describe the period 1953–1957 as simply a "preparatory" stage for the events that were to occur in the early '60s; nevertheless, in a very real sense that was what it was. But it was preparatory in a very particular way. The concepts of latent learning and docility will help to explain what I mean. Latent learning, in our context, may be defined as the formal addition of new responses to an organization's repertory. Such learning is actually cognitive (or formal) rather than contextually meaningful (or substantive). Docility is a distinctive but closely related phenomenon. It refers to purposive behavior. Following Simon, I use it in its "proper dictionary sense of 'teachability'." It involves an organization's observance of the consequences of its movements and in light of these its adjustment to achieve its desired purpose.[1]

---

[1] On latent learning see O. Hobart Mowrer, *Learning Theory and the Symbolic Process* (New York, 1960), pp. 12, 45 ff. On docility see Herbert A. Simon, *Administrative Behavior* (New York, 1961), p. 85.

The period 1953–1957 can be described as one of marked latent learning and limited docility for the Romanian Workers (Communist) Party elite. This was due in great measure to the nature of the Soviet bloc in 1953, particularly the Soviet Union's monopoly over all major policy and ideological initiatives and its requirement that satellites emulate these stances. Primarily for reasons of self-interest, the Soviet elite in 1953 began a series of obligatory and authoritative ideological redefinitions which were to have substantial implications for the development of the socialist community of nations: unintentionally, the Soviet elite itself started the "disintegration of the monolith" and the Romanian "independent course." Between 1953 and 1956 East European elites were confronted with the Soviet demand for "collective leadership," the attempted Soviet rapprochement with Tito, the "spirit of Geneva," the withdrawal of Soviet troops from Austria, de-Stalinization, the doctrine of "many roads to socialism," the stress on peaceful coexistence, and the denial of the inevitability of war.[2] All the East European elites and regimes were confronted by this series of "redefinitions," but since my primary concern is with Romania, I shall isolate the aspects of these redefinitions" which comprised the critical core of the Romanian elite's latent learning experience. The first was the Soviet declaration of fallibility in its relationships with its socialist neighbors. On October 30, 1956, the Soviet government admitted to "many difficulties, unresolved problems and downright mistakes, including mistakes in mutual relations among the socialist countries—violations and errors which demeaned the principle of equality in relations among the socialist states."[3]

The second aspect of the Soviet-initiated redefinitions was in a sense the other side of the coin—that is, a positive statement describing the "relations of a new type" that were to be established

---

[2] See Robert Bass, "The Post-Stalin Era in Eastern Europe," *Problems of Communism* 12 (March–April 1963): 70. The Soviet invasion of Hungary would not have affected Gheorghiu-Dej's belief in the sincerity of the Soviet declaration inasmuch as he undoubtedly believed that the disturbances in Hungary were the result of national and international capitalist provocations.

[3] See David Floyd, *Rumania: Russia's Dissident Ally*, pp. 37–38.

among socialist nations. Under Stalin, the various members of the Soviet bloc were bound together in a sort of "pooled interdependence," a relationship in which all parts of the system were connected with the center but not necessarily with one another:[4] "On the one hand, the mutual relations between the peoples democratic countries and the USSR were intensified, on the other there was a clear increase of a kind of isolationism, of a people's democratic provincialism, marked by a lack of information on each side about the life of the other and by absolutely insufficient contacts among them, if any."[5]

Khrushchev envisioned a quite different sort of relationship, which was clearly set forth by the Chinese in the theme of the Bandung Conference: Sovereignty, Equality of Nations, Mutual Aid, and Non-Interference. Obviously these slogans had the formal approval of the Soviet elite, but the legitimacy of the new approach was born out by several particular aspects of Soviet policy. In 1954 the Soviets acted on their redefinitions by undertaking the elimination of the corporate structure of control with which Stalin had dominated the various East European regimes. In particular, the role of Soviet security personnel was diminished and in Romania between 1954 and 1956 the Sovroms (joint companies) were eliminated. This reduction, and in some instances elimination of the Stalinist corporate control structure was of great importance in creating a basic premise for the potential appearance of opposition to the Soviet Union from within the bloc. If the Soviet ideological "redefinitions" created the value premises for such opposition, the Soviet structural innovations created the political context in which it could develop.

The importance of this structural change can be demonstrated by reference to two highly relevant Weberian concerns: patrimonialism and feudalism.

Before 1954, the bloc was a patrimony ruled by Stalin and

---

[4] See James D. Thompson, *Organizations in Action* (New York, 1967), pp. 54–55, for a definition and discussion of "pooled interdependence."

[5] V. Kotyk, "Some Aspects of the History of Relations Among Socialist Countries," *Radio Free Europe*, October 30, 1967. Kotyk is a Czechoslovak intellectual.

controlled by the direct presence of a staff of officials — military officers, political advisers, and security personnel — responsible to him. The bloc was in effect a corporate group, an organization having at its head a recognized individual with authority and an administrative staff at his disposal.[6] In addition, the heads of each of the subunits ("satellites" or in Weberian terms, "benefices") were Stalin's "retainers." Except for Tito, the various leaders of the East European regimes owed their positions to Stalin.

Khrushchev significantly revised this structure; he partially transformed a patrimonial structure into a "feudal" one. The basis for bloc cohesion was to be "ideology." A hierarchical distribution of authority would still exist but it was to be more reciprocal and less coercive. As in all feudal systems, personal relationships would play a large role. Thus, the ties of a Gomulka, Kadar, or Zhivkov with Khrushchev were a sensitive part of the ties between the C.P.S.U. and the Polish, Hungarian, and Bulgarian regimes. But the really distinctive aspect of Khrushchev's redefinition of the character of bloc unity was the extent to which the Soviet elite was placing its authority and conflict-control resources in jeopardy. Under Khrushchev, the C.P.S.U. declared its fallibility and made compulsory the formal internalization of values (such as sovereignty and equality) which in a specific context might lead to opposition. In addition, it contributed to such a context by removing its own administrative staff from the subunits of the bloc[7] and allowing the elites within that entity to increase their control over their own administrative and political staffs. In other words, elites which during Stalin's tenure had been patrimonial retainers lacking effective bases of support were now, largely be-

---

[6] See Max Weber, *"The Theory of Social and Economic Organization,"* pp. 145–146, on the concept of a "corporate group."

[7] Under Stalin, the nature of the relationship between the Soviet Union and most of Eastern Europe actually tended to approximate Etzioni's definition of an empire. In his words, "The decision-making of blocs . . . tends to be consultative . . . Empires have a considerable amount of decision-making power that binds member-units — i.e. their decisions are enforceable. Their scope is larger than blocs [i.e., in terms of the functions which they control: K. J.]." See Amitai Etzioni, "A Paradigm for the Study of Political Unification," *World Politics* 15 (October 1962): 46.

cause of Soviet encouragement, becoming feudal vassals possessing significant resources of their own.[8] The potential for conflict within the bloc was correspondingly heightened. Khrushchev's perception that the increasing diversity within the bloc required the consideration of alternative definitions of unity was one thing; his belief that "singleness of command" could be maintained, that "all commands in [the] system [would be] consistent among themselves, whether they originate[d] from a single source [i.e., C.P.S.U.] or from several sources,"[9] was a conclusion of a different order, and it was based on the assumption that a common ideology existed and that political agreement on its definition was possible.

A major consequence, however, of decentralization and the deconcentration of power, both processes being involved in any redefinition of a "patrimonial" structure to a "feudal" one, is that "once the subordinate centers have been delegated some authority, and once they have been given their own facilities for storing memories [i.e., the possession of and control over their own administrative and political apparatus] these subordinate centers and memory pools will in the future receive only part of the input from the supreme government [i.e., the C.P.S.U.]."[10] In short, the probability that the several units (i.e., satellites) within a system (i.e., the Soviet bloc) will arrive at an agreed-upon definition of a common ideology (i.e., Marxism–Leninism) is not independent of the structural definition of unity which characterizes that system. Unintentionally, the ideological and organizational "redefinitions" initiated by Khrushchev increased the likelihood that East European elites would translate the formal values of equality, sovereignty, and noninterference into effective political action.

The notion of "Soviet initiation" is particularly striking in the case of Romania. Until 1959 in crucial respects Khrushchev was as much a "Romanian nationalist" as Gheorghiu-Dej, and one of the major if unintentional stimulators of the independent Ro-

---

[8] For a discussion of feudalism see Weber, *The Theory of*, pp. 373–381.

[9] Karl Deutsch, "Cracks in the Monolith: Possibilities and Patterns of Disintegration in Totalitarian Systems," in *Comparative Politics: A Reader*, ed. Harry Eckstein and David E. Apter (New York, 1963), p. 498.

[10] *Ibid.*, p. 502.

manian course. A comparison of the speeches given at the VIIth Romanian Party Congress (December, 1955) by Gheorghiu-Dej and Alexei Kirichenko, head of the Soviet delegation, bears this out. Kirichenko's speech may justifiably be considered an expression of Khrushchev's position since Kirichenko is thought to have been one of Khrushchev's most loyal allies.[11] Kirichenko credited the Romanian Party with having been the soul and the organizer of the historic uprising on August 23, 1944, which led to the liquidation of the Antonescu-fascist regime. Together, he said, the Soviet army and Romanian people had fought for national and social liberation. He declared that the Soviet Union's policy was based on reciprocal respect of territorial integrity, sovereignty, and non-interference in the internal affairs of others, and he praised both Gheorghiu-Dej and the history of the Romanian Party. For his part, in December no less than in August at the time of Khrushchev's visit, Gheorghiu-Dej referred to the liberating mission and role of the Soviet army; he quoted Khrushchev on the connection of peaceful coexistence and noninterference — an emphasis that was directed more at the West than at the Soviets, given the Romanian elite's anxiety over the stability of its regime — and spoke of Romania's independence as being closely bound up with the socialist camp and in particular the Soviet Union.[12] One can find little if anything in either of these speeches of Gheorghiu-Dej to suggest that he initiated Romania's independent course in 1955[13] or that the scope of Romanian initiative was anything but limited.

---

[11] See Robert Conquest, *Power and Policy in the U.S.S.R.*, p. 267.

[12] See Cuvîntul Tovarăşului Alexei I. Kiricenko; conducătorul delegaţiei P.C.U.S., *Congresul al II-lea al Partidului Muncitoresc Romîn* (Bucureşti, 1956), pp. 213–221.

[13] In August, 1955, at the time of Khrushchev's visit Gheorghiu-Dej began his speech with these words: "Today marks eleven years of Romania's freedom from fascist control. On August 23, 1944, this [event] took place in the context of the glorious Soviet army's victorious offensive which, dealing blows to the fascist armies, entered as liberators on our country's territory." (*Scînteia*, Aug. 23, 1955.) He also referred to the Soviets as initiators of peaceful coexistence. In his speech to the Party Congress exactly four months later Gheorghiu-Dej used the same terms as Kirichenko in stating that the victorious popular

Besides the statements and behavior of the Soviet elite, there were other sources of latent learning — of political lessons to be observed and political conclusions to be drawn though not acted on at that time — available to the Romanian elite or sections of it. Among them were the behavior of the Italian and the Polish Communist parties. Spurred by Khrushchev's criticisms of past relations and his new model of party relations, the Italians in 1956 began to emphasize bilateral meetings and to condemn centralized meetings, and they went on from Khrushchev's "many roads" formulation to legitimate a policy that would enable them to decrease their domestic political isolation. In choosing a rightist strategy they offered a rationale which the Romanians were to make use of in the 1960s: namely, that whatever furthered the interests of any one communist party furthered the interests of all communist parties. The Italians made these policies, stands, and interpretations available at least in the formal sense.[14] The Romanians would opt for them and act on them once the evolution of their own situation began to demonstrate the situational relevance and political meaningfulness of these "conclusions." Beyond that, however, it is my contention that the evolution of political life in Romania was in part shaped by the availability of conclusions such as those drawn by the P.C.I. In at least one respect, the Poles, too, contributed to the latent learning of the Romanian elite. Following the turbulence in Poland, in November, 1956, the Soviets made new agreements with the Poles on the stationing of troops and economic assistance. The Soviets did the same with the Romanians, but the Poles fared much better on both issues. As Ionescu relates: "the agreement on the presence of Soviet troops in Poland was far more specific and hedged with limitations dealing with numbers, disposition, movements, jurisdiction, etc.," and whereas

---

insurrection in 1944 occurred alongside the liberating mission accomplished by the Soviet army (*Rapport d'activité*, p. 29). It is difficult, therefore, to accept Fischer-Galati's statement about Gheorghiu-Dej: "The evidence irrefutably supports the contention that he and his associates formulated the essential arguments of 1964 in 1955." See "Rumania and the Sino–Soviet Split," in Kurt London, ed., *Eastern Europe in Transition* (Baltimore, 1966), p. 265.

[14] See Donald L. M. Blackmer, *Unity in Diversity: Italian Communism and the Communist World* (Cambridge, Mass., 1968), pp. 65–66.

the Soviets canceled Polish debts, they agreed only to postpone for four years the repayment of the credits granted to the Romanian People's Republic between 1949 and 1955.[15] In terms of bargaining power the lesson drawn then or later by some if not all of the Party elite must have been that a militant strategy might be more efficacious than a moderate one in achieving a workable equality with the Soviet Union.[16]

Although latent learning was the main characteristic of the period under study (1953–1957), there were areas of docility or purposive behavior as well, and they were of some importance in that they established precedents for autonomous action and provided experience in and some success with such forms of behavior. The purposive behavior was, however, mainly defensive in nature, an attempt to cope with the uncertain political environment created by Stalin's death and the succession crisis in the Soviet Union. Gheorghiu-Dej, struggling for political survival in this un-

---

[15] Ghita Ionescu, *Communism in Rumania*, pp. 273–274.

[16] To use an American analogy, the "militant-S.N.C.C." Poles had gained more than the "moderate-N.A.A.C.P." Romanians. It is precisely lessons of this order that made the period 1953–1957 particularly crucial in the future evolution of the Romanian Party. As Professor Montias asked: How do you think Gheorghiu-Dej felt about the stagnation in investments and the sharp drop in the rate of industrial growth of those years? Didn't the Rumanians deserve generous Soviet aid in view of their loyalty during the 1956 crisis? Was it fair, instead, to "reward" Hungary's disloyalty by large grants and loans in 1957–1958? (Private communication to the author.) There is no simple answer to this very pertinent question. One could argue that, as in the 1950–1952 period, the threat to the socialist system was used by the Soviets to rationalize the attention and aid devoted to the "weak link" Hungary (and Poland) and that such an argument continued to be somewhat effective in placating Gheorghiu-Dej. Too, the standing of the Romanian regime within the socialist system was raised above that of Hungary and Bulgaria, and Soviet troops were removed in 1958. Most importantly, Gheorghiu-Dej may well have been aided by Khrushchev in his fight with Constantinescu and Chișinevski and perhaps received Khrushchev's support for the economic plan announced in November, 1958. In any case, I have emphasized the "learning" quality of this period because the available lessons ensured that any future period of Romanian emulation of Soviet policy (like the one that began in 1958) would take place in a different context and with a different legacy from that of the period 1948–1952.

certain situation, supported Khrushchev's program of greater autonomy for the members of the bloc, and he increased his efforts
to create a political and administrative apparatus loyal to himself
and more likely to sustain its political coherence while adapting
to developments within the Soviet Union. In scope, Gheorghiu-
Dej's purposive behavior during this period had definite limits,
but the implications of his behavior were considerably broader
and more significant.

An analysis of the period of uncertainty that followed Stalin's
death will be useful in explaining some specific events that occurred
in Romania during 1954 and 1955. It will also provide an opportunity and an appropriate context for investigating Gheorghiu-
Dej's relations with Khrushchev — the nature of which is of fundamental importance in determining what Gheorghiu-Dej's immediate goals were and whether or not he perceived them as possible only in a context of opposition to the Soviets in general and
to Khrushchev in particular.

Ionescu's work on Romania refers to the fact that the Romanian Party was the only one in East Europe not to hold a New
Course Party Congress by the end of 1954; not until September,
1955, was the Congress date announced. This political hesitation
can be related to the uncertainty caused by the Soviet succession
conflict, to Gheorghiu-Dej's political preference as well as astute-
ness, and to opposition elements within the Romanian Party. During the spring and summer of 1954, Malenkov's position in the Soviet Union became stronger. In Romania, the combined post of
Party Secretary and Prime Minister was split, and Gheorghiu-Dej
took the latter post, placing a close ally, Gheorghe Apostol, in the
position of First Secretary and removing from the Secretariat certain individuals such as Chișinevski, Constantinescu, and Moghioroș [17] who might use that body as an oppositional base. During the

---

[17] At the same time Gheorghiu-Dej added several "retainers" to the
Secretariat: Nicolae Ceaușescu, Mihai Dalea, and Ianoș Fazekaș; see Ionescu,
Communism in Rumania, pp. 232, 350–352, 354, for biographical data on
these men. Ceaușescu, Fazekaș, and Dalea are all about the same age (early
fifties). Not much is known about Fazekaș, but Dalea and Ceaușescu apparently are antagonists. Dalea is a former ambassador to the Soviet Union, and his
links with the C.P.S.U. and possibly with elements in the R.C.P. elite that

course of 1955 it became evident that Khrushchev's power position was increasing at the expense of Malenkov's.[18] The Romanian elite's announcement of the Party Congress in September, 1955, may be interpreted as being largely a consequence of Khrushchev's visit to Bucharest in August. The withdrawal of L. G. Melnikov as ambassador to Romania and his replacement by one of Khrushchev's closest associates, A. A. Epishev, immediately before Khrushchev's arrival, was undoubtedly a signal to the Romanian elite that Khrushchev (and the Party *apparat*) had been the victors in the succession crisis brought on by Stalin's death.[19] In turn, Gheorghiu-Dej not only called the Congress but on October 5, 1955, resumed the position of First Secretary (giving the Premiership to Chivu Stoica), thereby reflecting the power situation in the Soviet Union and his own personal and organizational preference.

I would conclude from these events that during this period Gheorghiu-Dej saw Khrushchev as the most desirable candidate for leadership of the Soviet Union. I am aware that there are analyses that differ from mine, and since my position here is essential to the subsequent argument, I will develop the point further. Gheorghiu-Dej and Khrushchev shared a number of significant characteristics and commitments: both men were of the working class; both adopted or possessed a "paternal" orientation toward their

---

have recently been purged (Drăghici, Apostol, Stoica) may explain his recent removal from the Secretariat. In a list of Party notables that appeared in *Scînteia* on February 28, 1970, Dalea's name was conspicuously out of its proper order. The Party elite is usually listed in three tiers, the first ending with Verdeţ, the second with Ştefan Voitec; Dalea, former ambassador, former member of the Secretariat, and former head of agriculture, appeared out of alphabetical order and last in the third tier. Less than a month later, however, on March 20, it was announced in *Scînteia* that Dalea (along with Miron Constantinescu) had been elected a nonvoting member (*membru supleant*) of the Executive Committee. Dalea's basis of support and political ties are unknown. His staying capacity despite Ceauşescu's apparent opposition to him makes him worthy of some attention.

[18] On this point see Conquest, *Power and Policy*, pp. 254–255. Ionescu's conclusion (p. 231) that Khrushchev's ascendancy dates from 1954 does not appear to be substantiated.

[19] It is worthwhile to refer back to the comments on Melnikov, Epishev, Khrushchev, and their relation to the Ukranian and the Romanian Party; see p. 141, n. 22.

constituency; both, particularly at this time, were "tough" toward the intellectual community; both were champions of heavy industry, of domestic orthodoxy, and above all of the Party as the concrete ruling institution.[20] In addition, it was Khrushchev who initiated the redefinition of relations with the other socialist communities beginning with China. This is an important point, because those who see Gheorghiu-Dej attempting as early as 1954 to pursue a conscious-purposive policy of opposition to the Soviet leader argue that Gheorghiu-Dej emulated the Chinese in attempting to wrest concessions from Khrushchev.[21] In light of Khrushchev's innovations, particularly his strengthening of the Party, and his continued domestic orthodoxy, it seems much more plausible to assume that in 1954–1955 Khrushchev and Mao were allies. And indeed in the opinion of one China expert, Franz Schurmann, such an assumption is warranted.[22] If such was the case, then there existed between Romania (Gheorghiu-Dej) and the Soviet Union (Khrushchev) as well as between the Soviet union (Khrushchev) and China (Mao) a significant *congruence* of interests, definitions, and policies.

It is possible to relate Gheorghiu-Dej's preference for Khrushchev both to the individuals who opposed Dej in 1954 and 1957 and to the types of issues that served as the basis for this conflict. It appears that Miron Constantinescu was the major focal point of opposition to Gheorghiu-Dej between 1954 and 1957; most students of Romanian affairs would agree with this. Not all would agree, however, with my conclusion that Constantinescu was Romania's "Malenkov" and not its "Khrushchev."[23] Like Malenkov,

----

[20] These characteristics and commitments are not, of course, all of the same nature or political significance, but they are complementary, and in the case of Gheorghiu-Dej and Khrushchev they formed an integrated syndrome. Moreover, the two syndromes were highly congruent with each other — with significant implications for the positive relationship between the two leaders in 1955.

[21] Stephen Fischer-Galati, *The New Rumania*, pp. 49–52.

[22] Franz Schurmann, "Mao Tse-tung," unpublished manuscript, University of California, Berkeley, 1965.

[23] For example, see Fischer-Galati, *The New Rumania*, p. 59. To argue that Constantinescu's political orientation was closer to Malenkov's than to

Constantinescu was (and remains) a dedicated communist and a Party man. Nevertheless, both Malenkov and Constantinescu demonstrated an orientation which emphasized the state, rationalization, and a more flexible control (in Parsonian terms, regulative *vs.* authoritative) over intellectuals. Finally, and perhaps most significantly, although a Party man, Constantinescu appears, like Malenkov, to have opposed what Nicolaevsky has termed "the apparat's dictatorship over the Party."[24] Quite simply, a position such as Constantinescu's (or Malenkov's) was bound to be unacceptable to Gheorghiu-Dej. Constantinescu not only presented Dej with an individual political challenge but also represented an alternative definition of the Party's composition, role, and structure. In many ways Miron Constantinescu was a representative of what was to be the major challenge faced by the Romanian Party during the period 1955–1965 — the integration of the political elite and the new social stratum created by its significantly successful breakthrough and industrialization program. Constantinescu actually embodied and combined aspects of the new, loyal middle class and the technically proficient, ideologically committed Party cadre.

Khrushchev's defeat of the "anti-Party" group in 1957 and Gheorghiu-Dej's exclusion of Constantinescu (and Chişinevski) from the Politburo in the same year provide a useful cut-off point for our analysis. The period of intense political uncertainty was over. In the Romanian case the "lessons" of the period were in most respects latent though available. They were latent precisely because agreements seemed to exist between the C.P.S.U. and the Romanian Party as to what behavior and policies were appropriate for actors or units within the bloc. It was on the basis of this "agreement" that the Romanian elite entered into what we have chosen to call a period of emulation.

Khrushchev's does not suggest that Constantinescu did not utilize the anti-Stalin speech made by Khrushchev at the XXth Congress to challenge Gheorghiu-Dej's position in the Romanian Party. But one should not from this conclude automatically that Constantinescu was a Khrushchevite.

[24] Janet D. Zagoria, ed., *Power and the Soviet Elite: "The Letter of an Old Bolshevik" and Other Essays by Boris I. Nicolaevsky* (New York, 1965), p. 116.

14

A Period of Emulation 1958-1961

AMONG THE RECENT flood of articles calling for a subdiscipline of comparative communist studies, Paul Shoup has pointed out that there is notably lacking a "conceptual framework, such as the notion of pluralism or the process of modernization, which could unify and orient empirical studies of communist states along comparative lines."[1] Instead of a comprehensive framework, it seems to me that we need to work out concepts that are abstract enough to be of value in comparative studies and, particularly, to be relevant to comparative studies of communist systems. Emulation appears to be such a concept. Although it is not a systematically developed or widely used concept, in any other than an ad hoc sense, it is one that has been applied and defined in comparative terms by Gerschenkron and more recently by Reinhard Bendix.[2] In addi-

---

[1] Paul Shoup, "Comparing Communist Nations, Prospects for an Empirical Approach," *American Political Science Review* 62 (March 1968): 186.

[2] See Reinhard Bendix, "Tradition and Modernity Reconsidered," *Com-*

tion, and this is a rarity in communist studies, Glenn Paige has employed and developed it very creatively in an analysis of North Korea's political development.[3] It is with reference to this treatment of emulation that we shall begin our analysis of Romanian national development during the period 1958–1961.

Paige defines emulative behavior as being "purposive organizational behavior, the object of which is to reproduce the behavior patterns (including policies) of another organization."[4] He also specifies the conditions under which emulative behavior is likely to occur, and experience is among them. The less the independent experience of a given elite the more likely it is to adopt in detail the experience of what is considered a legitimate referent. Similarly, I have argued that the Romanian elite, having no "practical ideology," turned to the Soviet model. Using Paige's terms, objective conditions in the late 1940s and first half of the '50s, together with an external orientation (toward the Soviet Union) and external control (until 1958 in both North Korea and Romania when Chinese troops and Russian troops, respectively, were removed) resulted in emulative behavior by both the North Korean and Romanian elites.[5] The Romanians, for a number of reasons,

---

parative Studies in Society and History 9 (April 1967): 292–346; and Alexander Gerschenkron, ed., "Economic Backwardness . . . ," in *Economic Backwardness in Historical Perspective* (Cambridge, Mass., 1962), pp. 5–31.

[3] Glenn Paige, "North Korea and the Emulation of Russian and Chinese Behavior," in *Communist Strategies in Asia*, ed. A. Doak Barnett (New York, 1963), pp. 228–262.

[4] *Ibid.*, p. 228.

[5] As Michael Montias has observed, owing to the presence of Soviet troops in Romania until 1958, it is impossible in the absence of confidential internal information to establish definitely whether or not Gheorghiu-Dej's emulation of Soviet policy in the period prior to withdrawal (i.e., 1948–1952) was the result of conviction or lack of choice. But there are a number of considerations that lead me to think that, if we must choose between conviction or necessity, conviction was a major element in Dej's behavior. The uncertainty surrounding the breakthrough endeavor, the prestige and power of the Soviet elite, and Dej's dogmatic orthodoxy (expressed so clearly in the "Decision on the Improvement of Party Work and Relations of the Party with the Masses" adopted at the time of the August, 1953, Plenum: see Fischer-Galati, *The New Rumania*, p. 47) all give the "conviction" interpretation plausibility.

continued until the end of 1961 to demonstrate a very high degree of emulation in contrast to the Korean elite, which began to engage earlier in purposive behavior based on perceived self-interest rather than on the reproduction of a referent's behavior. An analysis of why the North Korean elite chose a policy of initiation can help us to appreciate the reasons why the Romanian elite continued its emulative pattern. This quite different behavior of these two elites may be related to one of Paige's major hypotheses — that the propensity to emulate may be correlated with the perceived success of such behavior in terms of goal achievement. For a number of reasons, the North Korean elite perceived sooner than the Romanians a need to initiate a new policy in order to achieve goals that were not being achieved by emulation. Among these reasons were the implications of the Soviet policy of peaceful coexistence, the high incidence of factionalism within the Korean Workers Party, the unique relationship with the Soviet Union and China, and the critical role played by Soviet–Korean personnel in the Korean regime. The primary goal of the North Korean elite was the reunification of Korea, and this was hardly compatible with a policy of peaceful coexistence. The Romanians, on the other hand, could accept the policy of peaceful coexistence, to the extent that it implied greater domestic flexibility and increased trade potential, and was related to the notion of noninterference, which at this time was interpreted by the Romanian elite as applying primarily to the West and not to the Soviet Union. A second element in the independent course taken by the North Korean party was party factionalism. Not only were there individuals in opposition to Kim, but they seem to have been reasonably well organized and unified in spirit. Kim had by 1955 eliminated the "do-

---

Dej's political choices further strengthen the plausibility of the "conviction" interpretation. The removal of Soviet troops in 1958 was not the first time Dej had been presented with a situation allowing for greater choice. Stalin's death and the threat to Khrushchev in 1957 were also situations allowing for political initiative. Dej took advantage of the first to liquidate the proponent of greater national independence, Pătrășcanu, and used the second to eliminate the man assumed to be a national-Stalinist, Constantinescu. In both instances, rather than assuming the mantle of national-Stalinist or using his position to pre-empt this claim by others, Dej attacked the nationalist positions head on.

mestic faction" led by Pak Hon-yong, but he was still faced with a "Chinese" faction and a "Soviet" faction.[6] Gheorghiu-Dej had no such internal opposition, either in terms of organization or in terms of diversity. Nor had Gheorghiu-Dej experienced anything comparable to the situation that involved Kim and his faction with both the Soviet Union and China as a result of the Korean War. Finally, although the Romanian regime had had the experience of being staffed with numbers of Soviet personnel, its experience and that of the Koreans undoubtedly differed in magnitude at least. In Korea, according to two experts, "the power and influence of the Russian faction was not confined to organization and propaganda within the party. The men from the Soviet Union were dominant in industry, agriculture, construction, education, and news media. The group from Kzyl Orda was particularly conspicuous."[7] The faction led by Kim Il-song saw that its major priority, reunification, was being jeopardized by the Soviet Union, and it was unable to satisfy its aspirations through "domesticism." Its awareness of the need for policy initiation and not simply emulation was heightened by its unique experience with tutelary rule by two superiors, by the threat to domestic control posed by organized and highly distinctive factions, and finally, but not insignificantly, by the limits that were being imposed upon even routine, domestic autonomy by the presence of a Soviet-oriented cadre of experts unwilling to abdicate their positions of responsibility. Considerations of this sort did not really apply to Romania. In 1960, Gheorghiu-Dej, at least, still had faith in emulation as the best way of achieving Party goals. This interpretation is supported if one looks at the two areas in which conflict might soonest have occurred — conceptions of the world communist movement and attitudes toward comprehensive industrialization.

In December, 1960, in reporting to the R.W.P. on the meeting of Communist Parties held in Moscow the previous month,

---

[6] On factions in the Korean Workers Party see Chong-Sik Lee, "Stalinism in the East, in *The Communist Revolution in Asia*, ed. Robert A. Scalapino, pp. 114–140.

[7] Chong-Sik Lee and Ki-Wan Oh, "The Russian Faction in North Korea," *Asian Survey* 8 (April 1968): 285.

Gheorghiu-Dej presented a formulation of bloc unity that was Soviet-initiated and traditional: "The unity and the ever growing forces of the socialist camp are a reliable guarantee for each socialist country against the attempts of imperialist reaction and ensure within the framework of the entire socialist camp, the complete victory of socialism."[8] The order here is clearly different from the Italian party's definition of what guaranteed unity, and different also from the present Romanian leadership's definition of what constitutes the basis of a "reliable guarantee"; and in 1961 Gheorghiu-Dej still believed that the strength of all was the guarantee of each. It was to be two or three years before he accepted the argument that the strength of each party and regime are the basis of the unity and strength of the whole. In 1961, Gheorghiu-Dej was quite explicit as to the nature of the communist movement: "The entire international communist and working class movement recognizes the role played by the C.P.S.U. as its leading detachment, which makes the chief contribution to the enrichment of the theoretical treasury of Marxism–Leninism at every stage of the evolution of history."[9] Another index of the Romanian elite's conformity to Soviet premises was the R.W.P.'s standing at the Soviet XXIst and XXIInd Congresses in 1959 and 1961. At both Congresses Romania was ranked fifth (in comparison with 1956 when it was eighth), ahead of both Hungary and Bulgaria.[10]

Domestically, there was equally little reason for Gheorghiu-Dej and his closest associates to abandon the emulative posture. The year 1958 is a particularly appropriate date to set as the beginning of a period of rather complete Romanian emulation based on what was a substantial congruence of interests between the

---

[8] Gh. Gheorghiu-Dej, "Report Delivered at the Penum of the C.C. of the R.W.P., Held on December 19–20, 1960, on the Moscow Meeting of Representatives of the Communist and Workers' Parties of November 1960," in *Articles and Speeches*, p. 128.

[9] Gh. Gheorghiu-Dej, "Speech Delivered to the Big Meeting of Moscow Dedicated to Rumanian-Soviet Friendship (August 11, 1961)," in *ibid.*, p. 203.

[10] See Alexander Dallin, ed., *Diversity in International Communism* (New York, 1963), p. 2. By way of contrast: Gromyko in his "accommodating" speech of July 11, 1969, placed Romania last in the ranks of those belonging to the Warsaw Pact.

Soviet Union and Romania. In 1958, in what Professor Montias describes as an "authoritative article," Ts. A. Stepanyan put forward the thesis of the "more or less simultaneous transition to communism and its relation to mutual aid in the bloc." Montias goes on to note that Khrushchev confirmed Stepanyan's thesis at the Soviet party's XXIst Congress in January, 1959.[11] All this could only have accorded with the industrialization goals of the Gheorghiu-Dej leadership, and Gheorghiu-Dej and his adherents were probably more than pleased by Khrushchev's remarks at the IIIrd (now VIIIth) Congress of the Romanian Workers (now Communist) Party, in particular by the references to the Romanian Party's economic-plan figures, in which Khrushchev compared them to a symphony, and by Khrushchev's statement that the Romanian Party, inspired by the great victories of the Soviet Union, had secured liberty and independence for Romania.[12] In utter sincerity, too, Gheorghiu-Dej could take note in his December, 1960, report to the Party of the "brilliant speeches made by Comrade N. S. Khrushchev" at the November meeting of Communist Parties in Moscow.

However, to argue that between 1958 and 1961 the Romanian elite engaged primarily in emulative behavior, with regard to the critical issues of position in the bloc, attitude toward the Soviet Union, and domestic priorities, is *not* to say (*a*) that there was complete harmony between the Soviets and Romanians, (*b*) that there

---

[11] J. M. Montias, *Economic Development in Communist Rumania*, pp. 197, 198.

[12] "Cuvîntarea de salut Tovarăşului N.S. Hruşciov," *Congresul al III-lea al Partidului Muncitoresc Romîn* (Bucureşti, 1960), pp. 194 and 197–198. Khrushchev did not, I think, take an unfavorable view of the course the Romanian Party initiated in November, 1958, although others, particularly more specialized elites such as some Soviet economists, may well have done so. It is of great interest in the period 1958–1961 to analyze the way in which loosely linked issues involving different sub-elites in the Soviet Union, Romania, and other East European countries were drawn together, gained in political salience, and had their content substantially redefined.

In this connection it would be interesting to investigate the role that Kosygin played after becoming head of Gosplan in 1959 in hardening the Soviet and in particular Khrushchev's posture toward the Romanian industrialization plans.

was a complete absence of purposive behavior by the Romanians vis-à-vis the Soviets, or (c) that there were not significant implications involved in the Romanian commitment to industrialization.

To develop the first point (a), one may posit a Romanian posture of emulation based on a perceived congruence of interests between them and the Soviets while still allowing for certain types of conflict. It is my argument, however, that those conflicts which existed during this period (1958–1961) were dealt with in two major ways: by problem solving or by persuasion. According to March and Simon, both these processes involve the recognition of those engaged in the conflict that at some level objectives are shared: "In problem-solving it is assumed that objectives are shared and that the decision problem is to identify a solution that satisfies the shared criteria," while "implicit in the use of persuasion is the belief that at some level objectives are shared and that disagreement over subgoals can be mediated by reference to common goals."[13] Conflict, then, between the Soviet and Romanian elites at this point did not revolve around issues that directly questioned the character of their political relations. In Selznick's terms, conflict was significant but routine. Given this appreciation of the specific character of Soviet–Romanian conflict at this time, the issue raised by some analysts as to whether or not Khrushchev, at the June, 1960, Congress, promised to aid the Romanian industrial endeavor at Galaţi becomes less important than our ability to define the nature of the conflict that probably did exist over this issue. By being able to define the nature of this conflict as "routine," — that is, as significant but not directly bringing into question the basic definition of interelite relations — we are saved from jumping to the unwarranted conclusion that conflict over this issue showed that already in 1960, the Romanian elite was "declaring its independence."[14]

The second point (b) is related to the first and concerns the

---

[13] James G. March and Herbert A. Simon, *Organizations* (New York, 1958), p. 129.

[14] Obviously, if the Soviet elite had categorically stated its refusal to contribute in any way to the process of Romanian industrialization, that would have been a critical issue.

type of conflict that can be associated with emulative behavior. In analyzing the Romanian elite's purposive behavior during this period, the question is not whether it existed or not, but what it was related to. It would seem that at this time the Romanian elite's major effort in terms of purposive behavior was its attempt to reinforce existing Soviet ideological and policy commitments precisely because they were in accord with Romanian aspirations. Consistently, the Romanians emphasized Soviet statements that involved a commitment to industrialization, a creative application of Leninism, and peaceful coexistence. The Romanian elite also tried to use statements of this sort to strengthen their own efforts to reach their goals: they tried to persuade the Soviets to commit themselves to the industrial complex at Galați on the grounds that it was consistent with the Soviet-defined principle of "mutual entry" to communism and the Soviet emphasis on industrialization.

Finally, with regard to the last point (*c*), the Romanian commitment to industrialization had significant implications for the evolution of Soviet–Romanian relations even during this period of congruence of interests. The emulative posture and "domesticist" political stance which had so long characterized the Romanian elite had seriously circumscribed the Romanian regime's autonomy throughout the period we are discussing. In such a situation of circumscribed autonomy Thompson's hypothesis seems applicable: "The more sectors in which the organization [i.e., R.W.P.] subject to rationality norms is constrained [i.e., by the C.P.S.U.], the more power the organization will seek over remaining sectors of its task environment [i.e., industrial sector]."[15] Particularly from 1958 on, the one area in which the Romanian elite felt autonomous, in good part because of Soviet sanction, was in its policy of industrialization. Within such a context it may be hypothesized that the Romanian elite tended to emphasize industrialization almost to the exclusion of every other goal and in fact tended to look upon industrialization as a summary expression of all its goals. The commitment to industrialization was not, however, based simply on the situational circumstance that within that particular policy domain the Romanian elite exercised a good deal

---

[15] James D. Thompson, *Organizations in Action*, p. 36.

of (sanctioned) autonomy. Rather, this situational circumstance reinforced an ideological commitment that was substantive in nature. The significance of this point for future (post-1961) Soviet–Romanian relations resides in the character of a substantive commitment. In Weber's terms, it is one which cannot be altered by any reference to the notion of economic calculation;[6] it is non-negotiable. As long as Soviet and Romanian interests were perceived as being congruent, the character of the Romanian emphasis on and commitment to its policy of industrialization did not become a salient factor. Its significance rested in its existence and in the possibility that at some time the Soviet elite would define its interests in a way that would conflict with Gheorghiu-Dej's most valued policy.

By 1961 the conflict that existed between the Soviet and Romanian elites was beginning to change in character. An appreciation of this change — of relating time periods, levels of conflict, and types of conflict resolution — has a great deal to do with the success with which one can locate and understand the various stages in the growing Soviet–Romanian antagonism which resulted eventually in the Romanian "independent course."

In his work on Romanian economic development Montias notes that beginning in 1961, "the public discussion of CEMA [Comecon] issues became more acrimonious," and he suggests that domestic economic setbacks within the Soviet Union were at the root of this new Soviet posture.[17] I would agree that 1961 was the year in which a new sort of conflict appeared between the Soviet and Romanian elites.

In 1961 there was a definite increase in conflict, and for the next year and a half the conflict was of a different sort from before. Where there had formerly been problem solving and persuasion, there was now bargaining (and persuasion). To refer to March and Simon, bargaining is used "where disagreement over goals is taken as fixed and agreement without persuasion is sought."[18] In my view, by the end of 1961 most of the Romanian elite had come to

---

[16] Max Weber, *The Theory of Social and Economic Organization*, p. 185.
[17] Montias, *Economic Development*, pp. 205, 209.
[18] March and Simon, *Organizations*, p. 130.

this position. There was still some attempt to use other conflict-resolving strategies, particularly persuasion, but bargaining was the preferred strategy.

This was true for several reasons. On the whole, the principle set forth by Hoffmann seems to have prevailed — that there are real limits to "the credit of ambiguity." [19] A highly congruent situation was being superseded by one in which Soviet and Romanian self-interest could not be adequately reconciled to the mutual satisfaction of their respective goals. Reflecting the legacy of bloc relations, in particular the hierarchical precedence of the Soviet Union and its consensual definition of bloc unity,[20] in 1961 the Soviet elite began to manipulate ideological definitions and policy decisions so as to secure Romanian compliance to the new Soviet orientation. Following the XXIInd Soviet Party Congress, Aleksei Rumiantsev, editor-in-chief of the *World Marxist Review,* made a statement which, though directed at Albania, had significant implications for bloc relations per se. Rumiantsev noted that the "qualitatively new forms of relations . . . [among] the socialist countries . . . are not limited to a recognition of equality and sovereignty." Rather, such relations involved "fraternal association" which was a condition of proletarian and socialist internationalism.[21] In short, the Soviets were reasserting their right to interfere directly in the affairs of other communist parties and states.[22] More specifically, in a speech printed in *Pravda,* December 2, 1961, Yuri Andropov commented on "The XXII C.P.S.U. Congress and the Development of the World Socialist System," and did not fail to quote Gheorghiu-Dej, alone out of all the possible Party leaders within the bloc, in suggesting that the Albanian party leaders had veered away from the general line of the communist movement reflected in the 1957 and 1960 documents. Andropov further suggested that in so doing they were "destroying

[19] Stanley Hoffmann, "Obstinate or Obsolete? The Fate of the Nation-State and the Case of Western Europe," *Daedalus* 95 (Summer 1966): 874.

[20] The "consensual" approach to unity and conflict is defined in Part I.

[21] For the Rumiantsev statement see Dallin, *Diversity,* p. 624.

[22] Rumiantsev was stating the doctrine of limited sovereignty quite clearly almost a decade before Brezhnev was credited with the formulation of this concept.

the fraternal cooperation of the socialist countries and of the Communist and workers parties." [23] In an indirect but nonetheless telling fashion, the Soviet elite was reminding the Romanian elite of its obligations and Soviet expectations, and of the potential consequences of noncompliance.

Thus by the end of 1961 the period of Romanian emulation seemed to be ending, and it was shortly to be replaced by something of a different order. But before we begin to analyze what it was that replaced emulation, we should take a closer look at what had occurred within the Romanian political-social system during the period 1958–1961.

The Socio-Political Character of the Romanian Regime

Beginning around 1958, the core problem facing the Romanian elite became the integration of a relatively new social stratum, which had been created as a result of the Party's emphasis on mobilization and industrialization. Romania's economic "take-off" [24] which started in 1958 acted as a stimulus to the growth and significance of this stratum, and the questions of its role, status, and power in the Romanian political system, and of its contribution and relation to the definition of a Romanian socialist political community, grew ever more important. The manner in which the problem presented itself is important. Since at least 1958 the Romanian political system has been distinguished by the coexistence of conflicting types of strategic social-political strata. A new middle class began to compete and conflict with (as well as accommodate itself to) an already established "new class" in an attempt to assert itself as the defining element of the new political community in Romania.

Interestingly, it was a former member of the Romanian Communist intelligentsia, Petru Dumitriu, who first reached an appreciation of the existence of "Two New Classes." Dumitriu makes a distinction that is not merely historical: the new-class, which

---

[23] For the Andropov statement see Dallin, p. 614.

[24] On the Romanian economic "take-off," see Montias, *Economic Development*, pp. 53–79.

appeared in 1944 and is now the "ruling class," was not, he thinks, created and conditioned by the forces of industrialization. Indeed, he says, "it is worth remarking that the intellectual approach of the new-class to economic and technological problems is of . . . [an] irrational and authoritarian kind. . . . The typical member of the new ruling class is intellectually a stranger to the rational utilitarian thought which produces industrialism."[25] In my opinion, this is only partly correct. So far as the process of industrialization required a major breakthrough, involving individuals with a high sense of urgency, little patience with obstacles,[26] and a strong commitment to the process itself, the new-class was simultaneously a condition for and a product of the particular type of industrialization that occurred in Romania, and in other Leninist regimes. On the other hand, Dumitriu is undoubtedly right in saying that this stratum lacked an appreciation of the economic and technological character of the process — which, paradoxically, contributed to their capacity to launch it with such enthusiasm and comprehensiveness. Rather than the new-class, it was the new middle class, Dumitriu says, that was "created by the process of industrialization" — a class of skilled workers, technicians, scientists, professional people, and low-level economic managers.[27]

---

[25] See Petru Dumitriu, "The Two New Classes," *East Europe* 10 (September 1961): 5.

[26] For vivid descriptions of this sort of orientation, see two novels by the Slovak writer Ladislav Mnachko: *The Seventh Night* (New York, 1969) and *The Taste of Power* (New York, 1967).

[27] Dumitriu, "The Two New Classes," p. 5; and see also Milovan Djilas, *The Unperfect Society: Beyond the New Class* (New York, 1969), pp. 205–206, where he notes that "in each East European country in a different guise and with varying intensity, ground has already been covered for the creation of a new social stratum, a special middle class recruited from all present day strata, from the top of the party oligarchy itself to skilled workers and well-to-do peasants. The sum and substances of this new stratum are specialists of all kinds." The rest of Djilas' comments concerning the political characteristics of this group are more debatable. Ionescu alone among those studying Romania has focused on the appearance of this professional stratum. As of 1960, he estimated that there were approximately 700,000 people in this category. Although some of his conclusions about their orientations are debatable, his statement is an important one. See *Communism in Rumania*, pp. 325–331.

Dumitriu also distinguishes between these two strata in the matter of how they view their position in the political community. To paraphrase Dumitriu, the new-class (actually the older) is highly class-oriented; it is extremely aware of its own identity and defines itself not in relation to other strata but in opposition to them. Such a hypothesis seems plausible if we take into account the origin of this stratum. The new-class is the product of and quite naturally the exponent of the breakthrough process and of a set of policies and orientations which placed the greatest emphasis on manipulation, mistrust, and reduction of commitments to individuals, groups, and strata that were regarded as not being fully committed to the breakthrough. The new middle class, on the other hand, Dumitriu says, on account of its historical formation, economic role, and social status, sees itself as the defining core of the new socialist nation.[28] Dumitriu's comments on the place and role of the new middle class are somewhat diffuse, but extremely perceptive: here is a class that is the product of the Romanian Party's own policies — an indigenous class oriented toward professionalism, and the potential nucleus of a new socialist community with a real claim for recognition.[29] If, as Binder has argued, the success of political integration and national development "depends upon the almost chance creation of social strata which are by virtue of the peculiarities of their socialization and education both willing and capable of presenting a behavioral and ideological synthesis of historical values and the values associated with modernity,"[30] then in Romania the emergence of a new middle class in the late 1950's significantly approximates this social type. But one further point can be added: although Leninist elites are the more likely to attempt the *conscious* forging of such a type, the

---

[28] "The Two New Classes," p. 33.

[29] The term recognition is particularly important. As used here it refers to the aspiration of a social class for significant socio-political status. It is this desire for socio-political status as opposed to a desire for remuneration or even power that distinguishes the new professional class. I shall elaborate on this point in a work currently in progress, "Political Integration in Leninist Political Communities."

[30] Leonard Binder, "National Integration and Political Development," *American Political Science Review* 58 (September 1964): 630.

policies associated with this attempt bring about the prior creation of a social type to which the Party becomes highly committed,
of which the Party is in many respects a part, and which perceives
itself as threatened by the new middle class; that social type is the
new-class. The socio-political character of the Romanian regime
and community is largely, though not exclusively, a function of
the conflict *and* accommodation that has occurred and is occurring
still between these two strategic strata and orientations.[31]

A related conflict which appeared in 1958 involved alternative modes of securing compliance or conflicting types of incentives. Until 1958, the distinguishing characteristic of the Romanian
regime's efforts to induce compliance from its public was the use

---

[31] Since I do not know of any clear or useful definition of the new-class,
I shall designate several aspects of this socio-political entity which can help
one to identify it and differentiate it from other strata.

   (A) Historically the new-class tended to possess the following objective
       characteristics: (1) worker or peasant origin; (2) little education;
       (3) rudimentary skills.

   (B) More generally, the new-class may be defined in terms of its major
       social and political orientations: (1) Command approach to prob-
       lems and socio-political relations; an approach that is congruent
       with the posture and behavior of "officials" in most of interwar
       Eastern Europe. (2) "Mock bureaucratic" values. Orientation to
       ascriptive-personalistic and diffuse criteria of competence — again
       congruent with interwar values and behavior, but in this case rein-
       forced by the structure and defining principles of the patrimonial
       breakthrough system. (3) A preference for a patrimonially defined
       political regime and for the dominance of the apparatus over Party
       and regime. (4) A preference that finds ideological expression in the
       new-class's commitment to the concept of the "dictatorship of the
       proletariat."

   (C) As for the relationship of the new-class to the Party *apparat*, as a
       specific set of political roles the Party *apparat* has an identity of its
       own with interests which overlap those of the new-class. However,
       to the extent that the new-class is defined not in terms of formal
       political roles but in terms of sociopolitical orientations (see B), those
       members of the Party *apparat* with orientations such as those noted
       in section B may be legitimately considered members of the new-class.
       See Petru Dumitriu's article, "The Two New Classes," for another at-
tempt to define the new-class.

of coercive methods. This reliance on coercion was partly due to the emphasis placed on breaking through, but it was also a consequence of the type of personnel recruited into the Party, the socialization (informal as well as formal) these cadres received, and the existence of an institution such as the security police which in a real sense found its rationale in the employment of coercion and terror; and it was also a consequence of Gheorghiu-Dej's somewhat unsophisticated vision of the outlines of the new Romanian political community. The year 1958 was in a real sense a turning point. Actually, during that year, the regime seems to have decided on the use of utilitarian incentives as the major means of securing public compliance. Reflecting its Stalinist character and internal conflicts, this new policy was accompanied by more traditional-coercive measures. In July, 1958, Decree 318 was issued, elaborating new crimes and punishments in the penal code, including imposition of the death penalty for such offenses as "dealing with foreigners for the purpose of engaging the state in a declaration of neutrality."[32] But also in 1958 there were some real improvements in the material life of the people. Starting that year and continuing through 1964, the Romanians "succeeded in raising their imports of foodstuffs by 50% and in nearly tripling their imports of manufactured consumer goods . . . with noticeable effect on the size and the variety of the fund of consumer goods available to the population."[33] The regime may have countered absenteeism, embezzlement, and theft by reactivating judgment councils in factories and meting out harsher prison sentences as well as imposing the death penalty for "embezzlement of socialist property," but by the end of 1958 it was ordering new wage increases, price reductions, and as Fischer-Galati goes on to say, a "considerable extension of social security benefits granted workers."[34] Why did this shift occur? The reasons usually given

---

[32] Ghita Ionescu, *Communism in Rumania*, p. 290.

[33] John Michael Montias, "Rumania's Foreign Trade in the Postwar Period," *Slavic Review* 25 (September 1966): 435.

[34] Stephen Fischer-Galati, "Rumania," in *East Central Europe and the World: Developments in the Post-Stalin Era*, ed. Stephen D. Kertesz (Notre Dame, Ind., 1962), pp. 159–160.

include the greater availability of material goods to use as utilitarian incentives, and the relative ineffectiveness of coercive methods. There are additional reasons, however. To begin with, there was the precedent of Stalinism, which had never forsaken material incentives but on the contrary had employed them invidiously. One can also assume, I think, that the new middle or professional class was of importance — that certain elements in the Party elite coalition were in favor of stressing utilitarian incentives as the best way of getting good performance from the new middle class. The appropriateness of such incentives, it should be emphasized, was very likely defined in terms of expressive as well as instrumental considerations. For certain individuals within the Party the appearance of a skilled stratum — a product of the regime's own efforts and a potential guarantee of the regime's efforts to create a new society — called for a new sort of approach which not only rewarded this stratum economically but also showed that the regime was aware, politically as well as ideologically, of its role, aspirations, and potential.

Nevertheless, despite the reorientation of incentives, the increasing prominence of this new stratum, and the attempts of certain Party notables to act on this new situation, the new-class, which had been recruited on the basis of ascriptive considerations, continued to hold and fuse positions of status, power, and economic reward.[35] The obvious question is how?

---

[35] That this situation has continued to exist at least within the socioeconomic realm is demonstrated by Ceauşescu's speech on June 20, 1968 (*Scînteia*), in which he criticized the holding of several positions by one individual — an individual usually not competent to perform specialized tasks, usually not even trying very hard, always receiving an income from all his positions, and acting as a barrier to the upward mobility of new, trained cadres. Since 1965, however, the political elite, partly because of its changed composition, has become more and more antagonistic toward the policies and orientations of the new-class, and their attitude is bound to have an effect on the type of individual and stratum that occupy high status positions within the regime and serve as a recruiting base for the Party. The extent and quality of the regime's receptivity toward the new middle class will be of great importance in determining how far this "objective" class will become aware of its existence as a collectivity and define itself in terms which challenge the Party's current definition of socio-political life.

Gheorghiu-Dej and Party Institutionalization

If it is true that the core problem confronting the Romanian elite since 1958 has been effective integration of a new social stratum which we have termed the new middle class, it is equally true that the Party was the major factor influencing the resolution of this problem. One must therefore clearly define this organization's political character, the type of institution it was in the period under discussion (1958–1961), and the type of institution it is becoming. We can proceed with two hypotheses; (a) that the character of a political community is a combination of the social definition of its major publics, the political definition of its elites, and the relation between them (i.e., whether the emphasis is on manipulation or reciprocity), (b) that the decisive factor in the formulation of this identity, at least in Leninist contexts, is the character of the political elite. To state the hypotheses another way, one can view national communities as sets of reciprocal relationships between elites and publics possessing a character which, in Leninist systems, is decisively influenced by the specific political-ideological nature of the elite itself. Implicit in this argument is the contention that the term communist or Leninist, though having meaning at one level of abstraction, should not be allowed to conceal the existence of several analytically coherent subtypes of Leninist elites and communities.

This theoretical discussion may be related to the question of how it was that by 1961 (and as late as 1967) the new-class had continued to monopolize economic perquisites as well as positions of power and status, despite the appearance of a broad indigenous stratum of highly skilled persons. The answer to this phenomenon is mostly to be found in the significant power exercised by the political sphere over the socio-economic sphere in Leninist systems. Specifically, the answer can be traced to the particular type of party and regime that Gheorghiu-Dej had created between 1947 and 1957 as well as in the support that he and his party accorded the new-class.

What sort of party was it? Gheorghiu-Dej, speaking at the June, 1960, Party Congress, traced a continuous development of inner-party democracy, involving the participation of all members, the strict observance of democratic centralism, and collective leadership. He made a similar point in late 1961 at the Party Plenum when he said that after the removal of the Pauker faction the Party witnessed the return of normal functioning in the Central Committee, Politburo, and Secretariat: "Leninist standards were re-established . . . and Party control over the activities of all state bodies . . . [was] strengthened." [36] In truth, however, the state of the Party was rather far from Dej's idealized version. The structural and political reality of Party life was patrimonialism. Weber defined patrimonialism primarily in terms of traditional systems, but the concept can, I think, as the Romanians might say, be "creatively applied" to related contexts. Drawing on Guenther Roth's discussion of this topic, one can characterize Gheorghiu-Dej's regime as "personal rulership" based on three things: (*a*) the degree to which the Party's authority had become essentially — though never completely — dependent upon and a reflection of Gheorghiu-Dej's authority; (*b*) Gheorghiu-Dej's personal staff, which was political, military, and administrative in nature (according to Weber, the possession of such an apparatus brings about the development of patrimonialism); and (*c*) the impersonal component of Gheorghiu-Dej's power, which was based on his supporters' concern with material goals and rewards rather than on any belief in his unique personal qualifications. [37]

It is possible further to specify the character of Gheorghiu-Dej's regime after 1957 as resembling Weber's notion of sultanism — a form of patrimonialism in which there is a high concentration of power in an individual who stresses the "sphere of arbitrary will free of traditional limitations." [38] In our case, we would say

---

[36] Gh. Gheorghiu-Dej, "Report of the Delegation of The Rumanian Workers' Party Which Attended the 22nd Congress of the C.P.S.U.," in *Articles and Speeches*, p. 286.

[37] See Weber, *The Theory of*, pp. 346–354; also Guenther Roth, "Personal Rulership, Patrimonialism, and Empire-Building in the New States," *World Politics* 20 (January 1968): 194–207. On patrimonialism see also Richard Morse, "The Heritage of Latin America," in *The Founding of New Societies*, ed. Louis Hartz (New York, 1954), pp. 123–178.

[38] *The Theory of*, p. 347.

it was Gheorghiu-Dej's will free of limitations that the Party might have wanted to impose. The argument that the process of party institutionalization under Gheorghiu-Dej was essentially patrimonial has received significant confirmation from the present head of the Romanian Party in a speech delivered on April 28, 1968. Indeed, the very attributes of Gheorghiu-Dej's rule especially noted by Ceauşescu in that speech are defining aspects of patrimonialism and sultanism. The first point refers to the establishment of Gheorghiu-Dej's authority over Party authority. According to Ceauşescu, in April, 1956, the Politburo decided to remove Alexandru Drăghici as head of the Ministry of the Interior, which had charge of security police and troops. However, "this measure was not applied because of the opposition manifested by Gheorghiu-Dej and Alexandru Drăghici."[39] The relationship here revealed between Drăghici and Gheorghiu-Dej is of some significance: Drăghici was Gheorghiu-Dej's most important "retainer" precisely because he controlled the personal military-administrative apparatus of the leader, Gheorghiu-Dej. The mode of operation characterizing this apparatus is also characteristic of a patrimonial staff. Ceauşescu accused Drăghici of preventing Party (i.e., corporate) control over the Security ministry and forces, of considering himself "above" the Party, and of establishing the police in a dominant position in all spheres of Romanian life — that is, so as to prevent the deconcentration of power and the appearance of semi-autonomous areas within the regime which might oppose Gheorghiu-Dej. To complete the picture, Ceauşescu accused Drăghici of believing that "he could do anything because of his connections with Gheorghiu-Dej."[40]

The events and circumstances that led to the patrimonial definition of the Party have already been enumerated (see p. 147). The point of consequence here is that each of these several factors contributed to the existence of a form of party institutionalization (patrimonialism between 1947 and 1957 and sultanism between 1958 and the early 1960s) which in critical respects was based

---

[39] See Nicolae Ceauşescu, "Cuvîntarea . . . la adunarea activului de partid din Capitală," *Scînteia*, April 28, 1968.

[40] *Ibid.*

upon, and was highly acceptable to, the stratum that Diljas has termed the New Class.

Nevertheless, though patrimonialism in its sultanist form was dominant in the Romanian Party at least from 1957 until 1965, it was not an unquestioned principle. There was a competing and conflicting definition of party institutionalization which, though clearly inferior in power terms, was ideologically legitimate, more or less coherent, and increasingly significant. It was perhaps best expressed by the present head of the R.C.P., Nicolae Ceauşescu. For what I believe to be both material and ideal reasons, Ceauşescu disagreed with the definition of the party espoused and imposed by Gheorghiu-Dej and Drăghici. In terms of material interest, Ceauşescu's opposition was natural, since in true patrimonial fashion Gheorghiu-Dej had placed Drăghici and Ceauşescu in a "mutual-check" position.[41] In addition, as Party Secretary in charge of cadres Ceauşescu was more likely to defend the interests of his institution, the party, against Drăghici's — the police. But there were also ideal considerations involved in Ceauşescu's opposition. There is evidence which suggests that Ceauşescu's vision of the Party is based on an image attributed to Lenin, an image which includes the notion of a "clear code of personal and collegial ethics" among senior members, adherence to Party rules, and institutionalization of the Party as an entity valued in itself and above any one leader.[42]

One important mechanism which increased the political weight of this alternative view of party institutionalization was elite recruitment, particularly into the elite nucleus of the R.W.P.

---

[41] See Myron Rush, *Political Succession in the USSR* (New York, 1965), *passim*. Rush develops the notions of (presumptive) heir and counterheir in his analysis of succession crises. In these terms, by the early '60s Ceauşescu had apparently become the (presumptive) heir and Drăghici the counterheir.

[42] See George F. Kennan's introduction to the book of essays by Nicolaevsky (edited by Janet Zagoria) for a discussion of party character. And see, for example, *Scînteia*, April 18, 1970, where Ceauşescu speaks about Lenin's loyalty toward his work comrades: "As is known, even toward those with whom he had controversies and sharp polemics, Lenin maintained a civilized attitude of consideration and respect."

The term is taken from Janowitz, who differentiates between an elite cadre (in a Leninist system this would refer to the Central Committee) and an elite nucleus (the Politburo and Executive Committee in Romania). Following Janowitz' analysis, individuals within the elite nucleus of an organization tend to have careers that are significantly unconventional (in terms of the organizational norm); they also tend to have innovative perspectives, a capacity for risk-taking, expectations of discretionary responsibility, and well-developed political skills.[43] Organizations existing in or entering into situations that threaten their power and values are likely to recruit individuals with these characteristics into the elite nucleus. Ion Gheorghe Maurer is such an individual. In 1958 he became a full member of the Central Committee, in 1960 a member of the Presidium, and in 1961, the year in which conflict with the Soviets gained a new dimension, Prime Minister. To argue that Maurer was "like" Ceaușescu is not to assume a priori any identity of specific views. But the two men probably shared innovative views on the Romanian Party's posture toward the Soviet Union, on the new Romanian professional or middle classes, and on the role of the police and coercion in the Romanian political system. If, however, the recruitment mechanism was one way of increasing the political weight of Ceaușescu's alternative definition of party institutionalization, there was a certain paradox involved: individuals such as Maurer (and later Bîrlădeanu) may have been selected for membership in the elite nucleus because they filled a genuine need in view of the changing character of Romanian–Soviet conflict, but they were also acceptable to Gheorghiu-Dej as part of the patrimonial system. Personal ties, in other words, associated with political obligation, dependence, and trust, mediated the recruitment of individuals who were, or became, opponents of this patrimonial form of party organization.

By the end of 1961, then, there was in the R.W.P. a dominant form of party institutionalization which we have called patrimonial and an alternative form which was more collegial and legal-rational in intent. That Gheorghiu-Dej's patrimonial definition was clearly

---

[43] Morris Janowitz, *The Professional Soldier* (New York, 1960), p. 8.

dominant can be seen by an examination of several indices of institutionalization.[44]

Leadership coherence By 1961 Gheorghiu-Dej had effectively removed any "fiefs" led by oppositional elements, but had replaced them with patrimonial benefices under his personal control, that is, like Drăghici's in the Ministry of the Interior.

Membership stability In contrast to the period 1944–1952, the rate of entry into the Party was fairly stable between 1955 and 1962, with approximately 300,000 members added in seven years.

Boundaries and autonomy Although there were no longer ministries, departments, and regions which acted as "fiefs," that is, semi-autonomous structures under the Party leader, the Party and the regime were still subject to police control at all levels, as Ceaușescu pointed out in his April, 1968, speech.

Complexity Organizational differentiation may be assumed to have increased owing to the elaboration and take-off of the industrialization program and also to the regime's greater (Soviet-sanctioned) operational autonomy.[45] Critiques currently available in the Romanian press indicate, however, that the criteria for recruitment into new positions often were ascriptive rather than achievement in character.

---

[44] This set of indices is a composite of those used by Selznick, Huntington, Moore, and Polsby.

[45] The term "operational" is used in the specific sense employed by Schurmann, i.e., the implementation of policy; see his "Politics and Economics in Russia and China," in *Soviet and Chinese Communism,* ed. Donald W. Treadgold (Seattle, 1967), pp. 298–299. Schurmann's concept of "operations" is congruent with Selznick's concept of "routine decisions," Kuhn's concept of "rule (*vs.* paradigm) change," and Brzezinski's concept of "domesticism."

The creation of an Executive Committee in 1965 was a recognition of the increased complexity of Party and national life. This is an intermediary elite body between the Central Committee and the Presidium. The existence of this body not only allows for status recognition of more elite members but also, ideally, for more effective representation of different issue areas and points of view, and more effective policy deliberation. On this point see Nicolae Ceaușescu's statement at the IXth Party Congress in July, 1965, in *Congresul al IX-lea al Partidului Comunist Romîn* (București, 1966), pp. 730–732.

Social base   By 1961 the Party had a dual base, though one, the new middle class, was more potential than real. Although neither of these "bases" — the new-class or the new middle class — was homogeneous in composition or outlook, they did hold quite different implications for the future development of the Romanian political system and community.

Interstitial role   The Party was still ideologically and politically situated in an explicitly dominant position over society. Coordination of that society was based primarily on utilitarian and coercive sanctions rather than on shared values and political reciprocity between the Party and at least major strategic publics.

Vision-program definition   In 1961 the program was still very specific and securely bound up with the concrete process of industrialization. Gheorghiu-Dej demonstrated little creativity in dealing with the notion of political community, in reinterpreting the process of breaking through under changing circumstances, or in assimilating the consequences of the success associated with the Party's initial attempts at industrialization.

At the end of its period of emulation in 1961 the Romanian party and regime were characterized by the existence of conflicting types of Party definition, leadership orientation, incentive policies, and of politically relevant social types. Three points can be made about the significance of these conflicts. First, one may posit a "strain towards an effective type."[46] In many respects the new middle class, a collegial party, and an incentive system based on utilitarian and normative incentives form a congruent pattern. Similarly the new-class, a patrimonial party, and an incentive system based on coercive and utilitarian incentives form a congruent pattern. It can also be said that the respective members of these social and political strata give evidence of appreciating this congruence.

Second, to posit a "strain towards an effective type" does not suggest that such a type will automatically occur in any given situation, nor does it suggest which of the types will be the politically dominant one. What can be suggested, however, is that there

[46] See Amitai Etzioni, *A Comparative Analysis of Complex Organizations*, p. 87, for the phrase "strain towards an effective type."

is such a "strain" within opposing syndromes of incentive systems, party definitions, and social strata and that the decisive conflict in deciding which "type" will be socially dominant has to do with party definition. There is, then, a reciprocal relationship between the conflict of social types ("new class" *vs.* "new middle class") and party definitions (patrimonial *vs.* collegial) but it is a relationship biased toward the decisiveness of the latter conflict.

Finally, one cannot appreciate the policy of initiation undertaken by the Romanian elite in 1962 without an appreciation of the existence of these conflicts, nor can one understand the nature of their resolution without an analysis of that policy itself.

15

A Period of Initiation, 1962-1965

THERE IS LITTLE DOUBT that the period 1962–1965 has been so far the most critical in the history of Romanian communism.[1] It is my contention that the Romanian independent course actually began in late 1962 and not, as some analysts have suggested, in either 1955 or 1945.[2] The process of initiation, or establishing

---

[1] J. F. Brown has written a number of very good analyses of the Romanian "independent course": see for example, "Rumania Steps Out of Line," *Survey* 49 (October 1963): 19–35; and "Eastern Europe," *Survey* 54 (January 1965): 65–89. Political scientists are fortunate in having the excellent work of J. M. Montias on the economic aspects of the Romanian "independent course." Besides his book, one should be aware of his "Backgrounds and Origins of the Rumanian Dispute with Comecon," *Soviet Studies* 16 (October 1964): 125–152. Stephen Fischer-Galati also devotes a chapter of his work, *The New Rumania*, to this time period.

[2] See, for example, Stephen Fischer-Galati, "Rumania and the Sino-Soviet Split," in *Eastern Europe in Transition*, ed. Kurt London, p. 265, and *The New Rumania*, pp. vii.

autonomy, was, I think, gradual and contradictory, but it was not simply a reflection of Gheorghiu-Dej's turning from one improvisation to another and then suddenly discovering that he either had to make his commitment to a policy of initiation explicit and definitive or continue an ambiguous policy of emulating the Soviets. The latter interpretation has been cogently argued by J. F. Brown,[3] and in a sense my interpretation resembles his. Through a more conceptually refined approach my argument here will, I hope, more adequately explain the complex development during this period.

The process of initiation undertaken by the Romanian regime may be taken as an example of what organization theorists call search behavior. In their work on this topic Cyert and March have made several points that are pertinent to my analysis: (*a*) Any theory of organization goals must deal successfully with the obvious potential for internal goal conflict; (*b*) Any organization, that is, its leadership, should be regarded as a coalition; (*c*) Goals change as new participants enter and old ones leave the coalition; and (*d*) Organizations engage in "problemistic search." Search is stimulated by what is usually a specific problem and is directed toward finding a solution to that problem.[4] Such search differs from "random curiosity" in that it has a goal, and it differs from a "search for understanding" in that it involves understanding only so far as understanding contributes to control. "A problem," the authors explain, "is recognized when an organization either fails to satisfy one or more of its goals or when such a failure can be anticipated in the immediate future," and as long as the problem remains unsolved the search will continue. At first, the search will follow two courses: "Search in the neighborhood of the problem symptom and search in the neighborhood of the current alternative." If such restricted search does not lead to a solution, the organization will very likely broaden its consideration of alternative solutions in order to increase goal achievement, or it will lower its goals.

One can analyze the elaboration of the Romanian indepen-

---

[3] "Eastern Europe," p. 68.

[4] See Richard M. Cyert and James G. March, *A Behavioral Theory of the Firm* (Englewood Cliffs, N.J., 1963), p. 121–122.

dent course within this same framework. Its use enables one to locate and appreciate the essential elements in the development of the Romanian position, and even more, it allows for the incorporation of additional, congruent variables, which are closely related to the historical and substantive dimensions of the development of the Romanian independent course.

For a number of reasons the year 1962 is a logical point of reference — most importantly, perhaps, because of the impact of certain international, as well as domestic, events that year on the Soviet elite and particularly Nikita Khrushchev. Richard Lowenthal has vividly recounted what he calls the Soviet elite's illusion-ending experience of 1962. According to Lowenthal, the period of illusion lasted five years, from early 1958, when the Soviet elite thought that the conditions existed for an international Communist advance. In Lowenthal's words, "that was the rationale for the worldwide, but carefully controlled, Soviet political offensive; that is the illusion that may have been buried in Cuba."[5] In 1962 not only was Khrushchev confronted with serious international problems — the deadlock over Berlin, the Cuban episode, the "demonstration effect" of the Common Market combined with Czech and East German pressure over the question of the bloc's economic integration, and the question of Soviet relations with Albania and China — but he also had to cope with the interaction of these issues and a number of significant domestic problems which threatened his position.[6] At home, Khrushchev was faced with opposition from the number two man in the Secretariat, Frol Kozlov, and as a consequence of his proposed party reforms presented in September, 1962, he was also faced with increased intraparty opposition.[7] Not

---

[5] Richard Lowenthal, "The End of an Illusion," in *Problems of Communism* 12 (January–February 1963): 1.

[6] For a discussion of this period see *ibid.*; also Carl Linden, *Khrushchev and the Soviet Leadership: 1957–1964* (Baltimore, 1966); and Michel Tatu, *Power in the Kremlin From Khrushchev to Kosygin* (New York, 1968).

[7] These reforms were adopted in November, 1962. For a discussion of the reforms see John A. Armstrong, "Party Bifurcation and Elite Interests," *Soviet Studies* 17 (April 1966): 417–431; and Tatu, pp. 249–260 and 432–434. Tatu's discussion is particularly good. He notes that the Presidium appeared to be in agreement on the division of the Party in 1962, but at the *raion* level and

only was this set of interacting problems, issues, and challenges a threat to Khrushchev but also it constrained and limited the ways in which he could attempt to secure his position, while simultaneously placing decisive action at a premium.

Up until October, Khrushchev was still the initiator. In June the meeting of Comecon issued a statement entitled the "Basic Principles of the International Division of Labor." Initiation was not the same thing as success, however. Although this statement was acclaimed in both Czechoslovakia and the Soviet Union as a major achievement in the movement toward regional integration, it really, as Montias says, "left the opposition parties in the dispute more or less where they had stood before," and Khrushchev's and Ulbricht's attempts at "persuasion" and at combining ambiguity and contradiction were not enough to dispel the Romanians' apprehensions about integration based on a supranational coordinating body.[8] Mutual intransigence was followed in August by Khrushchev's "integrationist" article, "Essential Questions in the Development of the World Socialist System."[9] The Cuban crisis in October altered the situation to the Romanian's advantage. However, the February, 1963, Comecon meeting was the scene of what was most likely another attempt by the Soviets, Czechs, and Germans "to reorganize CMEA into a supranational agency that would be capable of initiating and supervising the execution of specialization agreements."[10]

This was the chronology of 1962, the critical year in Romanian–Soviet relations; but there are four important questions that we must answer: How does one explain the Romanian opposition to Soviet expectations and demands over the question of regional integration? (One must here specify motives as well as opportu-

among traditional types in the apparatus the proposal caused resentment. Armstrong especially mentions the resentment felt by the older agricultural secretaries. In these areas of the Party, then, there was probably increasing, if scattered, opposition.

[8] J. M. Montias, *Economic Development in Communist Rumania*, pp. 212–213.

[9] See Fischer-Galati, *The New Rumania*, p. 89; and Montias, *Economic Development*, p. 211.

[10] Montias, *Economic Development*, p. 213.

nities,[11] and show the interaction of the two.) What types of conflict were involved in the Romanian–Soviet confrontation? What types of mechanisms were at work in redefining the conflict and in contributing to the surprising outcome of Romanian "autonomy?" What type of leadership did Gheorghiu-Dej provide during this period?

The Romanian Elite in Opposition: Motives and Opportunities

The main stimulus behind the Romanian leadership's expanding conflict with the Soviet elite was the Soviet position toward the Romanian Party's commitment to a policy of comprehensive industrialization.[12] This issue was by no means simply, or primarily, economic, and it was not, as some have suggested, a matter of ordering the Romanians to concentrate entirely on raw material production. Rather, as Montias has pointed out, it was a question of specialization by industry (the Soviet position) or within industries (the Romanian position).[13] The chief aspects of the issue were political and ideological. Khrushchev had brought about what can

---

[11] Max Weber has noted with reference to classes that "the differentiation of classes on the basis of property alone is not 'dynamic,' that is, it does not necessarily result in class struggles or class revolutions." *The Theory of Social and Economic Organization*, p. 425. This is a point with a broader analytic import. The existence of classes does not necessarily mean that they struggle with one another; in the same way, the existence of opportunities for action does not necessarily mean that they will be taken advantage of, or even recognized. Something more than the mere existence of opportunities is usually at work in a situation where significant action is undertaken. For this reason an investigation of political motives is important in understanding the Romanian "independent course."

[12] The Soviet threat to Romanian industrialization was the immediate and most specific stimulus behind the "independent course," but the causal nexus surrounding this "course" was more complex. As an example: for some members of the regime, Party sovereignty was in all likelihood a more fundamental and autonomous matter. So, too, for these individuals and others, the matter of state sovereignty was critical and distinguishable from industrialization, though interdependent with it.

[13] Montias, "Backgrounds and Origins of the Rumanian Dispute with Comecon," p. 150.

be called a state of dissonance within the Romanian leadership. Gheorghiu-Dej in particular was confronted with a demand from a source which had until then been considered authoritative and which was now demanding that the Romanian leader radically rearrange and redefine his value and policy priorities. The Romanian regime's past performance certainly offered adequate grounds to predict that Gheorghiu-Dej would comply; he did not.

Recent analyses of Gheorghiu-Dej's refusal to comply usually emphasize the importance of the maneuvering room that had opened up to the Romanian leader and party in the wake of the Sino–Soviet split; but one need not limit the definition of situational opportunity to that alone. All at once, the Soviet elite had to face the failure of the Cuban affair, Khrushchev was encountering increased domestic opposition, and the Soviets were attempting to arrive at another reconciliation with Yugoslavia. The combined effect of these problems increased the opportunities available to the Romanian elite to achieve a more autonomous position within the bloc. But as we have noted, opportunity does not necessitate action; there must also be motive. In 1962 Gheorghiu-Dej was placed in a state of intense dissonance with respect to his most cherished goal — industrialization. His was a very specific political-ideological vision in that the goal of industrialization seems to have been the concrete expression of his major aspirations: a powerful party and a socialist Romania. This vision and his commitment to it are at the root of his opposition to the Soviets, and in this instance the questions of attitude, attitude change, and resistance to such change are especially relevant.

Theorists of "cognitive dissonance" argue that individuals engaged in behavior that contradicts certain of their cognitions will revise their cognitions to restore a state of consonance.[14] For our analysis, what is of greater interest are theoretical statements that deal with the *refusal* to redefine one's attitudes or beliefs, or to engage in behavior that may involve a redefinition of values and priorities. One such statement, in *Attitudes and Attitude Change*,

---

[14] See Arthur R. Cohen, *Attitude Change and Social Influence* (New York, 1964), pp. 73–80, for a discussion of theories of cognitive dissonance.

is particularly applicable to the case of Gheorghiu-Dej: ". . . a closer look at the psychological implications of having a stand on an issue reveals that commitment to a stand on an issue of any importance is more than an isolated, transitory event." Further, "judgment of items on religious, political, and social issues on which a person has taken a stand has a context of warm personal import . . . . these stands . . . are ingredients in the experience of self-identity." [15] It is my contention that Gheorghiu-Dej's commitment to industrialization represented this sort of taking of a stand, in which there was a high degree of ego-involvement, but of a particular sort which combined personal, ideological, and political elements. Dej was a politicized individual, and there is little doubt that his personal, political, and ideological beliefs were highly integrated, with obvious implications for the intensity of his commitment to the industrialization program. In addition, Dej was able to draw on a number of reinforcing factors which were immediately available. Some of these may be located under the heading motive, others under the heading opportunity; and at least two of them shared both qualities. In the first place, there was the ideological sanction of Lenin concerning the importance of socialist industrialization. Second, there was the legacy of Khrushchev's support for the Romanian program, along with his emphasis on ideology and the legitimacy accorded "domesticism." Third, there was the diminution of the C.P.S.U.'s authority following the de-Stalinization campaign initiated in 1956 at the XXth Congress and reinforced five years later at the XXIInd Congress. Such a diminution of authority certainly made it easier for Gheorghiu-Dej to rearrange his hierarchy of political-ideological priorities, putting industrialization ahead of recognition of Soviet authority.

Probably the two most critical "reinforcing factors" available to Gheorghiu-Dej and affecting his decision to oppose the Soviets were party unity and social-political support for such a decision. Certainly party unity is the factor most mentioned by analysts of Romanian politics in their discussions of Gheorghiu-Dej's success

---

[15] Carolyn Sherif, Muzafer Sherif, and Roger E. Nebergall, *Attitudes and Attitude Change* (Philadelphia, 1965), p. 64.

in pursuing a policy of initiation in opposition to the Soviets.[16]
Two points should be made about party unity, however; (a) the
R.W.P.'s high degree of cohesion was not based on all members
of the elite being equally committed to a policy of initiation, nor
on their all agreeing on just what values and priorities were being
defended; (b) party unity not only created or added to the Romanian elite's opportunity to sustain a policy of initiation but for at
least certain elite members provided a motive for such a policy.

The latter point relates directly to the question of social-political support for Gheorghiu-Dej's "autonomous stance." Some
writers have argued that Gheorghiu-Dej's opposition to the Soviets
was predicated on some form of necessity — specifically, that is, on
the necessity of maintaining the loyalty of his party cadres. Another
argument along the same line is that Dej's reconciliation with the
Romanian population (i.e., the release of political prisoners and
the manipulation of national symbols and feelings) was based on
the need to secure visible public support for his defiant posture.
Both these explanations are, I think, too limited, in scope and in
detail. In both, the emphasis is exclusively on the necessity of finding public support and the elite's reluctance to do so. There was,
I am convinced, much more to the question of support than that.
To begin with, given its course of behavior, the regime undeniably
had an objective *need* for public support, and the release of political prisoners and other similar gestures were in part stimulated
by this need. Second, and I think more important, there was also
a large degree of public support *available*, and not simply an anti-
Russian nationalist sentiment. The new-class of functionaries and
apparatchiks could, of course, be counted on to support a policy
that would increase their power, status, and material well-being,

---

[16] A policy of initiation, in contrast to one of emulation, involves decisions made on the basis of premises which an elite and organization autonomously and autocephalously provide for itself. To use Weber's definition:
"Autonomy means that the order governing the group [i.e., Party] has been
established by its own members on their own authority . . . autocephaly
means that the chief and his staff [Gheorghiu-Dej and the Secretariat] act by
the authority of the autonomous order of the corporate group [i.e., the Politburo and Central Committee] itself . . . not under the authority of outsiders." Weber, *The Theory of*, p. 148.

and by the same token to resist a policy that threatened Romanian industrialization, a source of much of their self-legitimation. Of greater importance, it may be hypothesized, was the support of the new middle class for a policy of autonomy, not only because their major roles were intimately connected with the process of industrialization, but because their pride and assertiveness could also be engaged. A third point to be made, I think, is that certain members of the elite coalition (i.e., Ceaușescu, Maurer, Bîrlădeanu, and perhaps Bodnaraș) did not act so much on the need for public support as on their *confidence* that such support was available and that the consequences of relying on it would be more positive than negative.[17] To these same members, opposition to the Soviet Union was as much a necessary condition for the elaboration of an effectively institutionalized political party and regime as it was a condition for maintaining the loyalty of party cadres. Briefly stated, the motives for eliciting public support were different in character. For Gheorghiu-Dej and some of his supporters the motives appear to have been primarily instrumental and manipulative. For others, these aspects, though present, were combined with other motives of a more expressive character involving ideas on the nature of the party as a political institution as well as more particular questions of political integration and the legitimacy of the regime.

Romanian–Soviet Confrontation: Types of Conflict

As a consequence, then, of the Romanian elite's commitment to industrialization, the threat posed by the Soviet position to this commitment, the "opportunities" available in the international

---

[17] Not surprisingly, there is little detailed information available on the subject of elite behavior in communist systems. Even so, the policy that Ceaușescu and Maurer have carried out since 1965 emphasizing socialist democracy and "going to the people" does seem to support my contention that these two men, at any rate, were confident that support was available. Bîrlădeanu, who had close ties with the progressive intelligentsia and was trusted by them, must also have been aware of this and in favor of a more trusting posture toward the populace. Bodnaraș' position is the least clear, and my inclusion of him is the most speculative.

environment, and the "reinforcing" domestic factors, the leadership of the Romanian Party expanded its search activity and changed its form. The period 1958–1960 had been one in which problem solving and persuasion were the main conflict-resolving procedures; in 1961 there came increasing bargaining between the Soviet and the Romanian parties, and this posture became dominant after June, 1962.[18] In 1963 the two sides turned to what March and Simon call "politics." "Politics," according to these authors, is a "process in which the basic situation is the same as in bargaining — there is intergroup conflict of interest — but the arena of bargaining is not taken as fixed by the participants."[19] With its Iron Gates agreement with Yugoslavia, its commercial agreement with China, the publication of China's "twenty-five points" of disagreement with the Soviet Union, and the sending of a Romanian ambassador to Albania, and above all, the assumption of a mediating role between the Soviet and Chinese, the Romanian elite was quite explicitly redefining and expanding the arena and nature of the conflict. The arena was bloc-wide and overt, with the Romanians "making the running" and not simply responding defensively to moves initiated by the Soviets.[20]

The role of mediator was mixed in character and implications. It did a great deal to enhance the status of the Romanian Party both at home and abroad, but it was as best a fragile role and more than anything else it illustrated the real limits of Gheorghiu-Dej's leadership. One observer has described Dej's behavior during this period as "daring shrewdness." Without denying Gheorghiu-Dej's ability or success, one might also say that his posture of "daring shrewdness" was an index of his operating style, which had definite limitations. Dej was a Stalinist, adept at manipulation and bureaucratic politics and reluctant to significantly redefine the rules of the game. At first glance his tactics — that is, acting

---

[18] Fischer-Galati, *The New Rumania*, p. 87.

[19] James G. March and Herbert A. Simon, *Organizations*, p. 130.

[20] Furthermore, in this changed context the diversified trade patterns which the Romanian elite had begun in the late 1950s and the gestures toward the West Germans and French took on more significance, enlarging the dimensions of the "politics arena."

as mediator between C.P.S.U. and the C.C.P. — seem to make good sense politically. The role of mediator would allow, one might think, for Romanian initiative and increased status, and at the same time it would offer the system of socialist states a mechanism for dealing with its most difficult problem, the Sino–Soviet split, and provide the Soviets with a structural device to absorb Romanian aspiration for greater autonomy and influence.[21] But this is only a superficial view, as I think certain members of the Romanian elite undoubtedly concluded. For a wide range of reasons, the Romanian Party's role as mediator was short-lived. To begin with, the C.P.S.U. in allowing the Romanian elite to become the mediator in the Sino–Soviet conflict was quite aware of the fact that it was entrusting Soviet interests to a political entity that was far from neutral. Second, the issues of contention between the R.W.P. and the C.P.S.U. were not simply routine; rather, they were critical in that they had a direct bearing on the definition of bloc unity, the definition of the Romanian political system, and the distribution of political power within both the Soviet and the Romanian elites. Third, the Romanian–Soviet conflict, unlike the conflict between Poland and the Soviet Union in the mid-1950s, was not ameliorated at this point by the major personalities involved. In contrast to Gomulka's relationship with Khrushchev, by 1962 Gheorghiu-Dej's does not appear to have been one that could in any way have brought about a resolution of the conflict between the two parties.[22] Also in contrast to the Poles, there was no "German threat" to act as a constraint on the Romanian's behavior. Fourth and finally, in the context of the points already made, I would suggest that certain members of the Romanian Party elite were aware of the dangers involved in attempting to

---

[21] For a discussion of protest-absorbing units and strategies see Amitai Etzioni, *A Comparative Analysis of Complex Organizations*, pp. 246–247.

[22] The reported personality clash between Gheorghiu-Dej and Khrushchev in no way obviates the earlier point concerning Gheorghiu-Dej's support of Khrushchev in the mid- and late 1950s. Political leaders do not have to like one another to support one another, nor does mutual support necessarily mean that there is not conflict. One has only to look at the Soviet–American alliance during the Second World War for an analogous situation in which these points are vividly illustrated.

secure autonomy primarily by manipulating critical issues without first establishing a coherent position and program.[23] Only if it had a clearly defined position and a workable program could the Party really hope to increase the costs to the Soviet Union of transgressing clearly stated norms and boundaries, and in the long run disengage its fate from the outcome of such issues as the Sino–Soviet dispute. It was considerations of this order that provided the basis for the new Romanian position announced in the Statement of April, 1964. This position with its emphasis on sovereignty was not at all a mere change in the rules of conflict within essentially the old setting. The April Statement signaled a new course for the Romanian Party, one in which "daring shrewdness" was to be supplemented by (and with Gheorghiu-Dej's death replaced by) an increasingly coherent and explicit defense of an indigenously arrived at set of political definitions and principles. This new course was to receive its clearest exposition at the IXth Party Congress held in July, 1965, under the auspices of Nicolae Ceaușescu.

Mediation and "Independence"

It would be a major (though not unprecedented) mistake to assume that an explanation of the Romanian "deviation" has now been provided. There is an unfortunate tendency in political analysis, similar to that in poor detective stories, to assume that once an outcome has been specified (whether it be a particular crime, or

---

[23] At one point in *The New Rumania* Fischer-Galati notes: "On April 22, 1964, Gheorghiu-Dej declared his own and his party's independence at a time when his own and his associates' future was in greater jeopardy than that of his country. The unequivocal and exclusive identification of the party with Rumania was both premature and unrealistic." (pp. 102–103.) On the contrary, it seems to me that the elite's and Party's full identification with the national community was the most appropriate and necessary basis for any effective declaration of independence. Rather than being premature and unrealistic it was timely and insightful. The unrealistic component of Dej's move was his belief that he could have his political cake and eat it too, that he could declare independence from the Soviets and secure support from his own population without making any substantial commitments to it, i.e., by simply limiting his regime for the most part to the manipulation of nationalist symbols and performance achievements in the economic field.

an increase or change in the type of conflict between certain units) and once a set of motives and opportunities have been located and defined, the "case" is solved. Not only is this incorrect, but also it leads to faulty (and consequential) conclusions, with scant appreciation of the intricate, rich, and open process whereby motives and opportunities are related to specifiable outcomes. The analysis thus far has, I trust, helped to show precisely what these motives, opportunities, and outcomes — in the sense of forms and changes in the character of Romanian–Soviet conflict — were. We must now go on to concentrate the analysis, drawing in from the stimuli (motives-opportunities) and the responses (forms of conflict) to get at the "black box" in the center — that is, the decisive element shaping the distinctive way in which a given elite (organization or individual) will respond to motives and opportunities. One mechanism that has been suggested as playing a significant role in relating motives and opportunities to outcomes is search behavior. To specify that as the mechanism in the case of Gheorghiu-Dej is important, for it implies that the broadening of conflict was incremental and not based primarily on purposive-comprehensive behavior, that is, on an already existing plan aimed at achieving independence from the Soviet. If my analysis is correct, the goal of independence was not a major aspiration of Gheorghiu-Dej until sometime in 1962 or later. Furthermore, if Gheorghiu-Dej was reluctant rather than eager to assert Romanian independence, one should try to explain more specifically how he effected a policy toward which he was ambivalent, and the implications of which he did not fully comprehend. For such a task the notion of search behavior is too general and mechanistic. The notion of mediation, on the other hand, can be very helpful, because it emphasizes that certain individuals, issues, and policies can affect conflict situations having a decision-inducing character. By studying the effect of mediation, we can learn a great deal about the setting and process that led to the Romanian independent course.

By late 1962 the position of the Romanian elite was defined by three clearly marked characteristics: the changing intrabloc environment in which Gheorghiu-Dej's alternatives were becoming fewer and more polarized, Gheorghiu-Dej's continued strong commitment to industrialization, and, by no means the least, the changing composition of the Romanian elite nucleus. It is my belief that Gheorghiu-Dej's policy of initiation, the Romanian "independent course," came about as a result of the manipulation of Gheorghiu-Dej's orthodox orientation and specific policy-ideological definitions by certain members of the Romanian elite nucleus (Ceauşescu, Maurer, Bîrlădeanu, and Bodnaraş) who had bona fide credentials as Romanian communists and were close followers of Gheorghiu-Dej, but who were also men distinguished by innovative careers, perspectives, and ideological conceptions. It was within this circle of the elite that Gheorghiu-Dej, reluctantly at first, made critical policy decisions which affected Romania's position and role within the bloc as well as the character of political life within Romania itself. A threatening situation, the need to make significant decisions, and the presence of trusted but innovative advisers made it possible for significant changes to occur, quite beyond what Dej expected or desired. Such an argument deserves elaboration.

Maurer became Prime Minister in 1961, and Alexandru Bîrlădeanu, the chief Romanian negotiator during the Comecon controversy, was made an alternate member of the Politburo in November, 1962.[24] Since Gheorghiu-Dej still refused to redefine his commitment to industrialization and since Soviet pressure was increasing, the changed composition of the elite was a source of potential innovation. To refer to Krech *et al.*, one can expect that "the modifiability of an attitude will be related to the degree of group support which the attitude has."[25] By the end of November, 1962, there existed within the Romanian elite nucleus a considerable amount of support for a substantial redefinition of attitude toward the Soviet Union and the character of the socialist bloc. It is safe to assume that recruitment to the elite nucleus was based mainly on Gheorghiu-Dej's personal opinion of the candidates, and persons, such as Maurer, who were elevated to policy-influencing positions usually were considered loyal. Cohen has

---

[24] See Fischer-Galati, *The New Rumania*, pp. 82, 91.

[25] David Krech, Richard S. Crutchfield, and Egerton L. Ballachey, *Individual in Society* (New York, 1962), pp. 223–224.

suggested that when the credibility of the communicator(s) has been established, "the greater the discrepancy between the subject's [i.e., Gheorghiu-Dej] position and the one advocated [i.e., by Maurer and Ceauşescu] the greater the change."[26] In other words, an emerging consensus among "credible innovators" within the Romanian elite may have been an extremely critical factor in the redefinition of Gheorghiu-Dej's posture toward the Soviet Union and toward the place of the Romanian political system within the socialist bloc. To say this does not necessarily imply (a) that there was a conspiracy against Gheorghiu-Dej, though it does not deny the existence of some form of conspiracy; (b) that there was an identity of views among the "marginals," that is, Bîrlădeanu, Maurer, Bodnaraş, and Ceauşescu; or (c) that they manipulated Gheorghiu-Dej's rigid orthodoxy because their own beliefs were in every instance diametrically opposed to their leader's. Undoubtedly, some of the "marginals" within the Romanian elite nucleus did substantially disagree with Dej; but the areas of agreement existing within the elite nucleus as a whole were equally important, for the existence of these areas enabled the "marginals" to effect what was to be a classic example of qualitative change through a type of "reformmongering." Nor does such an explanation imply that Gheorghiu-Dej (or individuals such as Stoica) simply resisted suggestions of initiating policies in opposition to the Soviet Union. My explanation does imply, however, that the understanding of those policies and initiatives differed among the members of the elite; that the manipulation of understanding was critical to securing Gheorghiu-Dej's support for certain initiatives; and that such manipulation was dependent on the existence of a group of mediators within the Romanian Party elite, individuals familiar to Dej and known to be loyal, and dedicated Romanian communists.[27]

---

[26] Cohen, *Attitude Change*, p. 30.

[27] There is a fourth point, which I shall state briefly, though it deserves a fuller treatment in a work with a slightly different set of concerns. As an instance of "reformmongering" (to use Hirschmann's term) the "manipulation of understanding" which occurred within the Romanian Party elite nucleus was not a one-way or clear-cut process which resulted in the innovators

This, then, is the general framework within which the process of mediation occurred; the process itself took many forms and appeared in several areas of political life at different times.

Forms and Areas of Mediation

Perhaps the first important instance of the process of mediation was the rapid completion of collectivization (or as the Romanians say, cooperativization) in early 1962. There were several possible reasons for this campaign: (*a*) if, as has been reported, Khrushchev expressed opposition to such a program, Gheorghiu-Dej by defending his orthodox commitments may very well have presented Khrushchev with both a fait accompli and a rather explicit "statement" about how far Khrushchev's authority extended; [28] (*b*) collectivization may also have been intended to demonstrate to the Soviets the Romanians' willingness, ability, and resolve to mobilize all available internal resources for their intended industrialization efforts. Certainly if the Romanians were to continue with the industrialization program, control over the agricultural sector would become increasingly critical, a point of which they were undoubtedly well aware; (*c*) collectivization may in addition have been motivated by a desire to increase the control of the Party over its national base, so as to reduce the number of issues that might

---

such as Bîrlădeanu achieving all their goals. As in all instances of "reform-mongering" that involve ambiguity, the outcome is in good measure beyond the control of the reformer. This is so because the object (individual, elite, or organization) to be "manipulated" has resources of its own, and interpretations of its own which can be backed up by those resources. In this instance, Gheorghiu-Dej had decisive control of the Romanian Party's political resources and was in a position to enforce his own understanding of what the Romanian independent course entailed — a fact which undoubtedly helps explain the hostility currently expressed toward him by Ceauşescu and some others in the regime. Only Gheorghiu-Dej's "timely" death in 1965 prevented the appearance of a critical intra-elite conflict over the "political meaning" of the Romanian independent course.

[28] Khrushchev was not the "sultanist" ruler of a Stalin-like patrimony but rather, as Gheorghiu-Dej's initiative on collectivization demonstrated, a feudal lord who was in continual conflict with lesser lords over the boundaries of their respective (policy) domains.

divert resources and allow more flexibility in dealing with immediate or future issues.

Whatever Gheorghiu-Dej's reasons for completing the collectivization effort so rapidly, it was a point of major consequence that he did so. It was an important act of initiation either in the sense of having been an act of emulation opposing Khrushchev's wishes (emulating Stalinist practices after the XXth and XXIst Soviet Congress was in effect an act of initiation), or if Khrushchev did not actively oppose Gheorghiu-Dej's decision, an act of voluntary rather than enforced emulation with regard to an issue that was critical rather than routine. The central element mediating this act of initiation was the rationale of protecting and adhering to orthodox-authoritative policies. This rationale facilitated a policy of initiation with regard to agriculture and at the same time constrained the Soviets' response — after all, socialist agriculture was a desired goal for everyone — and, not the least, it provided a precedent for a possibly more ambitious policy of initiation.

A second example of the mediation process may be found in the interaction of certain issues and individuals. The direct defense of the industrialization program was the setting for the ambitious policy of initiation which the Romanian elite under Gheorghiu-Dej explicitly began in 1963 and which culminated in the Statement of April, 1964. In this instance, the value placed on industrialization mediated a response of increasing opposition to the Soviet Union, and the initiation of a policy stressing the goals of Party and State sovereignty.

To understand how the issue of industrialization may have been handled so as to mediate Gheorghiu-Dej's support of a policy of party and state sovereignty it might be useful to reconstruct a relationship that may well have existed within the Romanian elite in 1962–1963. The relationship I have in mind is one that may have existed between Gheorghiu-Dej and Alexandru Bîrlădeanu — Party member, economist, and Romanian representative in Comecon — with respect to the issue of industrialization. This specific relationship is only one of several that were relevant to Gheorghiu-Dej's decision to support a policy based on party and state sovereignty, but in examining one plausible relationship closely we can, I think, draw out some significant aspects of the process that culminated in the Romanian Workers Party's "declaration of autonomy" in April, 1964.

Alexander Bîrlădeanu is a good example of the communist "marginal" who was co-opted into increasingly responsible political positions because he had experience that was applicable to the conflict in which the Romanian Party found itself beginning in 1962. In November of 1962, Bîrlădeanu was made an alternate member of the Politburo, and in July of the following year he accompanied Gheorghiu-Dej to Moscow for the "crucial meeting of the first party secretaries of the Comecon member countries at which the Romanian position appears finally to have carried the day." [29] Bîrlădeanu's political rise to the elite nucleus was part of the changing composition of the elite coalition led by Gheorghiu-Dej. Although Bîrlădeanu was made a part of this coalition essentially because of his expertise, his membership in the elite nucleus afforded him a context which to some extent obligated and allowed him to offer suggestions, present his views, and share in the definition of policy. He was, in other words, co-opted into the Romanian Party elite nucleus, but because of the hostile position of the Party vis-à-vis the Soviets and, in addition, the decision-making nature of the Politburo, he was very likely given the opportunity to expand his role. Together with Maurer and Ceaușescu, Bîrlădeanu may well have tried to urge certain changes on Gheorghiu-Dej: the need to recognize the value of state sovereignty in order to protect the immediate commitment to industrialization; the need to redefine quite substantially what the Soviet bloc should be, and what Romania's international role should be, pointing to the necessary interdependence of party-state autonomy and a continuing program of comprehensive industrialization. Presumably, because of Bîrlădeanu's background in economics and his commitment to the Party, Gheorghiu-Dej would be inclined to accept the arguments calling for a wider scope of initiation, going beyond the specific question of industrialization to the much broader question of sovereignty.[30]

---

[29] "Eastern Europe's Communist Leaders," *Radio Free Europe*, September, 1966, p. 11.

[30] As interesting as Bîrlădeanu's role was during this period, there is one other regime figure whose role was probably more interesting as an instance

A third, and more general, instance of mediation may be found in the changing composition of the Romanian Workers Party as a whole which had been occurring since 1955. Richard V. Burks has called this process the "Romanization" of the R.W.P.[31] — referring specifically to a process of ethnic redefinition — but I think the term can be used even more appropriately to describe a certain change in social identity. Between 1962 and 1964 the Party grew at a rate of almost 200,000 members a year. Undoubtedly, a significant proportion of those recruited were motivated by anti-Soviet nationalist sentiments, and by the hope of the material perquisites and general advantages associated with Party membership. But there were other new members, many drawn in by recruitment drives, who had more ambitious motivations. These were members of the new middle class, among the best educated and the most technically proficient elements of the population. Their material involvement with the process of industrialization and aspirations or demands for recognition, status, and influence could be expected to produce a climate of opinion within the Party in support of more elite innovation and initiation.[32]

So far, as examples of the mediation process within the Romanian elite nucleus, and especially as it affected Gheorghiu-Dej's posture, we have looked at the role of collectivization, the interaction of issues and individuals such as industrialization, Bîrlădeanu and Gheorghiu-Dej, and broader influences such as the Party's social composition. A fourth example relates solely to the part that one key individual may have played in encouraging Gheorghiu-Dej to engage in a policy which, though understood differently by different members of his elite coalition, was essentially one of initiation not emulation. I refer to Emil Bodnaraş, a man whose career in the Romanian Party deserves attention in

---

of mediation between the progressives and the Stalinists. I am referring to L. Răutu, the *èminence gris* of the Dej regime. Unfortunately, there is even less information available on Răutu than on Bîrlădeanu.

[31] See R. V. Burks, "The Rumanian National Deviation: An Accounting," in *Eastern Europe in Transition*, ed. Kurt London, p. 102.

[32] As Philip Selznick has argued, social composition is a critical factor in shaping the character of an institution; see *Leadership in Administration*, pp. 46, 57.

its own right. Bodnaraș occupied what some organization theorists have called a "boundary role." Kahn *et al* define a boundary position as one "for which some members of the role set are located in a different system."[33] Bodnaraș apparently held a boundary position between the Soviet and Romanian elites.[34] Under Stalin, there were individuals holding boundary positions of this sort in all the East European regimes, as part of the prevailing pattern of "pooled interdependence" whereby each unit in the bloc communicated with the center rather than with one another. To employ an analysis from Thompson: "when organizations [such as the C.P.S.U. under Stalin] employ standardization which cuts across multiple groupings [i.e., East European regimes] they also develop liaison positions [i.e., boundary roles] linking the several groups [i.e., the Romanian Workers Party] and the rule-making agency [i.e., the C.P.S.U.]."[35] So much for the origin and nature of Bodnaraș' position. The theoretical work dealing with the concept of boundary position also provides us with material for hypothesizing about Bodnaraș' personality and political posture. Persons who hold boundary roles seem to deal readily with the rather high degree of conflict associated with their positions, and they have been found to be "more oriented" than others toward the achievement of status. It is also to be noted that positions "at the organizational boundaries are directly exposed to changing external requirements, and that the occupants of such positions become proposers of organizational change."[36]

Combining these general aspects of boundary role positions with specific knowledge of Bodnaraș, we can learn a good deal not

---

[33] Robert L. Kahn, et al., *Organizational Stress: Studies in Role Conflict and Ambiguity*, p. 101.

[34] The boundary role function was important also at an earlier period in Romanian history. During the Phanariot Regime, Romanian leaders used to keep "a resident envoy at Constantinople, known under the Turkish title of Bash-Kapukihaya." Moscow replaced Constantinople, and the envoy's place of residence varied, but the same structural relationship obtained and the critical nature of the role was the same. See Robert Seton-Watson, *History of the Roumanians* (London, 1934), I, 31.

[35] James D. Thompson, *Organizations in Action*, p. 61.

[36] Kahn et al., pp. 105, 126.

only about Bodnaraş' career but also about his influence on the mediation process that occurred within the Romanian elite nucleus. We can, I think, assume three things at the outset: that Bodnaraş was not easily bullied; that he was ambitious; and that, more than most of the other members of the R.W.P. elite nucleus, he quickly grasped the implications of the Sino-Soviet dispute and the changing attitudes of the Soviets toward the Romanian program of industrialization, and toward the R.W.P. leadership in general. But why did Bodnaraş opt for Gheorghiu-Dej and not for Khrushchev? It is an interesting question, particularly if, as has been reported, Khrushchev was trying to draw Bodnaraş into a scheme to replace Gheorghiu-Dej. A number of reasons probably influenced Bodnaraş' decision to identify himself exclusively with the Romanian party and leader: (a) Bodnaraş may well have shared the commitment to the specific vision of a powerful industrialized (socialist) Romania. His early army career would tend to support such a national view. (b) He, of course, interacted more with members of the Romanian elite, particularly Gheorghiu-Dej and Ceauşescu, than with members of the C.P.S.U., which would lead one to expect a greater tendency to identify with the R.W.P.[37] (c) The C.P.S.U. had been losing prestige under Khrushchev, and that was hardly a point in its favor. (d) Quoting March and Simon: "the greater the number of individual needs satisfied in the group, the stronger the propensity of the individual to identify with the group."[38] Bodnaraş, though ambitious, may at the same time have realized that he could not hope for a better position of status and power than the one he held under Gheorghiu-Dej, and he of course had the advantage of being able to compare experiences under both the Soviets and Gheorghiu-Dej.[39] (5) Kahn says that role senders (i.e., Khrushchev) usually have an inadequate understanding of boundary positions, and for that reason one who holds a boundary role is often pressured rather

---

[37] See March and Simon, *Organizations*, p. 66, on "interaction."

[38] *Ibid.*

[39] No doubt, too, Bodnaraş knew that if Gheorghiu-Dej were removed, he could not expect such good treatmnt from an Apostol, or a Drăghici, or any of the other members of the "native worker" contingent.

clumsily from both ends (i.e., from Khrushchev and Gheorghiu-Dej). But boundary role occupants, especially successful men like Bodnaraș, have a considerable amount of self-esteem, and there is evidence that individuals with high levels of self-esteem are more likely than others to reject threatening appeals.[40] With that in mind, I suggest that beginning in late 1962 and particularly in 1963, because of increasing difficulties, Khrushchev made blunt suggestions to Bodnaraș, while Gheorghiu-Dej may have been more sensitive to the difficulties of Bodnaras' position and less clumsy (though no less direct) in his dealings with him.[41] Dej's possibly more adept handling of Bodnaraș was not due simply to good-will, understanding, or friendship, although these may well have entered in, but also to his having greater domestic control and a narrower range of problems than Khrushchev, and, I think, to his recognizing the true nature of Bodnaraș' political position. In any case, Gheorghiu-Dej's "handling" of Bodnaraș may have been a significant if not decisive factor in Bodnaraș' decision to support him.

Assuming that Bodnaraș' position, behavior, and personality were in accord with what we know about the occupants of boundary roles, we may now turn to the matter of how his choice of loyalties was related to the process of mediation that went on in the elite nucleus of the Romanian Workers Party. I have already mentioned that Bodnaraș, for reasons now made clear, was in a position to quickly grasp the implications and "opportunities" latent in the Sino–Soviet conflict and sense the changing attitude toward Gheorghiu-Dej and the Romanian industrialization

---

[40] See Cohen, *Attitude Change*, p. 45.

[41] Apropos of Gheorghiu-Dej's "understanding" of Bodnaraș' position, see Bodnaraș' comments in *Scînteia* (Feb. 11, 1964) on the occasion of his own sixtieth birthday. Referring to Gheorghiu-Dej's qualities as a leader, Bodnaraș especially praises his human understanding ("*profundă înțelegere omenească*"), a quality which has marked him as an outstanding leader ("*însușiri care l-au consacrat conducător de seamă*"). This may, of course, be no more than the usual sort of homage, but coming when it did — only two months before the Romanian "declaration of autonomy" — and in view also of Bodnaraș' exposed position and other characteristics which we have noted, the statement may well have been inspired by Gheorghiu-Dej's adept handling of his position.

program. What actually occurred we do not know, but we can, I think, construct a situation that perhaps approximates the real one. During this period Gheorghiu-Dej had sustained his commitment to certain policies in the face of increasing Soviet opposition and an increasing number of suggestions by members of the elite nucleus — the composition of which was noticeably changing — to launch a policy of greater opposition toward the Soviets. Suggestions of this sort were, we can hazard, greatly strengthened by certain information given to Bodnaraș, or available to him. In particular, Bodnaraș may have had information on the weakness of Khrushchev's political situation at home, and he may well have had personal messages from Khrushchev suggesting that Gheorghiu-Dej be removed from power. Obviously, the credibility of such information would have had a great deal to do with Gheorghiu-Dej's acceptance or rejection of it,[42] and Bodnaraș's credibility must have been substantial, for many reasons. Bodnaraș' Soviet ties would make the possession of such information plausible, and his boundary role would make him the natural one to approach in this sort of conspiracy.[43] Also, Bodnaraș' general credibility with Gheorghiu-Dej may well have been high because of their relationship in 1944 prior to the coup, and because of Bodnaraș' loyal support in Dej's conflict with Ana Pauker. Furthermore, Bodnaraș most likely had the support of other trusted members of the elite, including that of Ceaușescu, who had worked under Bodnaraș in the Political Administration of the Army in the early '50s.

One final example of mediation has to do with the increased value the Romanian elite placed on the nation-state. During the period 1945–1955 the nation-state was looked upon mainly as a "vehicle for progress," but between 1962 and 1964 the nation-state took on an additional aspect. Increasingly, the Party treated the nation-state as a shield behind which it could pursue self-defined

---

[42] See Cohen for a discussion of the role of credibility in his chapter on "Characteristics of the Communicator" (p. 24): "Change of attitude in the direction advocated by the communication was greater when it originated from the highly credible source than when it came from the low one."

[43] This is particularly so in light of Bodnaraș' long association with the Romanian military.

interests. Sovereignty became more and more the condition of Party and program autonomy, and sovereignty could have political meaning only in terms of the nation-state. Shoup formulates a similar view of the nation-state: "A second form of nationalism manifests itself in the belief that there exists a fundamental need — arising from fear, lack of understanding, or the unpredictable nature of international politics — for the maintenance of a considerable degree of national independence and for giving priority, in most cases, to one's own immediate national interests." [44]

From one point of view the commitment to industrialization mediated Gheorghiu-Dej's increasing appreciation of the nation-state. In turn, the "conditioned" value placed on the nation-state (by reason of its relation to continued industrialization) provided both an increased legitimacy for the nation-state and a core around which other socio-political forces, having a more complete appreciation of the role and value of the nation-state, could gather. [45]

Gheorghiu-Dej as Statesman

It is no exaggeration to say that the Romanian elite's Statement of April, 1964, was an "irrevocable decision," one which not only created a new situation but also subsequently influenced other important decisions. [46] Yet one of the remarkable characteristics of the Romanian decision was its fundamentally defensive or negative rationale.

The Romanian Party's assertion of autonomy did not grow out of a well-elaborated "practical ideology" — a coherent political vision combining historical experiences and well-defined goals. Obviously, it bore some relation to past difficulties with the Soviet

---

[44] Paul Shoup, "Communism, Nationalism, and the Growth of the Communist Community of Nations After World War II," *American Political Science Review* 56 (December 1962), 888.

[45] The word "complete" is not used here in a value sense. It refers to the greater number of dimensions and roles that were attached to the nation-state as a political unit by some members of the regime in contrast to others who viewed it almost entirely in instrumental terms and valued it mainly for the relation it bore to industrialization.

[46] On "irrevocable decisions" see Herbert A. Simon, *Administrative Behavior*, p. 66.

Union, to the immediate problems over industrialization, and to Gheorghiu-Dej's commitment to the policy of industrialization. But these specific considerations merely underline the absence of a broader (not necessarily more abstract) set of concerns and definitions, and, consequently, Gheorghiu-Dej's notable lack of skill as an institutional leader. At no point was Gheorghiu-Dej able to create a synthesis of his various initiatives — industrialization, bloc position, sovereignty, national renaissance, and national reconciliation. It is only fair to say that there had perhaps not been enough time for him to do so, but other things, such as the nature of his political and ideological beliefs, were probably much more decisive.

Marxism–Leninism is in many ways a relatively closed system of thought, but it is quite clear that certain versions of it are more closed than others. The Stalinist version may be said to be more dogmatic, and analytic — that is, capable of breaking down problems and suggesting specific solutions — but not synthetic — that is, capable of reconceptualizing problems and relating them in a new way.[47] Dej's Stalinist political identity formation, his limited education, and his personality (insofar as we know anything about it) all seem consistent with a highly specific, compartmentalized, tactically flexible, strategically rigid, and analytic type of political and ideological vision. A new synthesis, a new posture or perspective or appreciation, relating immediate issues "to their long-run implications for the role and meaning of the group,"[48] was hardly likely in such a man. With his orthodox commitments, including a strong faith in the "dictatorship of the proletariat," and his narrow definition of what such commitments involved, Gheorghiu-Dej was incapable of effectively relating his specific initiatives to the basic task of integrating national and ideological commitments and concerns. One major instance of this incapacity was his response

---

[47] This distinction between dogmatic belief sets (or ideologies) with analytic capacities, and open belief sets (ideologies) with synthetic capacities is taken from Milton Rokeech's excellent work, *The Open and Closed Mind* (New York, 1960). Applied to organizations, and specifically communist parties, Rokeech's dogmatic-closed category would include men like Novotny, Rakosi, and Gheorghiu-Dej, and his open-synthetic category, men like Tito, Dubček, and perhaps Ceauşescu.

[48] Selznick, *Leadership in Administration*, p. 37.

to the changing Romanian social environment. As I have pointed out, this environment was increasingly marked by the growth of the stratum that Dumitriu has called the "new middle class." As a new social element, it posed a question as to how it would be accommodated politically and ideologically by the Party elite. Since at least 1958 the question has been more or less open. In the first half of the 1960s the important issue was how Gheorghiu-Dej would relate to this increasingly strategic social stratum — whether he would approach it in such a way as to integrate its national orientation with a commitment to a Leninist political system or whether he would by his approach dichotomize *or* confuse the two — nationalism and Leninism — thereby either strengthening their mutual antagonism or denying their integrity as distinct political imperatives. It is of greatest importance to note that the situation at that time was "open": the opportunity existed to secure the loyalty of a strategic stratum and to define its commitment to the regime in such a way as to create an amalgam of national and Leninist definitions. But Gheorghiu-Dej, true to his Stalinist identity, failed to take advantage of the situation in this way. Instead, he dealt with the question of public support almost entirely in terms of manipulation, a posture based on a fundamental and typically Stalinist mistrust of his constituency. As a result, support from the new middle class for Gheorghiu-Dej's policies probably remained instrumental and selective: on the one hand heavily dependent on material payoffs from the regime, and on the other receptive to nationalist appeals but not to their supposed socialist character.

Not only did Gheorghiu-Dej fail to take advantage of the existence of a stratum which could have contributed greatly to the growth of a viable and coherent Leninist political community (had it been politically and ideologically accommodated rather than manipulated), but also, by trying to manipulate historic national symbols in a bid for easy support, in exchange for which the regime made no fundamental commitments, he endangered the Marxist–Leninist identity of the regime. Dej's behavior made the danger of opportunism very real. Selznick says that "opportunism" involves "making short-run, partial adaptations, the greatest danger [of which] lies in uncontrolled effects on organization[al] character."[49] Given the highly concrete, rigid, hence superficial nature of Gheoghiu-Dej's Marxist–Leninist beliefs, there was a strong chance that his regime could become nationalistic in the style of historic Romanian nationalism. Indeed, Gheorghiu-Dej, freed from a number of Soviet constraints and facing a situation that demanded character-defining decisions, and operating with a rigid, situationally undefined ideology, launched a set of policies which, however he may have intended them, did in fact give an increasingly chauvinistic national slant to the regime. Together, the strong anti-Soviet sentiments and the manipulation of quasi-mythical symbols stressing the Dacian past resulted in the attenuation and confusion of the regime's political and ideological identity. All these developments were directly related to the quality of Gheorghiu-Dej's understanding of the ideology to which he was committed and to the political stance he adopted. Gheorghiu-Dej never got beyond Stalinism, and it is extremely doubtful whether he accepted even in a formal sense the possibility, not to mention viability, of a communist system that was not Stalinist.

It is important that we understand these limitations on Gheorghiu-Dej as a statesman or institutional leader, for three reasons: It is to be expected that he will be accused (*a*) of not having seen the necessity of effecting a new political-ideological synthesis within Romania and of having resisted the various initiatives proposed in this direction during the period 1962–1964, and also (*b*) of having been at first very reluctant to make an explicit declaration of Romania's autonomy and, following that, of having failed to integrate the theoretical and policy implications of such a stance. More important than these considerations, however, is (*c*) our ability to differentiate Ceaușescu's leadership from Gheorghiu-Dej's.

Nicolae Ceaușescu as Statesman: A Preliminary Statement

The ideal institutional leader is an individual who is capable of relating current issues to an institution's identity and goals and who grasps the need for innovating as well as preserving, for under-

---

[49] *Ibid.*, p. 144.

standing the difference between critical and routine decisions, for selecting the proper social base, and so on. Clearly, no leader can live up to this ideal in all its details, but there are some individuals who, in one way or another, come close. Ceaușescu, especially in comparison with Gheorghiu-Dej, is one of these. This is not to say that Ceaușescu's vision of the ideal Romanian socialist political community has no political and ideological limitations, nor that he has a perfect ability to synthesize. But there is no doubt that since his assumption of power, Ceaușescu has demonstrated quite clearly that he should be considered a member of the category of leaders whom Hoffmann calls statesmen [50] and whom I, along with Selznick (and Barnard), would describe as institutional leaders. Any understanding of the recent political development of the Romanian regime and community must be based on an awareness of the difference between Ceaușescu's leadership and his predecessor's. There are, I think, some questions that arise naturally from such a contention. First of all, why was it Ceaușescu who succeeded Gheorghiu-Dej? And how, exactly, does Ceaușescu differ from Dej in matters of style, skills, and vision? And last, why does he differ? We can attempt some answers.

Djilas in his work on the New Class makes an interesting, if somewhat obscure, statement about the rise of political leaders: "The leader who succeeds in getting to the top along with his assistants, is the one who succeeds in most logically expressing and protecting the interests of the new class at any given time." [51] The statement actually is tautological, and it assumes that which has to be demonstrated — that the "new class" (or any collectivity) will act in unison during a critical situation; nor does it necessarily apply in a setting where the new-class faces legitimate competition from other strata such as the new middle class, who are also products of the regime. Nevertheless, Djilas has expressed what is perhaps the most significant explanation of Ceaușescu's ability to succeed Gheorghiu-Dej. The succession of course involved a number of elements. Most observers emphasize Gheorghiu-Dej's supposed

---

[50] See Stanley Hoffmann, "Paradoxes of the French Political Community," in *In Search of France*, ed. Hoffmann et al. (New York, 1963), pp. 1–118.

[51] Milovan Djilas, *The New Class* (New York, 1957), p. 81

blessing of Ceauşescu. Also, Ceauşescu had a dominant position within the *apparat* after a long tenure as party secretary in charge of cadres. Another element is the very real fear which most members of the elite coalition probably had of allowing Drăghici, the head of the security police, to obtain leadership of the Party. But the main reason was Ceauşescu's success in getting support from the varied set of individuals, cliques, and possible factions within the Party: as Thompson says, in an "organization with dispersed power, the central power figure is the individual who can manage the coalition."[52] Ceauşescu was the only figure who could effectively relate to and elicit support from the disparate elements comprising the Party elite (Central Committee and Politburo) and regime. His credentials with the new-class were established by his close ties with Gheorghiu-Dej and by his career in the *apparat*, while his policy stands in such matters as relations with the Soviet Union and the rationalization of Romanian economic life, together with his conception of the Romanian political community, may be presumed to have secured the support of the "marginals" in the elite nucleus, innovators within the Party *apparat*, and members of the new middle class.

Ceauşescu has shown himself to be very different from Gheorghiu-Dej in the one quality most valuable in a leader who is required to make decisions that could have an effect on the fundamental character of an organization: the ability to perceive, relate, and act on a wide range of problems. This might be called political imagination.

Ceauşescu's qualities are best demonstrated in the increasingly coherent political-ideological synthesis that has been elaborated since he came to power. This synthesis was first stated comprehensively at the IXth Party Congress in July, 1965, held under Ceauşescu's auspices. Ceauşescu, aware that reality is not infinitely malleable, has not approached the process of political and ideological

---

[52] Thompson, *Organizations in Action*, p. 142. In a patrimonial system such as existed in Romania (and the Soviet Union in 1953), the death of a leader means an immediate dispersal of power. The retainers, among whom the leader has delegated power in such a way as to maximize his own, confront one another as usual except for one critical factor: they are now in possession of substantial political resources.

synthesis and innovation simply or directly. He has had to deal both with *self-imposed* political and ideological constraints and with domestic as well as bloc-wide opposition. Nevertheless, he has been consistent in his efforts to give concrete expression to a comprehensive redefinition of Romania's place in the world socialist system and of the relation between the Romanian regime and the Romanian community.

Several things can be suggested to explain Ceaușescu's "synthetic" leadership capacity. Not the least perhaps is his identity-forming experience as a party member. One critical element in that process was his membership at sixteen in the Party-sponsored Anti-Fascist League, an experience and milieu that had a lot to do, I think, with his more developed capacity to combine Leninist and national commitments. Far more than Gheorghiu-Dej, he has shown himself capable of integrating the two rather than simply manipulating one for the purposes of the other. A second element may be related to Ceaușescu's position in the Party elite until 1954–1955. The fact that he was somewhat outside the elite nucleus until that time may have made it possible for him to maintain some degree of critical detachment from Gheorghiu-Dej's policies (unlike Drăghici, whose critical position in the Ministry of Interior, even before his admission to the Politburo in 1954–1955, demanded a more intense involvement and acceptance of Dej's perspective and policies). This detachment perhaps gave him the chance to consider new directions — along with such individuals as Constantinescu and Niculescu-Mizil — to reach fresh understandings and formulate alternative approaches to the problems that confronted the Party and the regime. The course of Ceaușescu's career may in fact be a clue to his apparent preference for political solutions as opposed to coercive or simply administrative solutions. Ceaușescu's long tenure in the *apparat* and more importantly in the Party may have been a matter of choice and not simply of assignment: an indication of a relative preference for the program-defining and relational aspects of the Party's role in the social system rather than for its program-imposing and command aspects. A fourth element in the particular quality of Ceaușescu's leadership is, of course, his personality. This is something we know very little about, although its puritanical and achievement components, with at least two related characteristics — an emphasis on organization and (controlled) risk-taking — are quite evident.

Whatever the reasons, however, under Ceaușescu's leadership the Romanian Communist Party is attempting and in certain respects has achieved a synthesis of perspectives, commitments, and policies in two vital areas: its relation to and place in the world socialist system, and its relation to its national constituency.

*A Period
of Elaboration and Synthesis:
July 1965-July 1969*

16

"On" Time and Synthesis

Two GENERAL REMARKS are necessary before we proceed to the major concerns of Part IV. One has to do with the time period discussed, and the other with the notion of synthesis.

The purpose of this work has been to provide an analysis of nation building in Romania during the period 1944–1965. The reasons for going beyond that "limit" should be made clear. It is not my intention to undertake a comprehensive analysis of domestic Romanian political life since 1965. Rather, I wish merely to extend the analysis of Part III to show how it applies in particular areas. I have argued that the leadership of Nicolae Ceaușescu is significantly different from that of Gheorghiu-Dej, that his conception of political community is different, that the regime's political and ideological point of view is more flexible and sophisticated, and that the leadership's innovative capacity is greater, although limited by self-imposed as well as exogenous constraints. If all this is true, then these features of the Ceaușescu regime should be evident in areas relating to its position in the world socialist system and in its ideological approach to the nation as a political entity. It is on this assumption that I shall proceed to analyze the behavior of the Ceaușescu regime.

The second remark concerns the title of this section. By no means do I wish to suggest that by July, 1969, Romanian political history had reached some sort of glorious Hegelian apex. One does not have to be a Marxist to appreciate the fact that every synthesis is partial, contradictory, and changing. Bearing in mind this understanding of what synthesis means, we can turn to an analysis of the two areas I have specified: the Romanian Party's statement of its position in the communist world and its ideological view of the nation.

17

The Romanian Communist Party
and the World Communist Movement:
A Redefinition of Unity

DAVID FLOYD has written of the Statement issued by the Romanian Workers Party in April, 1964, that "by far the most important and original of the sections for the communist world as a whole was the one dealing with political relations between the communist countries, though it was the statement on Comecon which attracted most attention at the time."[1] There is no doubt that the Statement struck especially at the whole matter of intrabloc relations. Henceforth the formal basis of relations enunciated by Khrushchev in 1955 was to become the real basis of relations among socialist nations: relations were to be based on "the principles of national independence and sovereignty, equal rights, mutual advantage, comradely assistance, non-interference in internal affairs, observance of territorial integrity, [and] the principles of socialist internationalism." Further, "The strict observance of the basic principles of the new-type relations among the socialist coun-

---

[1] David Floyd, *Rumania: Russia's Dissident Ally*, p. 113.

tries is the primary prerequisite of the unity and cohesion of these countries and of the world socialist system performing its decisive role in the development of mankind."[2]

Two other major points were contained in the section on the "World Socialist System"—and they were later to be reiterated at the Conference of Communist Parties held in Moscow in June, 1969. One of these, already familiar, was that "in the nature of the socialist system there are no objective causes for contradictions between the national and international tasks of the socialist countries," but that "on the other hand, no specific and individual interests can be presented as general interests, as objective requirements of the development of the socialist system." The second point declared that "it is up to every Marxist–Leninist Party, it is a sovereign right of each socialist state, to elaborate, choose or change the forms and methods of socialist construction."[3] In light of the division within the communist world and the traditional character of its organization, the position adopted by the Romanian Party in its Statement held important implications for the future character of the world communist movement.

Our main concern is with the political elaboration and ideological synthesis undertaken by the Romanian Communist Party between 1965 and 1969, as a result of Ceauşescu's leadership, which changed the Romanian concept of its position within the bloc and its concept of what the world communist movement ideally should be. This broad area can be broken down into specific topics: (1) the "consensual" legacy and orientation which have dominated conceptions of bloc unity; (2) the Romanian Party's acceptance of a new conception of and position on bloc unity; (3) the elements involved in this Romanian initiative; (4) the consequences of such a position for conflict resolution within the bloc; (5) a consideration of several factors that have reinforced a traditional (i.e., "con-

---

[2] "Statement on the Stand of the Rumanian Workers' Party Concerning the Problems of the International Communist and Working Class Movement (April 1964)," in William E. Griffith, *Sino-Soviet Relations, 1964–1965* (Cambridge, Mass., 1967), p. 284.

[3] *Ibid.*, p. 286.

sensual") definition of bloc unity among certain ruling parties; (6) a case analysis of events demonstrating the Romanian position, an essential in revealing that such a position, or synthesis, has not unfolded logically within a political vacuum but instead has come about amidst domestic and international conflict and opposition; and (7) a consideration of the Romanian Party's future relationship to the world communist movement.

Aside from the relevance of such an analysis to our argument concerning Ceaușescu's leadership capacity, there are at least two other considerations that justify an intensive study of the Romanian elite's international behavior. First, the nature of the Romanian regime's relation to the socialist system of nations and in particular the Soviet Union has been a significant element in shaping the character of party institutionalization, the elite's conception of political community, the character of its industrialization policy, and the degree of flexibility used in breaking through, especially in the areas of mobilization and recruitment of personnel. Second, the Romanian elite's posture vis-à-vis the socialist system of nations is *reciprocally* related to its internal political evolution. Thus one can hypothesize that the stress on diversity within the communist world so characteristic of the Romanian Party's bloc position since 1964 is in part related to its decision late in 1967 to reorganize the party and governmental apparatus so as to take account of domestic diversity. Certainly, no one-to-one relationship is suggested; however, certain stances and policies in one area may bear some relationship to policies and stances in other areas. Much depends on whether or not the same person or persons are responsible for policy in both the domestic and international arenas and whether there is the leadership capacity to draw related policy conclusions from similar premises in different arenas. The direction of influence may of course work both ways, from nation to bloc as well as vice versa. For example, once the nation has become the major referent, the attitudes expressed toward bloc unity may be determined by the role assigned to the nation. In fact, as we shall see, this is what has happened in Romania.

Consensual Legacy and Orientation

For more than forty years prior to the Romanian Statement of April, 1964, interparty relations within the communist world bore a very distinct character. Brzezinski has called them "integral relations"; while Thompson's notion of "pooled interdependence" emphasizes their hierarchical nature.[4] One might also use the term "consensual relations." Under Soviet hegemony, relations among the various communist parties within the bloc were based on the ideological imperative of internal agreement expressed in terms of shared perspective and a common set of norms as well as values. Agreement referred to the content of behavior, and differences among the regimes were ideally to be abolished.[5] The 1957 Moscow Declaration, for example, asserted that "the exchange of opinions revealed *identity* of views of the parties on *all* the questions examined at the meeting and *unanimity* in their assessment of the international situation."[6] At this time, a relationship based on consensual premises was defined as the prerequisite of each unit's sovereignty: "The solidarity and close unity of the socialist countries constitute a reliable guarantee of the sovereignty and independence of each."[7] Gheorghiu-Dej repeated this formulation — apparently quite sincerely — in his report to the IIIrd (now VIIIth) Party Congress in June, 1960, and a year later he again praised solidarity saying that "between the R.W.P. and the C.P.S.U. there have always been the closest fraternal relations and that complete understanding and unity of views have prevailed, never overshadowed by anything, on all fundamental problems."[8]

One could object that since, in 1961, conflict between the R.W.P. and the C.P.S.U. had been redefined from persuasion to bargaining, these statements of faith by Gheorghiu-Dej were an

---

[4] See James D. Thompson, *Organizations in Action*, pp. 54, 55, 61, 64.

[5] See Irving Louis Horowitz, "Consensus, Conflict, and Cooperation: A Sociological Inventory," *Social Forces* 41 (December 1962), 187.

[6] "The 1957 Moscow Declaration (Text)," in G. F. Hudson et al., eds., *The Sino-Soviet Dispute* (New York, 1961), p. 47; my italics.

[7] *Ibid.*, p. 51. See also Gh. Gheorghiu-Dej, *Articles and Speeches*, p. 94.

[8] Gheorghiu-Dej, *Articles and Speeches*, p. 204.

implied expression of conflict over "less than fundamental" problems. Such a conclusion would be warranted. A conclusion of greater import given our concerns, however, is that despite this conflict the traditional formulation was still perceived as the only possible and legitimate one, and that the Romanians as well as the Soviets still adhered to the consensual tradition.

Perhaps the single most revealing index of the Romanian Party's attitude toward interparty consensual relations is its position on the Comintern. In May, 1961, on the fortieth anniversary of the Romanian Party, Gheorghiu-Dej was quite explicit in stating that "it was only thanks to the political assistance given by the Executive Committee of the Communist International that the factional struggles could be put to an end, and the unity of the Party's ranks could be re-established."[9] The redefinition of unity within the communist world was to place a completely different value on the Comintern's activity. Ceauşescu demonstrated this very forcefully, as we shall see, in the speech he delivered at the forty-fifth anniversary celebration of the Party in 1966. It revealed his resolve to act on the implications of the April, 1964, Statement, to maintain the initiative of his regime, to elaborate a defense of its sovereignty, and to attempt to shape its environment. Ceauşescu's major goal has been, and still is, to redefine interparty relations on a cooperative rather than a consensual basis.

From Consensual to Cooperative Relations: "Adam Smith" vs. the Monolith

In undertaking a redefinition of the nature of interparty relations, Ceauşescu was presenting himself and his regime with a momentous task. Essentially, though he never used the phrase, nor even the word cooperative, he hoped to establish the legitimacy of cooperative interparty relations. Horowitz, from whom I am borrowing the concepts "consensual" and "cooperative," says of cooperative relations that they "make no demands on role uniformity but only upon procedural rules; cooperation concerns the settlement

---

[9] Gheorghiu-Dej, "Forty Fighting Years Under the Victorious Banner of Marxism-Leninism (May 8, 1961)," in *ibid.*, p. 169.

of problems in terms which make possible the continuation of differences and even fundamental disagreements." [10] The word cooperative can in this sense be fairly applied to Ceaușescu's political
orientation, aspirations, and demands in the area of interparty relations. One of the major convictions of the Romanian Party in its
position within the bloc prior to, during, and after the June, 1969,
Moscow meeting of communist parties has been that "under no
circumstances must these differences [within the bloc] have an
effect on relations among socialist states." [11]

A party's attitude toward the Comintern, I have suggested,
may be an index of its attitude toward "consensual" relations. Five
years after Gheorghiu-Dej expressed faith in the Comintern as a
unifying force, Ceaușescu made it clear that the Romanian Party
no longer accepted the Comintern as being beyond reproach. In
discussing the original decision to become a member of the Comintern, Ceaușescu was careful to point out that certain Romanian
delegates, "expressing their adhesion to the Leninist principles
with regard to the party of a new type, "raised a series of objections to the assessment made by the Comintern of the situation in
Romania . . . They also objected to interference of the Comintern in establishing the composition of the leading bodies of the
C.P. of Romania." At the Congress that ratified the decision to
create a Communist party, Ceaușescu said, other delegates expressed "reserves as to the obligatory nature of the decisions taken
by the Communist International for the component parties." [12]
Furthermore, he declared, it was the Romanians themselves, not
the Comintern, who had solved the problem of intraparty factionalism. The changed attitude toward the Comintern reflected not
only a new perspective on the kind of unity currently appropriate
among communist parties but also on the kind of unity that was
necessary for the effective institutionalization and political success of these parties within their respective countries. At the root

---

[10] "Consensus, Conflict," p. 187.

[11] Nicolae Ceaușescu, quoted in *Scînteia*, June 10, 1969.

[12] Nicolae Ceaușescu, *The Romanian Communist Party — Continuer of
the Romanian People's Revolutionary and Democratic Struggle, of the Traditions of the Working Class and Socialist Movement in Romania* (Agerpress,
May 6, 1966), pp. 28–29.

of this new perspective has been the Romanian elite's redefinition of the position of the Soviet Union in the world communist movement. What this position ought to be was made explicit in an article that appeared in the theoretical journal *Lupta de Clasă*, in April, 1968, under the heading, "Proletarian Internationalism and the Contemporary World":

> In the period between the two world wars, when the Soviet Union was the only socialist state, [when] the holy duty of the international working class, of all progressive forces in the entire world was the defense of the U.S.S.R. . . . the idea that the fundamental criterion of internationalism is the position taken toward the Soviet Union was broadly accepted. In our days, when socialism has become a world system . . . when in the world . . . [there] takes place anti-imperialist movements for national and social liberty, for democracy and social progress, *the criterion of internationalism has broadened*, has gained a richer content, corresponding to the great world-wide revolutionary process, extremely varied in its mode of manifestation, [a fact] which characterizes our epoch of man's transition to socialism. *Essential in affirming socialist internationalism today is the fight for assuring unity of all socialist countries of all* communist workers parties, *and of all anti-imperialist forces* . . . of solidarity with *all* who fight for independence.[13] (Italics added)

Essentially, the Romanian elite was arguing that the effective as opposed to formal recognition of diversity demanded a new conception of unity, and a new set of decision premises[14] and policies for each bloc member, particularly the Soviet Union. The Romanian argument was not original, but it was significant as being part of their elaboration of a specifically Romanian position within the bloc. For the world communist movement, it was noteworthy in that for the first time such a position was being forcefully expressed by a ruling party whose credentials as a bloc member, though attenuated, were still more acceptable than those of Yugoslavia, China, or the P.C.I. (Italian Communist Party). The Romanians made it very clear that no one center or number of

---

[13] The author was Ion Şerbănescu; p. 30.

[14] For a discussion of decision premises see the excellent book by Herbert A. Simon, Donald W. Smithburg, and Victor A. Thompson, *Public Administration* (New York, 1964), pp. 57–59.

centers is appropriate within the world movement. Because of the great diversity of national settings within which the Leninist parties must operate, centers will only lead to political errors — presumably to an even greater extent today than in the "Comintern past."

The argument of diversity provided a point of departure for the Romanian elite's criticism of the pattern of relations among communist parties for the past forty years, and for a suggested alternative. Ceauşescu formulated the essence of the alternative in his speech at the IXth Party Congress in July, 1965: "The development and flourishing of each socialist nation, of each socialist state, equal in rights, sovereign and independent, is an essential requirement upon which depend the strengthening of the unity and cohesion of the socialist countries, the growth of their influence upon mankind's advance toward socialism and communism."[15]

Clearly, this formulation completely reversed the old conditions of unity. The strength of all — which implied the domination of the Soviet Union — had been the condition of the strength of each; now, Ceauşescu was saying, it was to be just the opposite. Communist unity — bloc and world wide — was now defined as being primarily dependent on the strength and unity of each national constituent.[16] The Romanian redefinition of unity has replaced the notion of a monolithic unity with a concept that is highly reminiscent of Adam Smith's "invisible hand." As the Romanians see matters, in the resolution of major domestic problems and in international efforts the contributions of *each* Leninist party will result in a unity that is far more stable and genuine than

---

[15] Nicolae Ceauşescu, "Raportul Comitetului Central al Partidului Comunist Român cu privire la activitatea partidului în perioda dintre Congresul al VIII-lea şi Congresul al IX-lea al P.C.R.," in Nicolae Ceauşescu, *România pe drumul desăvîrşirii construcţiei socialiste*, I, 62.

[16] This position was included in the statement issued at the close of the Moscow meeting of communist parties in June, 1969; see "Sarcinile luptei împotriva imperialismului în etapa actuală şi unitatea de acţiune a partidelor comuniste şi muncitoreşti, a tuturor forţelor antiimperialiste," *Scînteia*, June 19, 1969. This did not mean, however, that the Soviets accepted the argument — simply that it was the price they were willing to pay to have the Romanians attend and sign.

anything that has until now passed for unity. Under Ceaușescu the Romanian elite has explicitly opted for a "branch" approach to international unity, whereby each Leninist party "independently establishes its political line, tactics, and strategy in such a way to apply creatively the general truths of Marxism–Leninism in terms of the concrete conditions in which it acts." In true Lindblomian or Adam Smith fashion, the consequence is not only the good of the "individual" but also of the "collectivity." Thus, "the way in which communist parties in socialist countries resolve the problems [associated with] the construction of the new order, [and] mobilize the resources and creative forces of the nation . . . has a distinct importance not only for the respective country, but also for the growth of the forces of socialism and communism." [17]

If, as Crozier has suggested, "in the long run power will tend to be closely related to the kind of uncertainty upon which depends the life of the organization," [18] then it seems clear that the Romanian elite led by Ceaușescu has attempted to define one locus of that uncertainty in terms of national diversity and to argue that only local Leninist parties can deal with it effectively — and by so doing legitimate and add to the power and autonomy of each national party. Importantly, however, the R.C.P.'s redefinition of unity has *not* depended on or originated primarily from the argument that diversity requires greater local power.[19]

The Question of Causation

The major element behind the Romanian elite's redefinition of bloc unity has been its belief in and assertion of the Romanian Party's "political maturity." By maturity the Romanians seem to mean much the same thing as political scientists do when they speak of party institutionalization. In the Statement of April, 1964,

---

[17] Întărirea unității mișcării comuniste și muncitorești — indatorire supremă," *Scînteia*, February 28, 1967.

[18] Michel Crozier, *The Bureaucratic Phenomenon* (Chicago, 1964), p. 164.

[19] The political stance that Brzezinski has termed "domesticism" is based on the argument that diversity requires greater local power. The Romanian argument goes beyond domesticism.

the opinion was expressed that "in their historical development, the socialist countries have become stronger economically, politically, and socially, the communist and workers parties of these countries have matured and their capacity of solving various problems pertaining to construction at home and the international relations of their countries has grown."[20] Three years later this view was elaborated in an authoritative article published in *Scînteia*, February 28, 1967: "The force of the communist movement finds expression in the growth of the level of maturity of the communist parties, in their organizational and political-ideological consolidation, in their capacity to elaborate their own political line and to successfully conduct a revolutionary struggle on the basis of applying the general truths of Marxism-Leninism to the concrete conditions of each country."

For the Romanians the whole question of unity is not, in other words, primarily one of the *need* to *allow* national parties more power and autonomy in order to cope with environmental diversity; rather, it is a question of right — the *right* of national parties to have full power and autonomy because they have the *ability* to deal with diversity. The final element in this particular synthesis is the Romanian Party's conclusion that the development and strengthening of such an ability is only possible if cooperative norms define interparty relations. Thus, the norm of noninterference (*neamestec in treburile internă*) has become the critical element in interparty relations. Given the Romanians' experiences with the Soviets and the Comintern, it is natural for them to single out "interference" as the greatest threat to a Leninist party's political maturation. "Interference" has indeed been referred to in every major Romanian article on "socialist internationalism" since 1964. Particularly striking in this respect were Ceausescu's remarks in a speech of April 13, 1968 (printed in *Scînteia*), when he said explicitly that the divisions within the communist world "have not fallen from the sky" but are rather the result of infringements of the principles which should be at the base of relations among socialist countries. The method Ceausescu suggested for removing

---

[20] "Statement," in Griffith, *Sino-Soviet Relations, 1964–1965*, p. 285.

these divisions made clear what principles he had in mind: "In our opinion, the liquidation of interference of any kind in the affairs of other parties and socialist countries is the way toward removing the differences, toward international unity and collaboration."

The reasons for the Romanian elite's comprehensive condemnation of interference were fully outlined in a major article entitled, "The Responsibility of the Communist Party Toward the Nation." The author, Dumitru Popescu, referred to the Romanian bête noire, the Comintern, and argued persuasively that interference by an outside party or agency results in ideological confusion, organizational incoherence in the form of factionalism, "errors in attitude toward certain social and political strata, and lessening of the [Party's] influence with the masses." [21]

Conflict Resolution Within the Bloc

The Romanian political synthesis concerning the character of the bloc, with its stress on coordination through mutual adjustment rather than standardization [22] owes more to Adam Smith's conception of unity than to Stalin's, and it has not been unopposed within the bloc. This is hardly surprising if we recognize the critical implications that such a synthesis must have for the bloc's political-ideological identity and the domestic position of several of the elites within it. Perhaps the most useful way of illustrating the nature and extent of opposition to the Romanian stance is by comparing the Bulgarian approach to the questions of bloc unity and conflict with the Romanian. Here we may consider the Romanian posture as fairly representative of the Yugoslav, the Italian, and the Czechoslovak position (until August, 1968); the Bulgarian position stands

---

[21] *Scînteia*, April 2, 1968. At the Xth Party Congress Popescu was made a member of the Secretariat. The analysis presented in his article is a good example of the error involved when any absolute statement is made concerning the theoretical incapacity of ideologically committed individuals. Popescu's article is analytically sophisticated. For an excellent discussion of the relation between theory and ideology, see Clifford Geertz, "Ideology as a Cultural System," in David E. Apter (ed.), *Ideology and Discontent* (New York, 1964), pp. 47–77.

[22] Thompson, *Organizations in Action*, pp. 54–82.

in the same relationship to that of the East Germans, Poles, Soviets, and Hungarians.

The Romanians have been consistent in drawing and integrating the conclusions associated with a cooperative definition of intrabloc relations. They have accepted the consequences of such a definition and have demonstrated this acceptance by their explicit and unvarying stands on the issue of conflict resolution within the bloc. In their view, conflict can best be handled by a policy of voluntary attendance at bilateral and multilateral meetings the main purpose of which is the distribution of information. Nonattendance at such (multilateral) meetings should in no way reflect upon the existing relations among the various parties within the communist world nor should it place in question their credentials as Leninist or anti-imperialist political forces. At these informational meetings, the topics considered should be as concrete and manageable as possible. Participants should abstain from any action that might threaten agreement and they should emphasize any real or probable areas of agreement. The autonomy of each participant should be recognized and guaranteed by accepting certain prerequisites such as the agreement not to condemn any party's leadership or domestic or foreign policy, not to exclude any party from consultations which affect that party in any way, and not to bias the outcome of any such meetings by requiring that decisions of former meetings (such as those in Moscow in 1957 and 1960) be considered programmatically binding.[28] The Romanians also argue that the objective as well as subjective bases of conflict within the bloc be recognized — that different levels of socio-economic development and the right as well as ability of each party to elaborate policy will inevitably create some conflict. As a consequence of this position the Romanians argue for patience (*răbdare*) in dealing with conflict. Finally, the Romanians have argued for the inclusion of *all* communist parties and anti-imperialist parties in any meeting concerned with adopting a position toward imperialism.

Boris Velchev, a member of the Politburo and Secretariat of

---

[28] For an exposition of these points see "Cuvîntarea Tovarășului Nicolae Ceaușescu la Consfătuirea Internațională a Partidelor Comuniste și muncitorești," *Scînteia*, June 10, 1969.

the Bulgarian party, outlined the Bulgarian position at the February–March, 1968, preparatory meeting of parties in Budapest. Although the Romanian party like the Bulgarian party "appreciates" the aggressiveness of imperialism, the Bulgarians particularly stressed the need to fight the international class enemy, and they put special emphasis on the threat posed by imperialism. As for the Third World anti-imperialist forces, Velchev made it clear that the Bulgarians favored assimilation rather than coalition: "the various revolutionary forces in the developing countries . . . already call, not only for struggle in common with the socialist countries . . . *but also for an ideological rapprochement on the basis of scientific socialism."* [24] On party equality and autonomy, the Bulgarian position emphasized each party's right to be sovereign but it also asserted the need to criticize some parties when their positions or behavior jeopardized effective coordination within the system. This stance is related to two others. Whereas the Romanian party has redefined internationalism to mean unity of all anti-imperialist forces, the Bulgarians adhere to the traditional definition. During the Budapest meetings in March, 1968, Velchev commented: "Georghi Dimitrov said that the attitude to that great country [the Soviet Union] is the touchstone of the sincerity and honesty of every labor leader, every working-class party and working people's organization . . . *These words are as valid as ever."* [25] [Italics added] The Bulgarian position recognizes only "subjective" differences among bloc members, differences based on leadership errors in policy and ideological interpretation, and will not admit the existence of major objective differences. The Bulgarians demand unanimity on all issues on the premise that all *genuine* Leninist parties can reach such agreement. To the Bulgarians, sustained differences are an indication that some parties are not genuine, and this leads them to the conclusion that they must not be allowed to prevent the occurrence of a meeting of the genuine parties.

It can thus be seen that the Bulgarian position emphasizes the uniqueness rather than the distinctiveness of communist parties

---

[24] *Information Bulletin* (Toronto, 1968), p. 106.
[25] *Ibid.*, p. 110.

and demands that the parties reach agreement on major issues before meeting with other anti-imperialist forces. To the Bulgarians,
the world communist movement is something more than the sum
of all communist parties and regimes, and this means not only that
the decisions reached at multilateral meetings must therefore be
binding on all the participants, but that all decisions reached at
previous meetings are also binding.

For a moment, let us consider the differences between these
two syntheses and stances — the Romanian and the Bulgarian — on
a more abstract level. In terms of bloc unity and conflict resolution,
the Romanians are willing to "satisfice," [26] whereas the Bulgarians
maintain a traditional belief in optimizing: that is, the Romanians
are willing to accept some degree of disunity, whereas the Bulgarians believe that complete unity is possible almost immediately.
The Romanians appreciate diversity; the Bulgarians demand unity
and define it as uniformity. The Romanians accept bargaining as
a legitimate and necessary means of resolving conflict whereas the
Bulgarians still insist on persuasion or problem solving.[27] One
values initiation; the other sees initiation by any party other than
the Soviet as opposition, "splitting."

It is also possible to locate the areas that provide the clearest
indicators of a given party's position. These areas are an elite's
estimation of the ability of imperialism to achieve its objectives
(all parties agree on its nature), the place of the Soviet Union within
the world communist movement, and a party's confidence in its

---

[26] James G. March and Herbert A. Simon, *Organizations*, pp. 140–141.
"Satisficing" means choosing a satisfactory as opposed to the best alternative.

[27] There are a number of concepts in the field of organizational theory
that involve the same thing that March and Simon have in mind when they
use the term persuasion. Thompson and Tuden's notion of "computational
decision making" and Simon's "analytic" approach to conflict are examples.
Louis Hartz's notion of "dogmatic liberalism" is also much the same. All
these concepts refer to an approach to conflict resolution which demands
unanimity and assumes that it is possible, and explains its absence in terms
of the misperception, lack of information, or alien nature of the antagonist
in the conflict situation. Those who adopt a "computational" approach to
all conflict refuse to admit the structural basis of conflict or its legitimacy.
This is equally true of a Brezhnev and of a Mayor Daley.

capacity to deal successfully with the development of its national base. The contrast between the Romanian and Bulgarian positions is perhaps best revealed in terms of elite confidence. The Bulgarian emphasis on the threat of imperialism, its dependence on the Soviet Union rather than a united front of forces, and its defensive domestic posture are all in contrast to the Romanian position, most clearly enunciated by Ceaușescu in his June 10, 1969, speech in Moscow, when he contrasted the dangers of imperialism to the strength and ability of socialism:

> Imperialism did not succeed in stopping the way to socialism when the latter was victorious in only one country or in the first years after the war when the workers' and peasants' power in the socialist countries was not consolidated, when there still existed an exploiting class who possessed important economic and political positions. So much the more today when socialism represents a living reality in our countries, when the people are masters of their countries' destiny and have at hand every means of defense, when there exists a powerful world socialist system, it is inconceivable that any force . . . would be able to turn the peoples of the socialist countries from their path, stop their victorious march forward.[28]

Definitions of Bloc Unity and the Question of "Party Maturity"

I have already suggested that the variable that can best explain the new Romanian conception of bloc relations and conflict resolution is party institutionalization, or as the Romanians call it, party maturity. In fact, the Romanian term is analytically the more useful because it directs one to the particular aspect of institutionalization that is most responsible for the attempts of the Romanian elite to formulate a new political and ideological synthesis. The aspect of institutionalization that I am referring to is adaptability. Huntington says of adaptability that it is, "in a rough sense, a function of environmental challenge and age . . . The more challenges which have arisen in its environment and the greater its age, the more adaptable [an organization] is . . . Old organiza-

---

[28] *Scînteia*, June 10, 1969.

tions and procedures, however, are not necessarily adaptable if they existed in a static environment."[29] The concept of adaptability as here defined can help us to see why certain parties such as the Romanian have begun to elaborate a new synthesis while others, like the Bulgarian, have maintained their commitment to Stalin's.

In Paige's study of emulation, he suggests that the propensity to emulate may be correlated with the degree of success in goal achievement experienced by an elite that has engaged in emulation.[30] It would be interesting to see how this can be applied in the Romanian–Bulgarian comparison. One major difference between the situation of the Romanian elite under Gheorghiu-Dej and that of the Bulgarian elite during the same period (1961–1964) was that the Romanian elite was obliged to oppose the Soviet Union in order to pursue its goal of industrialization, whereas the Bulgarian elite was able to pursue the same goal through compliance and emulation. In fact, the Bulgarian elite was able to adopt and maintain this posture in part because of the oppositional stance adopted by the Romanians. In much the same way as Guinea's resistance to France in 1958 shaped France's more benign or at least cautious attitude toward Mali, Romania's opposition contributed to the Soviet Union's positive attitude toward industrialization in Bulgaria. I do not mean to suggest that the difference in treatment by the Soviets has been the only reason, or even the major reason, for the difference in policies adopted by the two regimes; the most important reason perhaps has been the character of the Romanian and Bulgarian elite coalitions and the extent to which each of the parties has been organizationally coherent. But it is nonetheless true that the absence of any immediate or intense need for the Bulgarian elite to engage in critical forms of search behavior — a situation which contributed to and reinforced the defensive, relatively incoherent character of the Bulgarian party and elite — was related to the positive pos-

---

[29] Samuel P. Huntington, "Political Development and Political Decay," in *Political Modernization*, ed. Claude E. Welch, Jr., p. 215.

[30] Glenn Paige, "North Korea and the Emulation of Russian and Chinese Behavior," in *Communist Strategies in Asia*, ed. A. Doak Barnett, p. 246.

ture the Soviet elite adopted toward the Bulgarian party's industrial program.[31]

In contrast, when it found its chief goal of industrialization threatened, the Romanian elite with its relatively high level of organizational coherence began to engage in critical forms of search behavior on general questions of sovereignty and autonomy. Thus the two elites have followed different paths. The Bulgarians in the short run have maximized the degree of certainty surrounding their industrialization program, but they have at the same time jeopardized a more fundamental goal, party institutionalization; the Romanians, in the short run at least, endangered their program of industrialization, but they made possible an impressive growth in party institutionalization.

In February, 1963, the Romanian elite successfully handled the challenge posed by Khrushchev on the issue of a supranational Comecon body; in April, 1964, it issued its statement on party sovereignty; and between March and July it successfully handled its first succession crisis. One may presume that the elite's skillful handling of challenges has had a definite effect on party maturity or institutionalization and has increased the Party's confidence in its ability not only to respond to challenges but also to define its environment.

From this comparison of the Romanian and Bulgarian parties several points emerge. First, it is clear that the Romanian elite's capacity for political initiative and ideological redefinition is not something innate; I have already commented on Gheorghiu-Dej's reluctance and limitations as an innovator. In one respect the Romanian case is one of "to him who has it is given," whereas the Bulgarian case is an "avalanche of failure." The Romanian regime possessed a relatively united elite, a coherent organization, and elite members concerned with and capable of manipulating specific issues (such as industrialization) to achieve more basic goals (such as party autonomy). Possessing a political character of this order, it accepted the conflict over industrialization as an opportu-

---

[31] Similarly, the lack of a struggle with France may in part explain the inability of Modibo Keita to establish his leadership and control over the Malian regime.

nity, with the result that the Romanian party was strengthened in its capacity to exercise political and ideological initiative. In Bulgaria, on the other hand, where the party is characterized by a relatively fragmented elite and incoherent organization,[32] the absence of conflict over the issue of industrialization removed a potential source of power redistribution within the elite as well as of political initiative and ideological creativity.

But, it should not be forgotten that the specific composition of the Romanian elite nucleus has been an integral part of the way in which situations have been interpreted and acted on. To some extent a situation is defined by the behavior of those who figure in it, and this the Romanian elite seems to appreciate far better than the Bulgarian.

A second point to be drawn from this analysis is that the possibility exists that the Bulgarian elite (or any such elite) may itself engage in a policy of initiation. This conclusion is not based on the "it's happened before" principle. Rather, there are dynamic reasons — namely, the coaligning nature of elites, the continual bargaining over goals, the power of example (such as the Romanian and Czechoslovak), the impact of international events, and the process of mediation.

There is a third point which indirectly emerges from this comparison. I have suggested that one of the indicators that certain party elites are resisting a new political and ideological synthesis of the world socialist system in general and the bloc in particular is how successful a given elite feels it has been in its attempts at "socialist construction," that is, in effectively breaking through and then reintegrating the new political system with a new set of

---

[32] Students of East European politics are indebted to J. F. Brown for his recent work, *Bulgaria Under Communist Rule* (New York, 1970), for this country has been one of the most neglected by Western scholars. See particularly ch. 6, "Party and State, 1958–1962," and ch. 8, "Politics Since the Eighth Congress, 1962–1968." Brown describes in detail the factionalism and prolonged period of political instability and incoherence that beset the B.C.P., focusing on the purges in early 1961, the purge of Chervenkov in November, 1961, Khrushchev's overt interference in Party affairs, and the dramatic purges (of Yugov, Tsankov, and Chervenkov) at the VIIIth Party Congress in November, 1962. He also analyzes the April (1965) conspiracy involving members of the Bulgarian military.

publics. In view of the broad span of Leninist systems, however, this point warrants a more differentiated formulation. One can argue that parties with low levels of political confidence are emulating parties: they define proletarian internationalism in terms of Soviet superiority and maintain a dichotomous world view stressing the power of the international imperialist class enemy. In other words, a lack of political confidence reinforces emulation, which in turn threatens the level and character of political confidence.

Such parties as the Bulgarian, Polish, Hungarian, and East German fit into this category. In these parties, low political confidence may be related to indecisive national breakthroughs and/or rigid conceptions of what a breakthrough involves. Parties of this type actively oppose the synthesis offered by Romania and Yugoslavia. On the other hand, the synthesis can also be opposed by parties with relatively high levels of institutionalization and success in breaking through. China is a case in point. Before the cultural revolution, the C.C.P. was in favor of a more hostile though not aggressive posture for the world communist movement. The reason, however, was not the C.C.P.'s lack of a political synthesis and vision of its own or a low level of political confidence. Rather, it was the nature of the political and ideological vision that lay behind the Chinese emphasis on greater bloc unity and the dangers of imperialism. To Mao, if not to individuals such as Liu Shao-chi, the tasks of breaking through and political integration are more than interdependent: they are almost synonymous. System building and community building must be carried out simultaneously; cultural redefinition must be an integral and critical aspect of breaking through and system redefinition, not simply a by-product of mobilization and industrialization. Mao's criteria of success in breaking through are thus much more ambitious than those held by Stalin or Khrushchev or most of the present East European elites. In Mao's eyes, the breakthrough cannot be considered decisive until there is clear proof of an expanding process of cultural redefinition, affecting the way in which human beings interact socially, think ideologically, and behave politically.[33] One aspect

[33] For Soviet and East European elites, a decisive breakthrough means the creation of a democratically centralized party, the removal of the threat of

of Mao's more comprehensive and ambitious definition of success has been the Chinese demand that international accommodation be avoided, because it is a threat to the continued and necessary sense of urgency about reaching the goal of a decisive breakthrough. Thus, *for different reasons*, both the Chinese party with its political and ideological fusion of the breaking-through and community-building processes and the Bulgarian party with its system-oriented and rather rigidly defined breakthrough could oppose aspects of the Romanian vision of the bloc and its relationship to the rest of the world.

Three Case Studies of the Romanian "Position"

It will no doubt have been understood from the analysis thus far that the Romanian elite's redefinition of its place in the bloc — that is, its political-ideological conception of membership in the bloc — and its attitude toward the bloc were not arrived at synoptically. Quite the contrary. It was a matter of gradual elaboration, undertaken amidst domestic and intrabloc conflict, in response to numerous challenges. An examination of three of these challenges should help to bring out how extremely concrete and open-ended the process of elaboration has been under Ceaușescu's leadership, and it will also illustrate Ceaușescu's skill in coping with opposition to the new position on party and national sovereignty.

On July 25, 1967, Ceaușescu delivered a significant speech on the Romanian party and government's foreign policy. On the whole, it has been viewed as a fairly mild speech compared with several other policy statements both before and after, but it is a good example of how competent Ceaușescu is as a statesman, and it gives a notion of the sort of historical and political context within which the Romanian synthesis has evolved.

The summer of 1967 was a critical time for the Ceaușescu regime in Romania. Its recognition of the West German regime and its defense of Israeli sovereignty had called into question its cre-

---

organized internal resistance, comprehensive industrialization, the creation of strategic support groups (i.e., skilled workers, state farmers, socialist intelligentsia), and (in the case of East Europe) alliance with the Soviet Union.

dentials as a legitimate Leninist leadership. Even if one rejects as unlikely the possibility that Ceauşescu and his closest associates had some misgivings about their "vision" and its policy implications, the condemnation of the bloc, and the opposition of certain domestic forces as well, must together have been a serious challenge to Ceauşescu.[34] Such a challenge both threatened his personal power and required him to define more clearly the intensity of his commitment to his vision of Romanian national development and of the conditions necessary for that development.

Ceauşescu's handling of this challenge in his July speech should be seen as an instance of successful statesmanship. Hoffmann has described the tasks of statesmanship as being those of: "selecting the most favorable interpretation of the facts whenever the lessons they carry are ambiguous, of choosing the most subtle and dignified form of submission, when the lesson is beyond debate; and most importantly of trying to change the facts whenever they are intolerable but it is in the nation's power to transform them."[35] A test of statesmanship, one might add, is whether or not it can avoid having a "lesson" considered "beyond debate." Second, a political leader might be considered a statesman to the extent that he is successful in extending the boundaries of his nation's power. Or, somewhat differently stated, a statesman is one who does not accept as fixed the power of his nation to transform "intolerable facts."

Ceauşescu's behavior in the summer of 1967 was an example of a leader's attempting to keep the meaning of a "lesson" open rather than "beyond debate," while at the same time making it clear that he recognized the necessity of accommodating his regime to the challenge it faced without, however, lessening its uncom-

---

[34] The question of Ceauşescu's power, like that of most political leaders' power, is usually approached in a zero-sum fashion. To evaluate Ceauşescu's power accurately, one must also take into account both the distribution of power within the Party elite and the changing character of the opposition he has faced continuously since 1965. Certainly in the summer of 1967 the presence of Drăghici, Stoica, Apostol, Dănălache, and others of similar orientation at middle and lower levels placed Ceauşescu in a rather touchy political situation.

[35] Stanley Hoffmann, "Paradoxes of the French Political Community," in Hoffmann et al., *In Search of France*, p. 74.

promising commitment to the synthesis and political program which gave it a distinctive identity. Recognizing the Romanian regime's isolated and exposed position, Ceaușescu made the basis of his speech a reaffirmation of Romania's "development of friendly relations and many-sided collaboration" with the countries belonging to the "world socialist system," which was, he emphasized, the "central objective of the party and government's foreign policy." [36] But he also reaffirmed his basic commitment to "cooperative relations" in saying that policy disagreements between socialist states should not interfere with trade relations or with the basic unity of all socialist systems. If in thus reaffirming the centrality of the world socialist system in the R.C.P.'s foreign policy Ceaușescu showed that his regime still faced certain limits or constraints, he also made it clear in his defense of cooperative relations that he was aware of the extent to which such limits were self-imposed and was committed to a new conception of international relations among socialist states. Ceaușescu's entire speech was a classic instance of "selecting the most favorable interpretation of the facts" and, implicitly as well as explicitly, a reaffirmation of his commitment to the R.C.P.'s conception of the world socialist system and its relation to the national development of all the members. Thus, although Ceaușescu criticized those who had underrated the aggressive nature of imperialism, he also began his speech with a section titled "the superiority of the forces of socialism, progress, and peace over the forces of reaction and imperialism" — making the most of the ambiguous statement issued by the Soviets in 1956 on the balance of world forces. Similarly, Ceaușescu stressed the importance of the socialist bloc, but he went on to note the importance of an anti-imperialist front of all progressive forces. A more subtle stroke was the manner in which he listed the regimes with which the R.C.P. had close relations. The Soviet Union came first, then Bulgaria, and then Yugoslavia. This relationship with Bulgaria, he seemed to be saying, was proof of Romania's commitment to the world socialist system. And by putting Yugoslavia third

---

[36] "Expunerea cu privire la politica externă a partidului și guvernului," in Ceaușescu, *România pe drumul*, II, 422.

he seemed to be saying that, although Romania's first attachment was to the bloc (i.e., as represented by its ties with Bulgaria), it was a particular sort of attachment and not without its own limits. Ceaușescu's demonstration of statesmanship was completed by the categorical defense of his regime's commitment to sovereignty, a defense which in policy terms involved the recognition of Israel's right to political and national existence.

The implied thrust of Ceaușescu's response in the speech of July, 1967, was accommodation without compromise over basic commitments, and he carried it off brilliantly, accepting the opportunity implicit in the challenge he had been confronted with. It was a test of his commitment to the conception of national development that had been formally articulated in April, 1964, and July, 1965, and it was a test of the ability of his coalition to steer an independent course — avoiding the mutually exclusive resolutions of such a challenge by neither acquiescing to Soviet demands on the West German and Israeli questions nor, like Yugoslavia, breaking ties with the bloc.

From another point of view, Ceaușescu's reply to the challenge in the summer of 1967 gave evidence of the continued existence and strength of a more traditional political and ideological vision within the Romanian Party. The more traditional element defined the process of party institutionalization in terms of limited member participation and/or influence and oligarchical rather than collegial rule; it accepted violence and coercion as necessary to the process, and it saw no need to redefine this process in terms of the specific problems associated with different stages of development, believing that the problems were as they had always been. Finally, those committed to such a posture continued to look upon the Romanian political community in terms of elite manipulation of popular support with an almost complete absence of political reciprocity between elite and public. The challenge and Ceaușescu's response in the summer of 1967 involved a definite manifestation of the open-ended conflict that existed within the R.C.P. between competing visions of national development; they demonstrated that there is no one necessary course which the process of national development will take and that the leadership function is critical in determining what course will be chosen and how it will be defined.[37]

A second example of Ceaușescu's ability to realize the opportunity latent in serious challenge has to do with the consultative meeting of communist parties which took place in February and March, 1968. For a wide range of reasons, the Romanian Party has been wary of multilateral meetings, but domestic pressures from "traditional" elements and pressure exerted by friendly parties such as the Italian (P.C.I.), together with what might be assumed to be the Romanian Party's desire to disprove the charges of national isolation which were directed against it combined to bring the R.C.P. to Budapest in February, 1968. The R.C.P.'s mode of participation, however, was much more significant than its decision to participate. Before sending delegates to Budapest, the R.C.P. sent members of the Presidium to two parties that were not attending: Gheorghe Apostol went to Pyongyang, and Emil Bodnaraș went to Havana. Both of these party regimes were known for their support of the principles of autonomy and sovereignty. The R.C.P. delegates, Niculescu-Mizil and Dalea, then appeared in Budapest as semi-official representatives of China and Cuba, two important regimes that were actively "confronting imperialism." At Budapest, the Romanian delegates repeatedly argued for the inclusion of all parties in such a meeting; they signified that they were against discussing and/or condemning the line of any party, against any kind of name-calling or interference, and against any tendency toward a new center for the world socialist system.[38] Finally, Ceaușescu effectively demonstrated his power and support within the R.C.P. by withdrawing his delegation from the meeting after the comments of the Syrian delegate concerning the R.C.P.'s policies.

---

[37] One thing should be clear. The composition and/or boundaries of the leadership sector is an extremely important variable affecting the leadership function — specifically, whether the leadership is restricted to a small and relatively isolated elite (as was the case in Hungary under Rakosi) or is broadened to include the party *aktif* and certain strategic publics (as occurred in Czechoslovakia under Dubček).

[38] Cuvîntarea Tovarășului Paul Niculescu-Mizil la întîlnirea consultativă de la Budapestă," *Scînteia*, February 29, 1968.

In the short time of its participation, the R.C.P. had gone on record as the spokesman of the parties that stood for party and national sovereignty and had argued this position forcefully; it had demonstrated vividly that it was willing to act on its commitments, and had given evidence of Ceaușescu's control over those commitments.

A third and final example of the political-historical context[39] within which the Romanian Party worked out its conception and definition of its relation to the bloc was the June, 1969, meeting of communist parties in Moscow. Shadowed by the political reality of the invasion of Czechoslovakia, the circumstances under which this meeting was scheduled were not the most auspicious from the Romanian point of view. Yet in a number of respects the meeting and the events that preceded are a striking example of the strength of Romanian initiative, of the political ability of the Romanian leadership, and of its intention and capacity to act consistently and yet not rigidly on its conception of the character of bloc relations and the prerogatives of individual communist parties.

To begin with, in April, 1969, two important articles dealing with the subject of unity within the socialist world appeared in the Romanian journal *Lumea*.[40] The main thesis, in some ways not strikingly new, was that unity within the "socialist world" is dependent upon the right of each socialist regime to initiate policy in the international arena as well as domestically. In essence, this was a reiteration of Ceaușescu's stand of the summer of 1967 — that all nations, small as well as large, have the right, ability, and obligation to pursue active policies in the international arena in the pursuit of international peace. But Corbu's argument, particularly in his second article, appears to expand the standard Roma-

---

[39] "Political-historical context" resembles "organization-situational factors," the term already familiar in this work, but it is more precise, less general. Not all organizational factors are political (they may in other instances be psychological), nor do all situational factors have to be historical (they may be sociological).

[40] See Nicolae Corbu, "Care este linia dominantă: Considerații asupra raportului de forțe în lumea contemporană," nr. 17, *Lumea* (17 aprilie 1969), 10–13; "Pentru ca forța socialismului să se manifeste din plin," nr. 18, *Lumea* (24 aprilie 1969), 9–12.

nian argument on sovereignty. It is in effect a denunciation of the utility and workability of "domesticism" — a political stance characterized by a refusal or inability to initiate policies in all issue areas on the basis of self-provided premises — for the real point is that policy in the international sphere should not be based on the emulation of Soviet policies but should rely on the premises shared by all socialist regimes and independently defined by each. Since the previous August, the question of the right of each party to engage in international initiatives had been increasingly criticized within the bloc, and Romanian statements had pointedly omitted any mention of it. On May 13, however, shortly after the appearance of Corbu's articles, the Romanian and Norwegian communist parties issued a joint statement in which they declared that unity should be reestablished within the movement on the basis of respect for the right of each party to establish its own policy on all problems, both internal and international.[41] In my opinion, the second Corbu article, which can be taken as an expression of the position of the R.C.P., does more than simply uphold the *right* of each party to make its own policy. It implies that it is their *obligation* to do so. The Romanian Party's argument, if my interpretation is correct, is that only if all parties assert and develop their capacities to contribute to the establishment of bloc unity and international détente will it be possible for any party to elaborate its own political skills, define its national base, and provide effective leadership domestically. According to the Romanians, then, the failure of the various Leninist parties to act in a sovereign fashion in the international sphere sustains their state of dependence on the Soviet Union, and this dependence makes them defensive and isolationist toward the rest of the world at precisely the time when they should be otherwise — when the relative strength of the socialist and anti-imperialist forces, the possibility and neces-

---

[41] Similarly in *Scînteia*, July 30, 1969, the "Decision [of the Central Committee of the R.C.P.] regarding the Romanian Communist Party's delegation to the international meeting of communist and workers parties," gave a particular interpretation to the statement of June 19, issued after the Moscow meeting, which stressed the coordination of foreign policy by socialist states; the June 19 statement was here interpreted as recognizing the "right of each party to decide independently about its internal and external policy."

sity of decreasing the chances of war, and the need to take part in the scientific-technological revolution all call for active international involvement.[42]

The Romanian position seems to me to suggest that "domesticism" weakens the bloc and all of its members by denying to the bloc and each national community the insights and contributions which are a function of autonomous, if interdependent, policy initiatives. The Romanians appear to be arguing that "partial sovereignty" contributes to a rigidity of thought, an inability to conceptualize problems in new ways and to seek fresh solutions, and this rigidity contributes in turn to the defensiveness and fragility of each party and regime. In short, the articles by Corbu were at a minimum an instance of drawing out and acting on the implications of previous statements such as the right and necessity of international initiatives by small nations made in July, 1967.

The Corbu articles also presaged political initiative, and this was immediately evident in the series of meetings the R.C.P. undertook with the Yugoslav, Australian, Italian, and French parties prior to the June meeting in Moscow. But even more significant were the R.C.P.'s decisions to participate in the Moscow meeting, and to invite the President of the United States to visit Romania in early August. The latter decision was certainly the strongest sign so far that the Romanians believe in the interdependence of ideological and political initiatives, accepting policy as a necessary intervening variable if ideological declarations (such as those on the sovereignty of all communist regimes and parties) are to become political realities.

I have previously made the point that the Romanian elite's political and ideological synthesis has taken place in a historical-political setting and not within a vacuum. This was certainly true for the Corbu articles, the behavior of the Romanian leadership at the Moscow meeting, and the invitation to President Nixon. The Corbu articles were undoubtedly stimulated by the meeting that was scheduled for June, 1969. And the Romanian decision to

---

[42] *Scînteia*, June 27, 1969; see Maurer's comments on the need for Romania to "involve" itself in the scientific-technological revolution. Also Corbu, "Pentru ca forţa socialismului . . ."

attend the meeting and the invitation to Nixon were in part determined by several events that occurred during the winter and spring of 1969: (a) the declaration of Warsaw Pact members in March, calling for a European security conference, which was for the Romanians a major policy success, not in the sense that they imposed it on the other bloc members but in the more limited sense that it was wholly compatible with their own concerns and positions, that is, *active* coexistence; (b) the meeting of Comecon in April, which did not result in demands for a supranational planning body, and which in general adopted a position with which the Romanians could agree; and (c) the meetings of the Romanian leadership with the Soviets and Poles in mid-May — in accordance with the sustained Romanian emphasis on direct bilateral talks between party and regime leaders to deal openly with major issues or differences. These three events paved the way for Romanian participation at the international meeting in June.[43] After these events, all of which involved policy successes for the Romanians, it would, of course, have been difficult for the Romanians to abstain from the meeting, but by the end of May at least the Romanians seemed determined to go. They had by this time stated their ideological position forcefully in the "Corbu articles"; they had consulted with their "allies" the Italians, Yugoslavs, Norwegians, and Australians; and they had consulted directly with the Soviet and Polish leaderships, and very likely had informed them then of the Nixon invitation.

The Romanians did participate in the meeting in June, and despite the criticism of China and other objections, they stayed to sign the final document. To a certain extent this may have been a gesture of reciprocity: presence at Moscow in return for the outcomes of the Warsaw Pact, Comecon, and bilateral meetings. But there is no doubt that the meeting gave the Romanians the chance to do several things in the way of bloc politics. First of all, by being there they could protect themselves against the criticism of others.

---

[43] See *Scînteia*, March 18 and April 27, 1969, for the statements on the Warsaw Pact and Comecon meetings, and R.F.E. *Situation Report* (Rumania), May 19, 1969, for a comment on the Ceaușescu trip to Moscow and Warsaw in May, 1969.

Ceaușescu could reply without delay, and in the presence of all parties, to Brezhnev, Zhivkov, Kadar, and Ulbricht on the topics of nationalism, the role of bloc organizations, the issue of "comradely assistance," and the character of international meetings.[44] Second, the Romanians could argue their position on important issues, as Ceaușescu did rather eloquently on June 10. Here again, in a most important context, Ceaușescu upheld the right of each party to decide policy in fact, not just in theory, and urged the participants to understand that internationalism is dependent upon respect for national prerogatives. This was the thesis of the Corbu articles, that internationalism was dependent on national-ism in the sense that for a party to contribute to unity within the movement, it had to exercise the right of initiative domestically and internationally. Without the exercise of this right, internationalism (proletarian) would be a fragile and exploitative arrangement; this position was formally communicated to those at the meeting and published in some form in the journals of the various parties in attendance. A third opportunity for the Romanians at the meetings was that of criticizing the decisions and behavior of others. Ceaușescu did indeed make clear the Romanian position on the Israeli's right to national sovereignty and on the criticisms of the Chinese. He also commented on the inappropriateness of the scheduling of the meeting. Finally, it was only by participating in the meeting to the end that the Romanians could have any hope of influencing the wording of the final statement. Absence would very likely have meant that decisions would have been reached and programmatically stated which would have been antithetical to their political and ideological interests. As it was, the final statement contained nothing that adversely affected Romania's status as a bloc member or as a socialist regime. It did not deal harshly with parties that did not attend, nor, in particular, was there any mention of excommunicating the Chinese regime from the socialist "family." Also, the statement contained a favorable theoretical

---

[44] For the statements of Brezhnev et al., see *Scînteia*, June 13, 14, and 15, 1969. Taken together, they include all the essential elements of a "consensual-orthodox" position.

argument on the relationship of national development and bloc unity.[45] Within the context of the Czechoslovak invasion, the pressure to have an international meeting, and the threat to the Romanian synthesis posed by the orientation of the Soviet leadership, the Romanian elite showed that it was aware of the real constraints which it faced and demonstrated once again an impressive ability to prevent the "lesson" from being "beyond debate."

Perhaps the most revealing aspect of the period surrounding the Moscow meeting — particularly indicative of the way in which organizational (political) and situational (historical) factors are interwoven — was the Romanian decision to invite the American president to Bucharest. My analysis so far has stressed the evidence of continued Romanian ideological and policy initiative and success within the bloc and the movement, and in the international arena. This stress has been legitimate; however, the success of the Romanians between March and July, 1969, was not due only to their skillful leadership or to their diplomatic and ideological finesse. Rather, it was due to an interplay of these (organizational) factors with a set of (situational) considerations that relate to the Soviet elite. The situational factor that provided the context within which an elite such as the Romanian, capable of exercising initiative and ready to do so, could exploit the advantages of a specific political reality, was related to the main priorities of the Soviet elite between March and July — which were significantly congruent with the behavior of the Romanian elite. Let us be clear as to what is meant by congruence. It does not mean the Soviets were satisfied or happy about the Romanian statements, policies, and initiatives. But, given their own prorities, the Soviets could not prevent the Romanians from exercising initiative, or from reinforcing the commitment to their own political-ideological synthesis without the Soviets jeopardizing their own policy aims. What

---

[45] For the Romanians' own perception of the positive aspects of the Moscow meeting as well as a general comment, see two articles in *Scînteia*, one by Mihail Telescu, "Coeziunea partidelor comuniste, cel mai important factor al unirii tuturor forțelor antiimperialiste," June 20, 1969, and in particular, "Sub steagul luptei antiimperialiste, pentru întărirea unității mișcării comuniste" (unsigned), June 21, 1969.

was the content of this congruence? First, the Soviets' success in imposing Husak on the Czechoslovak party decreased the dangers attached to a European détente. Second, in putting down the Czechoslovakian threat, the implications of the Romanian stance were also contained, since Czechoslovak revisionism, with Romanian, Yugoslav, and Italian revisionism, might together have comprised a politically critical mass within the bloc. Third, for whatever set of reasons (among which one might certainly mention Sino–Soviet relations), the Soviets had themselves been interested in at least a climate of conflict amelioration within the European context.[46] Fourth, the Soviet desire to hold an international meeting of communist parties increased the Soviet tolerance of Romanian statements and initiatives. The Soviet leadership quite clearly wished to demonstrate its tolerance of diversity and its "abhorence" of such "imperialist-concocted" notions as that of limited sovereignty.[47] For all these reasons, the situation was such that the independent-minded Romanian Party could accommodate itself to certain very real constraints — that is, to an implied pressure to attend the meeting, since not attending might have placed the Ceauşescu regime in a politically and militarily tenuous position — while at the same time displaying a remarkable capacity to derive the most from this situation. Thus the situation of congruence allowed for Romanian initiative, and the character of Romanian leadership, including its conception of the R.C.P.'s place and role in the bloc, of its ability and rights, and national obligations, made it probable that such a situation would be actively responded to — as in fact it was. One final comment, however, must be made about the situation of congruence that existed in the summer of 1969 between Soviet and Romanian concerns, and apparently still exists: we must remember that priorities can change. If the Soviets should reorder their priorities, the Romanian elite will continue to be in danger not only of having less freedom to elaborate and act on

---

[46] See Gromyko's speech, sections of which are published in *Scînteia*, July 11, 1969; and the "friendly treatment" afforded Titulescu by the Soviets (R.F.E. *Situation Report* [Romania], June 24, 1969) as two signs of the Soviets' (tactical) accommodative posture during the summer of 1969.

[47] "Cuvîntarea Tovărăşului L. I. Breznev," *Scînteia*, June 13, 1969.

their political and ideological synthesis, both within the bloc and internationally, but also of having to face the prospect of Soviet invasion. All statesmanship, even of the highest caliber, has limits, particularly when the state is small and is confronted by a hostile great power.

As of July, 1969, then, there were still no answers to the questions of what type of relations would define the "world socialist system," what form conflict resolution would assume, and in general what direction the political development of Romania would take. As for the future, one cannot, obviously, foresee in detail what relations will prevail even a year from now, nor to what extent it may be the R.C.P. that alters relations. Within certain limits, however, one can specify what might shape the future course of events within Romania and within the bloc.

The Romanian Communist Party and the World Socialist System

Haas has said that "a close study of negotiating processes in international relations suggests the prevalence of three types of compromise, each indicative of a certain measure of integration." These types of compromise involve accommodation "on the basis of the minimum common denominator," accommodation by "splitting the difference," and, most ambitious of all, accommodation on the "basis of deliberately or inadvertently upgrading the common interests of the parties." [48]

As part of its program of synthesis the Romanian elite has argued for all three types of compromise. In every statement concerning intrabloc conflict, the Romanian elite has reiterated the request that nothing should be done by any party to aggravate the conflict already existing within the movement. Along with this, it has stressed the importance of dealing with manageable problems, on which there is agreement, and of leaving in abeyance problems

---

[48] Ernst B. Haas, "International Integration: The European and the Universal Process," in *International Political Communities: An Anthology* (New York, 1966), pp. 95–96.

that appear to resist immediate resolution. Essentially, however, the Romanian approach to compromise within the bloc is based on an attempt to "upgrade the common interest" by redefining the fundamental conditions for bloc unity, so that the good of each unit guarantees the good of the whole rather than vice versa. By redefining the political situation so as to remove the structural and ideological binds which aggravate and prolong conflict, the Romanians argue, the common interest would be substantially enhanced.

The Romanians have met certain difficulties in trying to revise the premises for bloc decisions. These difficulties pertain to the decision issues that have occupied the attention of the Soviet elite, the procedures the Soviets (and others) have adopted in their attempts to resolve the conflicts within the bloc, and the difficulty of finding mediators.

To begin with the question of decision issues, the Soviet elite (along with several East European elites) has shown itself to be unsure of its position toward political innovation within the bloc.[49] This uncertainty over the legitimacy of certain innovations has been evident in the attitude toward the question of whether or not Yugoslavia is a socialist country. It was most evident in the Soviet attitude toward developments in Czechoslovakia, and it is still apparent in the Soviet attitude toward Romania. To the extent that bloc conflict during the period 1963–1968 has been related to "uncertainty over preference regarding possible [political] outcomes" on the part of several bloc members — namely, East Germany, Bulgaria, and the Soviet Union, as well as Poland and Hungary — one can say that it has been sustained by the procedures adopted within the bloc for problem solving.

According to Thompson, from whom I have borrowed the term *decision issues,* a strategy of compromise is the most suitable in a situation where parties conflict because of uncertainty over preference for specific outcomes — as was the case in 1968 when the Italians, Yugoslavs, and Romanians were ready to accept the political implications of Dubček's rule while the majority of War-

---

[49] See Thompson, *Organizations in Action,* p. 134, for a discussion of "decision issues."

saw Pact members reacted in the opposite fashion. However, the Soviets have for the most part refused to accept such a strategy. Instead, they have shown themselves at least reluctant to compromise. They have excluded those who disagree with them from discussions which have yielded critical decisions affecting conflict within the bloc. They have pressed for multilateral meetings of all parties or of only those amenable to their views. And they have jeopardized the efficacy of attempts at compromise within the bloc by maintaining a *pro forma* attachment to the procedures associated with the compromise strategy and by showing a willingness to break their commitments to compromises that have been reached. These points need some elaboration. At Dresden, the Soviets excluded the Romanian party from discussions pertaining to the position of the Warsaw Pact on Czechoslovakia. The Soviet Union and its closest allies firmly believed that a meeting of communist parties should be held without delay. This desire for a multilateral meeting was in many ways antithetical to a desire to reach an effective resolution of issues within the bloc, for, as Thompson points out, the "subtle processes of compromise cannot work with large numbers [such as attended the Moscow meeting in June, 1969]. . . . When power is widely dispersed, compromise issues can be ratified but cannot be decided by the dominant coalition *in toto*." [50] Insofar as the Soviet Union demonstrated a great degree of impatience to hold a multilateral meeting regardless of the preparatory work preceding it, those regimes within the bloc who were parties to one or more of the conflicts within the system had just cause to fear the outcomes and doubt the efficacy of a general meeting. For compromise to work as a strategy of conflict resolution, it is first necessary for a series of smaller agreements among small numbers to be arrived at, on the assumption that these will mesh at a certain level.[51] It would appear that by early 1968 the Soviets were at least recognizing the need for some preparation. The Budapest meeting was held first, in February and March, and several similar meetings were held between then

---

[50] *Ibid.*

[51] See *ibid.*, p. 134. In this as in many other instances, the current Romanian elite has demonstrated its organizational-theoretical abilities.

and June, 1969, some of which the Romanians participated in. The Romanians, quite sensibly I think, viewed these preparatory meetings with some reservations. First, it is not meetings per se that are important in effecting a compromise but the outcomes of such meetings — the extent to which they are successful in contributing to a partial resolution of outstanding issues. Second, by their behavior at Dresden and their actions after the discussions with the Czechoslovaks at Bratislava and Cierna, the Soviets betrayed their commitment to, and appreciation of compromise and patience. Finally, there was little evidence that the Soviets or their allies had revised their expectations or definitions of what would be considered desirable outcomes of a general meeting of parties.[52] For all these reasons, conflict within the bloc continued to remain high; and it is not likely that it will cease in the near future.

One other factor has contributed to the sustained atmosphere of conflict within the bloc, compounding the difficulties the Romanians face in trying to revise the premises for bloc decisions. This is the lack of effective mediators. It is in some ways a historical problem — a part of the Stalinist legacy in problem solving which is evident in the continued emphasis on a consensual approach to conflict within the Polish, East German, Hungarian, Bulgarian, and Soviet elites. A more immediate complication is that the main point of controversy within the bloc is the question of party and national sovereignty; naturally, a party such as the Romanian is extremely sensitive to any interference in its affairs and reluctant to accept as unbiased any mediator drawn from within the bloc itself. The two thus oppose each other: the consensual orientation toward conflict held by most of the bloc members lessens the probability that a mediator will be drawn from outside the bloc, such as the French or Italian party, while the sensitivity on the sovereignty question lessens the probability that

---

[52] Of greatest significance is the Soviet elite's sustained adherence to a traditionally Stalinist-consensual appreciation of bloc unity. Agreement between the Soviets and the Yugoslavs or the Soviets and the Romanians is still a matter of situational congruence — temporally rather than value-based coincidence of interest. For this reason the Romanians are rightfully cautious in accepting the Soviets' zigzag policy.

regimes such as the Romanian will allow any chosen mediator from within the bloc much scope for action. This near-impasse has not ruled out all mediation, as was shown by the role played by the Hungarian party during 1968–1969. Nor is it impossible that a party such as the French might assume a similar role. But there is no questioning the difficulties associated with the quest for effective mediators.

By the end of 1968 intrabloc conflict had assumed rather alarming proportions. The "decision issue" was no longer intrabloc uncertainty over outcome preferences — that is, the range of political innovations that would be considered legitimate. Rather, there was a polarization of positions on this issue and here developments within Czechoslovakia had a decisive influence.

The Romanian elite and world communism

Without attempting any sort of prediction as to what Romanian national development will be in the future, one can, I think, say something about how the Romanian elite may attempt to define its relationship to the world communist movement. My major hypothesis is that the tendency of the R.C.P. to move toward a significant redefinition of the boundaries of the world socialist system will increase as a function of the Soviet Union's tendency to act on a consensual definition of membership and unity within the system. At least two supplemental propositions can be added to this: (a) that the constraints working against any significant political or ideological redefinition of the bloc by the R.C.P. are not simply external but also endogenous — in other words, that the R.C.P. has ideological as well as practical reasons of political survival for wanting to maintain its position within the bloc; and (b) that a small state is particularly limited in the ways in which it can act on any given preference or tendency precisely because the question of political survival can so easily become a real issue.

Even before the Soviet invasion of Czechoslovakia, the Romanian elite gave real if limited evidence of a desire to redefine the boundaries of the world communist movement. In this, as in many other things, there was a certain element of latent learning involved, for it was Khrushchev, at the 1961 Soviet Party Congress, who first blurred the boundaries: "The tasks of people's democratic, national liberation and socialist revolutions are drawing closer together and becoming more intertwined in the present epoch. The logic of social development has caused all these revolutions to be directed primarily against one chief enemy — imperialism."[53] Today it is the Yugoslav party that is the most active agent in redefining the boundaries, and its policy finds some echo in the new Romanian ideological definition of proletarian internationalism. The Romanians enjoy very close relations with the League of Yugoslav Communists. In fact, at the time of Ceauşescu's visit to Yugoslavia in May, 1968, the Romanian press pointed out that Romanian–Yugoslav relations could serve as a proper model for relations among socialist nations. And it is important that one of the major foci of this visit was the question of alignment and the boundaries of the world socialist movement. In this instance, Ceauşescu's position might be described as being cautious but open. On May 4, several weeks before the visit, the Romanian Party paper *Scînteia* printed a detailed summary of an article that had appeared in the Yugoslav paper *Borba* under the title, "The Daily *Borba* on the Position of the L.Y.C. Toward the Meeting of the Communist Parties." This article frankly criticized the proposed meeting (finally held in June, 1969) for being limited to communist parties and pointed out that although the rationale of such a meeting was to create an effective anti-imperialist front, not all the anti-imperialist forces were to be invited. *Borba* then went on to ask: "do the communists, have, perhaps, unique interests in the anti-imperialist struggle?" *Scînteia* on May 28 also printed Tito's statement that "between our two countries and parties there exists full accord on the fundamental principles according to which countries must conduct international relations," and that "our points of view concerning many international problems are either very close or identical." In the same issue, Ceauşescu explicitly emphasized the *aligned* position of the Romanian Party and

---

[53] "Report on the Program of the Communist Party of the Soviet Union to the XXII Congress of the CPSU, October 18, 1961," in Alexander Dallin, ed., *Diversity in International Communism*, p. 37.

regime. In response to Tito's comments on the need for a high-level conference of nonaligned nations and to his combining the notion of a socialist nation with a policy of nonalignment, Ceauşescu noted that the R.C.P. and the Romanian Socialist Republic put the socialist system and, in particular, relations with the Soviet Union—"which with its tremendous material and human potential plays a remarkable role in the contemporary world, in the defense of peace and security."—at the center of their foreign policy. Continuing in this vein, the Romanian leader stressed the importance of Romanian relations with Bulgaria and Hungary.

In terms of my hypothesis, the Romanian elite's behavior prior to the Soviet invasion of Czechoslovakia in August, 1968, particularly its restrained response to Yugoslav statements on the relationship between the sovereignty of socialist nations and a policy of nonalignment, was the outgrowth of several interacting factors. (a) Soviet elite intransigence toward a cooperative as opposed to consensual definition of intrabloc relations was apparent as of July, 1968, but not decisive. The Czechoslovak "experiment" was still underway, and the somewhat ambiguous situation within the bloc gave the Romanian elite the latitude necessary to work for change within the existing system and helped to maintain the belief that revision of existing relations was possible within the current boundaries of the bloc. (b) The Romanian elite was operating under a number of self-imposed value constraints, such as the desire to remain a bona fide member of the bloc in order to preserve a context seen as necessary or supportive of its political and ideological identity. (c) The Romanian elite did not want to act in such a way as to bring the Czechoslovak experiment to an end. On the contrary, the Romanians thought they should avoid action that might jeopardize the Czechoslovak development as well as their own position. (d) Consequently, the Romanian elite decided on a "Rubashov" role,[54] acting on the premise that its greatest resource in shaping the evolution and definition of intrabloc relations was its presence as a bloc member. There were no doubt

---

[54] Rubashov, in Arthur Koestler's *Darkness at Noon* (New York, 1941), inspired by ideological and political motives, tries to change the Party's character from inside, i.e., while maintaining his membership.

other reasons also for the Romanians' reticence on the question of redefining the boundaries of the world communist movement and world socialist system, but essentially it was a combination of those I have mentioned: the desire to maintain its Leninist identity and its connections with other Leninist parties, the "openness" of the situation in Czechoslokavia and the bloc and the fear of giving support to those in opposition to the Czechoslovak developments, and the belief that its greatest resource in the battle for redefining the quality of bloc relations was its bloc membership.

The invasion of Czechoslovakia by the Soviet Union, Poland, East Germany, Bulgaria, and Hungary significantly altered the Romanian party's position as a member of the bloc, and in terms of our hypothesis it is to be expected that to the extent that the Soviet Union maintains or increases its dogmatic and aggressive posture, the Romanian elite will contemplate and engage in an *ideological* redefinition of the bloc's boundaries.[55] Assuming a situation of increased Soviet intransigence, one possible form of redefinition involves an ideological statement by the Romanian elite which defines radical anti-imperialist regimes as integral parts of the world

---

[55] As part of its continuing emphasis on sovereignty and perhaps in reaction to continued Soviet intransigence, on the 25th anniversary of Romania's liberation the Romanian Party initiated a distinctly new definition of that event and, by implication, of the Romanian Socialist Republic's status in the world community. At one and the same time, the Soviet army is given more attention and credit than has been the case in the past few years, while the role of "other United Nations" forces is also explicitly recognized. In addition, the activities of the Romanian Party in the period before the liberation, between 1940 and 1944, are elaborated in greater detail, and the role of the Romanian army after August 23, 1944, in helping to defeat the Nazis, and the recognition of this role by the major powers at that time, are particularly emphasized. This new interpretation is consistent with the argument of the Corbu articles, and with the stress placed by the Romanian elite on the need to eliminate "blocs" and substitute for them a world of equal nations, voluntarily choosing what commitments they shall make. It is also an index of the regime's increasing institutionalization, as is shown by the greater complexity associated with the Party's role in the early 1940's, and the greater emphasis on autonomy, in which the Party and the nation are lauded as major participants in international events, not merely as auxiliaries dependent on the Soviet Union. See Nicolae Ceaușescu in *Agerpress*, August 22, 1969.

socialist system. Such a statement would be consistent with the Party's definition of Proletarian Internationalism and its concern over party and national sovereignty. The Romanian elite's rationale in defending such a position could stress the need to include units within the system that were free from the Stalinist experience, legacy, and orientation and were therefore capable of stimulating "cooperative" relations based on the actual recognition of norms such as noninterference.

There are, however, two situational factors that still continue to influence the direction and content of the Romanian party's political stance vis-à-vis the bloc. The first is the real possibility of a Soviet invasion, which constrains any tendency within the elite to complete a significant redefinition of the ideological character of the bloc and, beyond that, to transform such an ideological statement into policy. Second, if for no other reason than the relative lack of elite coherence within the Soviet leadership, Soviet behavior is likely to oscillate rather than simply progress in one direction. In terms of my hypothesis, to the extent that Soviet behavior is characterized by a *less* intransigent bloc and international posture, as was the case during the spring and summer of 1969, the Romanian elite's tendency to redefine the bloc's boundaries will not be reinforced. Throughout the summer of 1969, in fact, this tended to be the case. On the one hand, the Romanians did not emphasize the meeting of nonaligned nations in Belgrade, and on the other, they limited their statements on the bloc to those stressing the importance of avoiding international isolation and of defining the world socialist system as one comprised of all ruling parties, not simply those with membership in Comecon and the Warsaw Pact.

The Romanian Communist Party
and the Nation

THE SECOND MAJOR AREA in which the Romanian elite under Ceaușescu's leadership has been creating a synthesis of perspectives, commitments, and policies is in its appreciation of the nation as a political unit. Under Ceaușescu, there has been an ideological acceptance of the nation as opposed to a simple political manipulation of it. Ideologically, there has been a continuous and conscious attempt to incorporate, recognize and control the idea of the nation. The present elite led by Ceaușescu has added an expressive appreciation of the nation to the former instrumental orientations which at first saw the nation as little more than an appropriate framework for power consolidation, industrialization, and system building, and, later on, as an effective and necessary protective device in the form of state sovereignty. This expressive appreciation reflects a "fundamental attachment to the values embodied in the national culture and history of [the Romanian] people." [1]

---

[1] This is the third type of appreciation of the nation which Shoup mentions in his article, "Communism, Nationalism, and the Growth of the Com-

At the IXth Party Congress in July, 1965, Emil Bodnaraş, a member of the Presidium, pointed out that "the nation as a historic entity, far from being surpassed, finds the condition for its full affirmation and development only in socialism, [only there does it find] the condition for the materialization of its entire capacity."[2] More recent comments suggest that the nation will have an important role for a very long time to come. In an authoritative article which appeared in *Scînteia* on January 24, 1968 ("The Development of the Socialist Nation and Proletarian Internationalism"), Nicolae Corbu and Constantin Mitea argued that a minimum condition for the fusion of nations was the worldwide victory of communism and after that a long period of gradually expanding international communist relations during which each nation would further develop itself in a dialectical sense. But the Romanian appreciation of the nation's role has not been limited to a recognition of its longevity.

During his visit to Romania, De Gaulle made a comment that must have found an immediate response among the Romanian elite. In discussing why the French and Romanians valued national autonomy, De Gaulle explained that it was not solely because of the pleasure involved in being master of one's house: it was also because "nations are those entities each with its own soul and body, which constitute in the last analysis [*în urma urmei*] the irreducible elements and indispensable sectors of universal life."[3] If we define as nationalist any individual, elite, or organization that accepts the view that the nation is an "irreducible" and in-

munist Community of Nations After World War II," *American Political Science Review* 56 (December 1962): 886–898. A word should be said here about the term "expressive." It may be conceived of as a "socio-emotional" dimension of thought, behavior, or institutions, as referring to the dimension of political sentiment. It does not imply a priori irrationality, fanaticism, or romanticism, nor is it the only path to irrationality or fanaticism: those with an instrumental approach to issues can be equally irrational and fanatical; see, e.g., the criticism of the Novotny regime in "Czechoslovak Action Program," *Radio Free Europe* (Czechoslovak Press Survey), May 20, 1968.

[2] Cuvîntarea Tovarăşului Emil Bodnaraş," *Congresul al IX-lea al Partidului Comunist Romîn* (Bucureşti, 1969), p. 647.

[3] Quoted in *Scînteia*, May 16, 1968.

valuable element of international life, there are definite indica-
tions that the Romanian elite can be considered a nationalist
elite.[4]

One indication is an article that appeared in the *Romanian
Journal of Sociology* in which the authors, G. Dolgu and M. Dulea,
argued that "the nation is a social micro-unit with its own structure: it has an independent existence, evolves on the basis of the
endogenetic factors and remains indivisible even in the conditions
of the sharpest internal contradictions, or of the most profound
transformations and evalutions."[5] On the credible assumption that
this argument is popular with Ceaușescu, Maurer, and certain
other members of the Romanian elite, it is possible to conclude
that the attachment of the present Romanian elite to the nation
is an essential part of its ideology, despite the partial contradiction between this and certain Marxist–Leninist tenets concerning
the nation-state as a historical-political entity.

Sources of the Romanian Elite's Political and Ideological Appreciation of the Nation

Three areas of explanation have already been considered in discussing the Romanian elite's new appreciation of the nation. These
included the need for public support in the controversy with the
Soviet Union, the confidence that support was available (from different social sectors for partially different reasons), and the Party's

---

[4] This definition of a nationalist is not meant to be exclusive, but merely
a fundamental part of a romantic nationalist stance.

[5] "The Concept of Sovereignty in a Sociology of Development," *Romanian Journal of Sociology* 4–5 (n.d.). Here, as in other instances such as
the Bodnaraș speech in July, 1965, the Romanian position toward the nation
greatly resembles the one formulated by two Austrian socialists, Karl Renner
and Otto Bauer. To use Pipe's words, in their study of the relationship between nationalism and socialism and in their attempts to reconcile the two,
these two men discovered that "the nation had to be recognized as a valuable
and enduring form of social organization," and they argued that under socialism the nation would become if anything a more significant political unit as
a consquence of the greater social mobilization and political-cultural participation of the mass of people. Richard Pipes, *The Formation of the Soviet
Union* (Cambridge, Mass., 1964), pp. 25–27.

confidence in its ability to control as well as elicit support. In addition, two other areas of explanation should be considered.

The first involves the relationship between beliefs and attitudes, specifically those related to the question of national diversity and sovereignty. It has been established by experiment that an "individual's attitude [predisposition to respond] can be changed by changing his beliefs about [an] object." It has also been established that the reverse can occur, that "beliefs [hypotheses about the nature of an object and the types of action that should be taken toward it] may also be viewed as consequences of attitude."[6] During the period 1955–1964, the Romanian elite gave increasing evidence of a firm belief in the notion of diversity and the concept of sovereignty, both of which, I suggest, contributed to a positive attitude toward the nation as a political entity. I further suggest that as a function of the increase and change in the conflict between the Soviet Union and Romania, this positive attitude contributed to the Romanian elite's positive belief in the basic value and importance of the nation. Moreover, one specific mechanism for translating this positive attitude toward the nation into a positive belief has been external criticism. The Romanian elite has faced considerable criticism of its ideological assertion of the concept of sovereignty and of the policies that have been associated with it.[7] It may be conjectured that such criticism has strengthened the Romanian commitment to the notion of autonomy and to the entity at which this criticism has increasingly been directed, the nation. But whatever specific mechanisms were involved, by 1965 the Romanian elite had elevated a positive appreciation of the nation to the point where it had become an element within what Brzezinski has called the philosophical component of Marxist–Leninist ideology.[8] In this respect the Romanian elite has made

---

[6] Martin Fishbein, "A Consideration of Beliefs, Attitudes, and Their Relationship," in *Current Studies in Social Psychology*, ed. Ivan D. Steiner and Martin Fishbein (New York, 1965), p. 119.

[7] This criticism has been sustained since 1961 and has covered the topics of economic integration, bloc unity, and international initiative (i.e., Romania's diplomatic-economic ties with West Germany, and its defense of Israeli sovereignty).

[8] In one of the most analytically sophisticated sections of *The Soviet*

a basic, character-defining value commitment, which contributes significantly to its distinctive identity and at the same time entails a set of constraints and opportunities that in large measure will provide the framework for the future development of the Romanian party, regime, and community.

The second explanation of the Romanian elite's new appreciation of the nation is interwoven with the emphasis placed by Leninist elites on consciousness and control, and with the problematic nature of the Romanian elite's success in producing the nucleus of a new socio-political type, a new professional or "middle" class. The appearance of this class provides the leadership of the Romanian Party with both a challenge and an opportunity; the way the Party defines its relationship to this class, which as I have pointed out is largely a product of its policies of breaking through and industrialization, will determine the nature and extent of the Party's control over the process of national community building. The Romanian elite, or at least the part of it that is committed to Ceauşescu, is certainly aware of the importance of the new middle class and is doing its best to assimilate it within the existing political-ideological framework.

Social mobilization in Romania has been significant more for qualitative than for quantitative reasons. According to one of the regime's leading intellectuals, "in absolute figures, the transfer of the inhabitants employed in agriculture to the other branches of the national economy amounted yearly to an average of 43,000 persons, in the period 1950–1964."[9] But it is not primarily the

Bloc, Zbigniew Brzezinski makes a distinction "between those aspects of the ideology which can be called its philosophical component [. . . the a priori assumptions which form the foundation stone of the ideology], those which can be called its doctrinal component [. . . historically contingent concepts of a strategic character], and those which might be referred to as its action program" (p. 489). This useful specification of the different levels of an ideology is similar to a more general treatment of belief systems by Milton Rokeech in *The Open and Closed Mind.* Rokeech distinguishes the central, intermediate, and peripheral regions of belief systems in a more general analysis which provides a useful framework for a comparative study of ideologies.

[9] Costin Murgescu, C. Grigorescu, G. Retegan, and V. Trebici, "Influences of the Process of Industrialization on Social Mobility — on Romanian

numbers involved or the shift from rural-agricultural to urban-industrial locations that is most striking, in Romania or in other Leninist countries. What may be of greater significance, as saying something about the nature of the mobilization effort, are the occupations and roles assumed by mobilized individuals. In turn, such occupations and roles are related to the type of mobilization Romania has experienced in the last twenty years. Mobilization, in Romania, has been primarily an outgrowth of rapid and comprehensive industrialization rather than of modernization.[10] One result of this has been that the "introduction of contemporary technical progress and . . . the growing complexity of the processes of production . . . [has] directed the process of professional diversification along the lines of changes towards professions that require a [higher] educational qualification."[11] That is to say, mobilization based on a policy of rapid and comprehensive industrialization has presented the Romanian elite with the task of effectively assimilating increasing numbers of individuals occupying or aspiring to professional or highly skilled occupations. Several suggestions can be made as to the character of this mobilized stratum: (a) to the extent that mobilized elements are peasant in origin, their propensity to value the nation will be high, partly because the breakthrough process is more successful in reshaping institutions than in reshaping values;[12] (b) to the extent that mobilized elements hold professional or skilled jobs, they will demonstrate much pride and assertiveness in their desire or demand for social status, eco-

---

Data," *Romanian Journal of Sociology* 4–5:138. More recently it has been stated that each year 100,000 peasants enter the working class; see Mircea Bulgaru in *Lupta de Clasă* (July 1969), p. 59.

[10] There is a significant difference between modernization and industrialization. On this see Reinhard Bendix, *National-Building and Citizenship*, p. 5; Charles Lindblom, "Has India an Economic Future?" *Foreign Affairs* 44 (January 1966): 239–253; J. P. Nettl and Roland Robertson, "Industrialization, Development, or Modernization," *British Journal of Sociology* 17 (September 1966): 274–291; and David Apter, *The Politics of Modernization*, pp. 1–80 and *passim*.

[11] Murgescu et al., p. 185.

[12] This point was confirmed in a recent symposium held in Romania on the country's social structure; see "Structura socială ă României,"*Lupta de Clasă* (July 1969), pp. 55–80.

nomic remuneration, *and* political recognition; and (c) to the extent that mobilized elements are peasant in origin and hold professional or skilled jobs — a common situation in Leninist systems that have experienced rapid and comprehensive industrialization — their propensity to fuse nationalistic feelings with demands for status and recognition will be very great.

This situation has presented the Romanian elite with a major challenge and opportunity, one to which Ceaușescu has responded quite differently from his predecessor Gheorghiu-Dej. The Ceaușescu regime's emphasis on foresight and control has contributed to the regime's conclusion that "the nation is the motive force of present-day development," and to a sustained concern with its ability, politically, ideologically, and organizationally, to shape the character of the nation.[13] Ceaușescu's interest in assimilating and defining mobilized elements within the Romanian system is appropriate for an institutional leader who is concerned with the "definition of his party's mission and role" and wants to decide what the character and direction of his polity ought to be. The degree of success that he and his supporters will experience is another question. The point here is that questions concerning character and direction are of the greatest priority for Ceaușescu. For the R.C.P. he has set the task of defining the political-ideological commitment of newly mobilized elements, those desirous of status, recognition, and responsibility, in a manner congruent with the self-assumed role and goals of the Party. In addition, he has apparently identified the two "conflicting imperatives" which must be clearly understood and integrated (rather than simply manipulated) if the Party is to maintain its role, relate it to the changes occurring in its national base, and beyond that, shape the character of those changes. These two imperatives can be termed nationalism and socialism. Following Apter, we may view them as two types of ideology which perform different functions within a given socio-political system.

---

[13] The most dramatic expression of this concern was the National Party Conference held in December, 1967, which was regarded by the Party as its most important undertaking since the 1965 Congress. At this conference the character of the Party, the territorial definition of the country, and aspects of its economic structure were significantly redefined.

Apter defines socialism as an ideology that emphasizes development goals "for which individuals must sacrifice" — a statement that certainly applies to the Romanian regime.[14] Furthermore, "Government is seen as the main source of development. Unity, represented in national citizenship, is the critical form of allegiance, with no other loyalties taking precedence over the state itself. Behind unity is the concept of society as a natural and organic body in which all the parts have their appointed functions, especially those linked to the development process." Socialism thus has two aspects: "In the content of its ideology, it defines modernity. In the application of its ideology, it defines social discipline manifested in solidarity groups whose raison d'être is functionally for development." As an ideology of universalistic and secular concerns, however, socialism is not quite able to perform a solidarity function within a given political community. Nationalism, on the other hand, "incorporates primordial loyalties in a readily understandable synthesis, taking up the 'slack' in identity and solidarity where socialism fails." Notably, "nationalism incorporates specific elements of tradition and employs them to bring meaning to the establishment of a solidly rooted sense of identity and solidarity."[15]

Under Ceauşescu the Romanian Party has sought to maintain the initiative in relating national and socialist foci so as to build the Party's authority. Ceauşescu has attempted to redefine the Party by emphasizing recruitment criteria which stress professional training, expertise, and youth and by emphasizing the collegial principle of decision making, thus allowing new professional elements greater participation and giving greater recognition to their skills and loyalty to the regime.[16] Ceauşescu's attacks on the "new class,"

---

[14] Note in this connection the statement made by Ceauşescu at the Xth Party Congress, "that the construction of socialism and communism requires work, order, discipline, and responsibility," a statement worthy of a regime with developmental goals whether it be socialist or Andrew Ure's England. See Nicolae Ceauşescu, *Report At the 10th Congress of the Romanian Communist Party* (Agerpress, August 6, 1969).

[15] See David E. Apter, "Ideology and Discontent," in *Ideology and Discontent* (New York, 1964), pp. 23–24.

[16] The new participation also has obvious instrumental considerations —

including the statement in March, 1968, that 30 per cent of the Party and State activists were to be transformed to production units and his criticism of persons in the regime who held several jobs,[17] were of significance politically as well as symbolically. Essentially, Ceauşescu hopes to bring about a more effective integration between strategic publics and the Party as well as a greater performance capacity for the regime.

Perhaps the clearest example of the different ways in which Gheorghiu-Dej and Ceauşescu have related to the nation and to the task of integrating nationalist and socialist premises lies in the area known as the "nationality question," which more than anything else has to do with the regime's orientation toward the Hungarian minority. There seems to be little doubt that both Gheorghiu-Dej and Ceauşescu have aimed at the assimilation of the minorities, but their approaches to the task do appear to be marked by important differences. Gheorghiu-Dej appears to have acted in an "integrally nationalist" fashion in his post-1957 efforts to assimilate the Hungarian minority. His policy was a perfect instance of a "breakthrough" mentality and strategy based on the most explicit forms of coercion and intimidation.[18] Under Ceauşescu the Romanian regime has continued with its attempts at demonstrating to the Hungarian population that they have no alternative but to become a part of the Romanian national community. However, though the regime has consistently moved to structurally reduce the potential political influence of the Hungarian sector, these moves have not been characterized by violence or chauvinism. Evidence on the latter point, including a series of articles by Michel Tatu in *Le Monde* and my own experiences in Romania in the summer of 1967, does not point to serious or centrally legitimated

---

i.e., to increase the performance of the system. These considerations are usually emphasized, and expressive considerations are not even recognized, so I have reversed the order somewhat.

[17] See Nicolae Ceauşescu in *Scînteia*, March 23 and June 21, 1968; also Ceauşescu's speech to the Cluj County Party Organization, *Agerpress*, July 14, 1969.

[18] See the article by George A. Schepflin, National Minorities Under Communism in Eastern Europe," in *Eastern Europe in Transition*, ed. Kurt London, pp. 117–145.

manifestations of an integral nationalist orientation toward the ethnic minorities.[19] Rather, along with attempts to reduce the political-territorial influence of the Hungarian minority there appear to be moves by the regime to allow for increased individual participation at the local level.[20] In short, Ceaușescu's policy so far shows signs of being a greater and more sophisticated effort to integrate nationalist premises with socialist premises — that is, to integrate a desire to eliminate the possibility of an effective withdrawal of political support from the regime at a critical moment by the Hungarian population with the desire to create a "solidary" society. A solidary society can be defined as one in which the various parts have similar levels of economic development, social development, and ethnic composition with differences allowed for and even supported rather than intimidated so long as they are individual rather than collective (or structurally expressed) and cultural rather than political.

A final example of the way in which Ceaușescu has sought to integrate national and socialist premises is in the realm of symbols. At the Party's IXth Congress in July, 1965, the Romanian People's Republic became the Romanian Socialist Republic. This change made it possible for all strata to join in a demonstration of pride — the Party, the assertive new class of professionals, and

---

[19] Michel Tatu in *Le Monde*, November 11–14, 1967.

[20] An instance of the former was the decision at the National Party Conference in December, 1967, to make the county (*judeţ*) rather than the region the basic territorial unity. This fragmentation plus the partial redistribution of population lessened the organizational base of the Hungarian sector of the population.

As instances of the latter, one must look at the increase in minority cultural activity. In a section entitled, "Expansion of Cultural Life Among The Hungarian Minority," *Radio Free Europe* (Rumania), July 31, 1969, in a report on cultural life in Romania, notes a recent issue of *Korunk*, the Hungarian-language magazine, as having described the increase in the number of provincial weeklies, contacts between Hungary and the Hungarian population in Romania, and the increased activity of the Hungarian intelligentsia in Romania. See also *RFE Situation Report — Rumania 29 August 1969*, p. 14. One must also note the formation of special worker councils for various nationalities within the Socialist Unity Front and the decentralization of the Writers Union.

the more traditionally nationalist but recently uprooted peasant-workers — and all within a symbolic context which quite explicitly defined the change in terms of socialism.

After all that has been said, one must still admit that it is entirely possible that Ceaușescu and the Romanian elite will fail in their attempt to emphasize the nation while redefining it in terms congruent with party premises. But it is nonetheless important to realize that the Party is making a serious effort to achieve this integration, and that together with industrialization it considers this its major responsibility.

In summarizing the Romanian Party's present position toward the nation, three related terms may be used: control, definition, and selectivity. The term control emphasizes the R.C.P.'s concern with consciously shaping political outcomes. As a Leninist elite it places a high premium on the comprehensive coordination and integration of developments within its "domain." Leninist doctrine, certainly adhered to in this detail by the R.C.P., would say that conscious political direction and not the operation of impersonal socio-economic forces stimulates the effective integration of a nation. This sort of attitude toward the political sector's active and defining role was expressed by Jerzy Wiatr, a Polish communist and sociologist, who believes that changes in the nature of the state "inevitably remodel the national nexus since . . . the state plays in it the central part of both a value and an institution which at first is a signal factor in the formation of the nation and then is the most direct expression of national life." [21]

However, because different Leninist leaders and parties have quite different perspectives on the notion of control, the critical and differentiating characteristic of the R.C.P.'s position is closer to the second term, definition. Under Ceaușescu the Romanian elite has not attempted to define control only in terms of the nation's importance as a symbol with high manipulative value for most social groups within its boundaries; nor has it lost control by in fact subordinating its socialist or Leninist identity to its national identity (as tended to occur under Gheorghiu-Dej). Rather, by emphasizing increased public participation, collegial

---

[21] "State and Nation," *Polish Perspectives* 11 (March 1963): 24.

decision making, the importance of respecting legal norms, and the decentralization (not deconcentration) of power, (i.e., to the county level), the Romanian Party has given some sign that it intends to revise significantly the old pattern of ideological manipulation and political domination in favor of a new pattern of increased political as well as ideological reciprocity with the nation.

Selectivity, the third term, is one of the mechanisms by which control can be made operational and by which definition can be given content. And the process of selection, the things selected, is a clue that can help one to ascertain the nature of a Leninist elite's nationalism. As an example, one can point to the position taken by the present Romanian elite in its statements about the semi-fascist Iron Guard movement which existed in Romania throughout most of the interwar period and into the early 1940s. In *Scînteia* on May 31, 1968, in an article entitled, "An Antinational, Obscurantist Movement of Sad Memory," Academician P. Constantinescu-Iași and Ion Spălățelu went to great lengths to argue that the Iron Guard was fascist, foreign to the "progressive humanitarian spirit" of the Romanian people, and antithetical to the Romanian nation. A week later a similar article appeared, under the title, "Two Important Moments in the Romanian People's Antifascist Struggle." The purpose of the two articles was not exactly the same, but at one level they both implied the same thing: that the nation per se is not the most valued referent for the Romanian Party. The regime has been careful to point out that it is interested in recognizing and incorporating only those elements from Romania's past that are in accord with, if not identical to, today's political-ideological definition.[22]

---

[22] Fischer-Galati's criticism of the regime's attempted synthesis of nationalism and socialism is, I think, imperceptive. He says: "This synthesis of Rumania's national and social aspirations into the new 'socialist nationalism' appears to be both incomplete and unrealistic. The quintessence of historic nationalism — doubtlessly an integral part of the Rumanian belief system — was anything but socialist. The nationalist tradition was bourgeois, stressing anti-Communism, anti-Semitism, anti-Magyarism, anti-Russianism, and above all, the Christian and Latin character of Rumanian civilization. The bourgeois nationalist legacy identified the ultimate national goal as the 'embourgeoisement' of the society . . . political control by a landlord-bourgeois

The Character of Romanian Nationalism, 1965–1969

I have so far suggested that under Nicolae Ceauşescu and since the IXth Party Congress of 1965 the Romanian elite has demonstrated an appreciation of the nation that differs from the version under Gheorghiu-Dej. This "appreciation" has occurred at two levels or in two domains — the ideological and the policy (political) — and its dominant characteristic has been an attempt to integrate socialist and nationalist premises. The rationale behind this attempt appears to be the belief that the viability of the Romanian regime is dependent on a greater incidence of reciprocity between elite and publics and a smaller incidence of domination and distrust.

I have also discussed several organizational factors — that is, the emphasis of Leninist elites on consciousness and control — and

---

oligarchy . . . in a superficially democratic structure" *The Socialist Republic of Rumania* (Baltimore, 1969), pp. 103–104.

As I have just pointed out, the present regime is obviously not interested in synthesizing every element of traditional Romanian nationalism with socialism. Particularly under Ceauşescu, it has shown itself to be selective in its use of the elements of traditional nationalism. Nor is it very convincing to argue that, despite this intention, the Romanian elite will fail because traditional Romanian nationalism exists as a well-integrated configuration which cannot be taken selectively, piece by piece. Certainly all treatments of history are selective; all national myths are in some ways "distortions," and a great many of these "distortions" are accepted and supported. More importantly, however, even if traditional Romanian nationalism existed as a tightly integrated set of symbols and beliefs, one may still ask who belonged to the interwar Romanian nation-state and who subscribed to its beliefs and what the quality of this commitment was. As Fischer-Galati himself points out, the regime was only "superficially democratic," and the nationalism was that of the middle classes. This does not mean that the peasant masses were *not* nationalistic, but one ought to investigate the conception of the nation that is held by nonparticipants in the political process, to see what the bases of their "nationalism" were and what changes the conceptions may have undergone as a result of their mobilization, mobility, education, change in reference groups, aspirations, and so forth.

The question of how unrealistic the regime's attempts are becomes more complex and interesting when posed in this context. Equally, the question about the incompleteness of the regime's synthesis of nationalism and socialism becomes different. All syntheses are incomplete; the question is whether they are successful.

situational factors — that is, the appearance of significant numbers of mobilized elements occupying or aspiring to professional
positions — which have contributed to this new appreciation of the
nation. What remains is to establish the quality of the nationalism
that has characterized the Ceaușescu leadership during the period
between the IXth and Xth Party Congresses.

Here my interpretation differs markedly from the usual ones.
One standard conclusion has been that the only difference between Ceaușescu's and Dej's nationalism is that Ceaușescu is a
more dogmatic or intolerant nationalist. Also, quite incorrectly,
Ceaușescu's nationalism has been described as social-fascist, much
like the Iron Guard. And in addition these observers have failed
to provide an analytical base from which one could try to determine the conditions that might turn the present brand of Romanian nationalism into something dogmatic and integral.

Under Ceaușescu, the nationalism of the Romanian regime, at
least through the summer of 1969, has been what Carlton Hayes
has termed romantic (liberal) nationalism.[23] There are a number
of indices one can use to justify this characterization: (a) the presence or absence of an Adam Smith sort of definition of world
harmony; (b) an emphasis on the value of sovereignty, that is, national independence; (c) identification with "oppressed" nations;
(d) an emphasis on the past which focuses on events and continuity rather than on a golden age or myth era; and (e) a view of
nations as the natural divisions of humanity.

Liberal nationalists, Hayes says, assumed that "each liberal
national state in serving its true interests and those of its citizens
would be serving the true interests of humanity at large."[24] As
I have shown, this is precisely the prescription the R.C.P. has
given for harmony and unity within both the world socialist system and the world. It is the very essence of the "cooperative"
stance assumed by the Romanian elite in international relations.
As for notions of independence, it is hardly necessary to demon-

---

[23] See Carlton Hayes, *The Historical Evolution of Modern Nationalism*
(New York, 1959), pp. 151–160, for a discussion of liberal nationalism and
romantic-liberal nationalism.

[24] *Ibid.*, p. 159.

strate the quintessential position this concept occupies in the Romanian elite's value hierarchy. Hayes also suggests that romantic-liberal nationalists "feel the liveliest sympathy with the nationalist aspirations and struggles of every 'oppressed' or 'enslaved' people." Although it is of course nearly impossible to sift out all the various motives behind a given act, one can point to behavior by the Romanians that appears to be based on the considerations Hayes mentions. The Romanian defense of Czechoslovakia's right to independent policy development and their censure of the Warsaw Pact invasion is one example. The sympathy with which the Romanians view the Vietnamese struggle against the United States, and the defense of the Israelis' right to political sovereignty are two other examples.

The fourth index is not used by Hayes but it can perhaps be of use here. Integral nationalists, I suggest, tend to take a diffuse view of history, emphasizing a golden age or a myth era, whereas romantic nationalists tend to emphasize the continuity of history and specific developments within that history.[25] In the Romanian case a stressing of the historical significance of the Dacians (except for specific purposes such as finding historical support for resisting infringements on one's sovereignty) might be taken as a sign that the regime is moving toward an integral nationalist posture (as was the case during Dej's last years in power). On the other hand, a certain emphasis on concrete events in the past would seem to imply a more romantic-liberal stance. Certainly in the last two or three years a good deal of attention has been given to specific events and persons, such as the career of Tudor Vladimirescu, the revolution of 1848 and the part Nicolae Bălescu played in it, the peasant uprisings of 1907, and the role of Titulescu in the interwar period.

As for the last index, the presence or absence of the view that nations (nation-states) are natural divisions of humanity, two types of "evidence" might be mentioned. The first is related to a subject we have already touched upon, selectivity. In its treat-

---

[25] The reasons for these different approaches to history cannot be elaborated upon here, but it may be noted that they are partly due to the very significant *anti* nation-state component of integral nationalism (i.e., Nazism).

ment of Romanian history the Party has singled out one figure above all others — Nicolae Bălcescu, a liberal nationalist of the nineteenth century. It is worthwhile looking at what Bălcescu thought about the nation. In his *Istoria românilor sub Michaiu Vodă Vitezul* (1878), in a fashion worthy of Mazzini, Bălcescu says that world unity is dependent upon the fullest expression of national diversity. The world is to be unified through a national division of labor. Each nation, he thinks, has an "evangelical mission" which consists of contributing to world harmony through the development of its national distinctiveness. Only independence can provide the framework within which each nation can make its contribution to world culture.[26] These ideas are reflected today in the current Romanian literature on the nation. Dolgu and Dulea, in the article earlier referred to, quote with approval the statement by D. Gusti that there can be no "talk of a pre-eminence of humanity, because although forming a unitary whole, this does not mean the dissolution of the nations but their raising to humanity through creative work, without losing anything of the independence of their originality. A humanity without the strong personalities of the nations which make up its unity would be anaemic, poor, and exhausted as it would lack the very multiplicity of sources which give it life and vigor."[27] This attitude toward the nation is precisely what Hayes has termed romantic-liberalism, which assigns a special role for each nation and sees the *independent* elaboration of *each* nation's distinctive identity as a condition of world development. In this respect, romantic nationalism is antithetical to chauvinism and imperialism and is fully compatible with the Marxist contention that no people who interferes with the freedom of others is free.[28]

But to say that the current Romanian elite position is one of romantic nationalism is not to imply that this position rules out

---

[26] See pp. 1–5 of the 1878 edition (Bucureşti).

[27] G. Dolgu and M. Dulea, "The Concept of Sovereignty in a Sociology of Development," p. 222.

[28] This Marxist and romantic nationalist tenet was used by the Romanian Party in its defense of Czechoslovak sovereignty; see *Scînteia*, October 7, 1968. My thanks to J. F. Brown and his staff for having located this statement for me.

the possible appearance of a more integral nationalism. In the first place, romantic nationalism has *several* components, some of which allow for or are congruent with an integral nationalism.[29] Second, the Romanian elite and regime are made up of individuals who, it may be presumed, do not all possess the same commitment to romantic nationalism or even any commitment to romantic nationalism. It is true that for the last five years the most consistent posture of the Romanian regime has been romantic nationalism — as we have seen in our analysis of the ideological appreciation of the nation developed by the Romanian elite and its political behavior — but some question may exist as to what this behavior signifies.

A romantic nationalist posture favors a policy of active interaction ideally on an equal basis with other nations. An integral nationalist posture works in the opposite direction. Within the world socialist system, the Romanian elite's policy of "active coexistence" is very consistent with the ideological postulates of romantic nationalism — just as the dichotomous view of the world and the assertion of Leninist uniqueness by the Bulgarians is congruent with integral nationalist postulates.

The behavior of the Romanian regime since July, 1965, has certainly been consistent with its emphasis on active coexistence. Since the IXth Congress the Romanian party has been host to delegations from forty-eight countries, and it has extended its commercial and political relations to regimes as different as West Germany, Israel, and those of the Latin American countries.[30] Clearly, if there is any one central component of Romanian foreign policy it is the prevention of Romania's isolation: politically, economically, technically, and culturally.

---

[29] As examples: romantic nationalists emphasize the distinctiveness of each nation. In certain situations distinctiveness may be interpreted as uniqueness, a change which involves a qualitative reordering of one's appreciation of the nation. Similarly, romantic nationalists believe that each nation has a "mission." Again under certain circumstances, a mission defined as each nation's contributions to the culture of an area or the world may be interpreted by a regime as being the right and duty to impose its "contribution" on that area.

[30] Ceauşescu, *Report to the 10th Congress*, p. 113.

Nonetheless, the argument can be made that such "involvement" is more formal than substantive. Take, for example, the Romanian interest in expanded foreign trade. Some have suggested that the new interest among certain elites in the nonindustrialized or industrializing sections of the world, "in expansion of international trade as a means of promoting development . . . represents an attempt to extend protectionist philosophy and methods beyond the limitations of the domestic market of the nation-state rather than a conversion of development theorists and policy-makers to a more free-trading philosophy." [31] Although the author of this statement, Harry Johnson, was not specifically directing his comments to Romania, it is fair to consider this argument as it applies to the Romanian elite's over-all posture toward the international sphere. One could argue that despite its greater range of global interactions, it has been engaged in a posture of national isolation. If this could be demonstrated, the argument(s) that Ceauşescu's Romania is dogmatically or integrally nationalist would be strengthened. The argument of "national isolation," however, does not hold up very well. It is certainly true that the Romanian regime has taken a protectionist posture — using the term in the broadest sense to cover the regime's political and ideological as well as economic policies. The meaning of that posture is not self-evident, however. Rather than seeing it as an index of closing off, as in aggressive nationalist regimes, I suggest that the Romanian "protectionist" stance may be regarded as a response to and index of the Romanian regime's recently acquired autonomy — as an attempt to elaborate a "practical ideology" issuing from a specific (Romanian) social reality.

As a posture or strategy, "protectionism," as Selznick has pointed out, may be essential for the defense of "precarious values" [32] such as the right to provide autonomously the major premises for and definition of domestic and foreign policy. In this sense

---

[31] Harry G. Johnson, ed., "The Ideology of Economic Policy in the New States," in *Economic Nationalism in Old and New States* (Chicago, 1967), p. 137. Johnson's first essay in this volume is one of the very few worthwhile discussions of the nation and nationalism.

[32] See Philip Selznick, *Leadership in Administration*, pp. 119–133.

the Romanian regime's posture, up to the present time, has been one of marked autonomy rather than isolation. It is a posture that seems appropriate in light of recent history, in which the Romanian regime has been making a sustained effort to acquire political autonomy and to establish its right to make decisions critical to its political identity. In the context of this history, the Romanian elite and regime's emphasis on protectionism or self-interest can be interpreted more appropriately in terms of its recently acquired and consistently elaborated policy of initiation rather than in terms of isolation or autarchy. To quote Weber, "one of the most important aspects of the 'rationalization of action' is the substitution for the unthinking acceptance of ancient custom [the analogue in this context would be the Romanian Party's mechanical emulation of Soviet decisions], of deliberate adaptation to situations in terms of self-interest"[33] — such as the so-called Romanian "independent course" or what I have called its policy of initiation.

This argument concerning the meaning of the Romanian regime's "protectionist" posture also helps to explain why the present Romanian elite has elaborated a national position so much in accord with Hayes's "romantic nationalism." It can readily be seen that the ideological postulates of romantic nationalism are compatible with the emphasis placed by Ceaușescu, Maurer, Bodnaraș, and others on the value of independence. These same postulates are also compatible with the Leninist belief that the party can develop only in a situation marked by the effective interaction of elite and public, where the political leadership respects and attempts to develop the distinctiveness of its national environment. Furthermore, the romantic nationalist postulates emphasize the illegitimacy of chauvinism, and this too is much in accord with the emphasis placed by the Romanian elite on the standard of noninterference.

As for the future development of the Romanian elite's appreciation of the nation and the character of its nationalism, some would argue that the logic of its current nationalism (which is not integralist) will lead to a more intense and chauvinistic posture. In

---

[33] Max Weber, *The Theory of Social and Economic Organization*, p. 23.

his discussion of liberal nationalism Hayes notes that "liberal nationalists were high-minded, optimistic, and devoted to the cause of peace," but that the logic of this nationalism "and its fine intentions were not sufficient of themselves to insure its triumph. Its needs must grasp the sword and slay its adversaries." In short, "in achieving its goal [it] suffered a transformation."[34] Such a transformation may indeed occur despite the desire of significant elements within the Party to prevent such a development. Whether or not it does is related to a more fundamental question concerning the character of the Romanian political community since 1965 — its leadership, its several publics, and the issue areas that are seen by both as being of most importance to the Romanian Socialist Republic.

---

[34] *The Historical Evolution*, pp. 161 and 163.

Agenda

THE PRIMARY ITEM on my agenda is to "complete" the analysis of national development that this study has begun. What is required is an analysis of the second critical aspect of nation building — the process of political integration and the creation of a viable political community. I hope I have made it clear that this aspect of national development is not separate from breaking through. Rather, at certain points and at different times certain actors within a society perceive the major social-political task as being the creation, support, and elaboration of political (in contrast to administrative) and, in general, expressive (in contrast to instrumental) relationships between elite and publics.

In the course of my analysis of the breaking-through process I have had occasion to refer to the process of integration and community building. What is required at this point is a more formal systematization and definition of those comments. A second study is necessary, one which will do for the concept of community building and political integration what this study has tried to do for the concept of revolutionary breakthroughs. This second study is now in progress, and it, too, is conceived of as a "theoretical case study," an analytical exercise integrating theoretical, comparative, and case study components. Specifically, it will try to define the concept of political integration, to develop a typology of political integration in Leninist polities, to compare several such polities within the framework of this typology, and finally to specify and increase our understanding of political life in Romania since the IX Party Congress. The same "dialectical" assumption that supported this study of revolutionary breakthroughs supports the one in progress — namely, that a theoretical case study is the most appropriate instrument for the simultaneous refinement of the theory and for an understanding of the distinctive conceptions and approaches to universal political concerns and issues that contribute to a given nation-state's particular identity.

Bibliography

Works in Comparative Politics and Organization Theory

BOOKS

Abdel-Malek, Anouar. *Egypt: Military Society*. Translated by Charles Lam Markmann. New York: 1968.

Almond, Gabriel and G. Bingham Powell. *Comparative Politics: A Developmental Approach*. Boston: 1966.

Almond, Gabriel and Sidney Verba. *The Civic Culture*. Princeton: 1963.

Apter, David. *The Politics of Modernization*. Chicago: 1965.

Aron, Raymond. *Démocratie et totalitarisme*. Paris: 1965.

Bendix, Reinhard. *Nation-Building and Citizenship*. New York: 1964.

———. *Work and Authority in Industry*. New York: 1956.

Blau, Peter. *Exchange and Power in Social Life*. New York: 1964.

Blau, Peter and W. Richard Scott. *Formal Organizations*. San Francisco: 1962.

Cohen, Arthur R. *Attitude Change and Social Influence*. New York: 1964.

Crozier, Michael. *The Bureaucratic Phenomenon.* Chicago: 1964.

Cyert, Richard M. and James G. March. *A Behavioral Theory of the Firm.* Englewood Cliffs, N.J.: 1963.

Dahl, Robert A. and Charles E. Lindblom. *Politics, Economics, and Welfare.* New York: 1953.

Dahrendorf, Ralf. *Class and Class Conflict in Industrial Society.* Stanford: 1963.

Deutsch, Karl. *The Nerves of Government.* New York: 1963.

Deutsch, Karl, and Foltz, William J. (eds.). *Nation-Building.* New York: 1963.

Easton, David. *A Systems Analysis of Political Life.* New York: 1965.

Eckstein, Harry. *Division and Cohesion in Democracy: A Study of Norway.* Princeton: 1966.

Emerson, Rupert. *From Empire to Nation.* Boston: 1960.

Erikson, Erik. *Young Man Luther.* New York: 1958.

Etzioni, Amitai. *A Comparative Analysis of Complex Organizations.* New York: 1961.

Finer, S. E. *The Man on Horseback.* New York: 1962.

Fitch, Bob and Mary Oppenheimer. *Ghana: End of an Illusion.* New York: 1966.

Gore, William J. and J. W. Dyson. (eds.). *The Making of Decisions.* New York: 1964.

Haas, Ernst. *Beyond the Nation-State.* Stanford: 1964.

Hayes, Carlton. *The Historical Evolution of Modern Nationalism.* New York: 1959.

Hirschmann, Albert O. *Journeys Toward Progress.* New York: 1965.

Huntington, Samuel P. *Political Order in Changing Societies.* New Haven: 1968.

Janowitz, Morris. *The Professional Soldier.* New York: 1960.

Johnson, Chalmers A. *Revolution and the Social System.* Stanford: 1965.
———. *Revolutionary Change.* Boston: 1966.

Johnson, Harry G. (ed.). *Economic Nationalism in Old and New States.* Chicago: 1967.

Kahn, Robert L. *et al. Organizational Stress: Studies in Role Conflict and Ambiguity.* New York: 1964.

Kolko, Gabriel. *The Politics of War.* New York: 1968.

Kothari, Rajni. *India.* Boston: 1970.

Krech, David; Crutchfield, Richard S.; and Ballachey, Egerton L. *Individual in Society.* New York: 1962.

Kuhn, Thomas. *The Structure of Scientific Revolutions.* Chicago: 1962.

McConnell, Grant. *Private Power and American Democracy*. New York: 1966.

Machiavelli, Niccolo. *The Prince and The Discourses*. New York: 1950.

Mansfield, Peter. *Nasser's Egypt*. Baltimore: 1965.

March, James G. and Herbert A. Simon. *Organizations*. New York: 1958.

Marx, Karl. *The Eighteenth Brumaire of Louis Bonaparte*. New York: 1963.

Moore, Barrington. *Social Origins of Dictatorship and Democracy*. Boston: 1966.

Mowrer, O. Hobart. *Learning Theory and the Symbolic Processes*. New York: 1960.

Nasser, Gamal Abdel. *Philosophy of the Revolution*. (n.p., n.d.)

Nettl, J. P. *Political Mobilization*. New York: 1967.

Padgett, L. Vincent. *The Mexican Political System*. Boston: 1966.

Post, Ken. *The New States of West Africa*. Baltimore: 1964.

Pye, Lucian. *Aspects of Political Development*. Boston: 1966.

Riggs, Fred. *Administration in Developing Societies: The Theory of Prismatic Society*. Boston: 1964.

Rokeech, Milton. *The Open and Closed Mind*. New York: 1960.

Selznick, Philip. *Leadership in Administration*. White Plains, N.Y.: 1957.

———. *The Organizational Weapon*. New York: 1960.

———. *T.V.A. and the Grass Roots*. New York: 1966.

Sherif, Carolyn; Sherif, Muzafer; and Nebergall, Roger E. *Attitudes and Attitude Change*. Philadelphia: 1965.

Simon, Herbert A. *Administrative Behavior*. New York: 1961.

Simon, Herbert A.; Smithburg, Donald W.; and Thompson, Victor A. *Public Administration*. New York: 1964.

Thompson, James D. *Organizations in Action*. New York: 1967.

Weber, Eugen. *Varieties of Fascism*. New York: 1964.

Weber, Max. *Economy and Society*, ed. Guenther Roth. Translated by Guenther Roth and Claus Wittich. 3 vols. New York: 1968.

———. *The Protestant Ethic*. Translated by Talcott Parsons. New York: 1958.

———. *The Theory of Social and Economic Organization*, ed. Talcott Parsons. Translated by M. Henderson and T. Parsons. New York: 1947.

Wildavsky, Aaron. *The Politics of the Budgetary Process*. Boston: 1964.

Wolin, Sheldon. *Politics and Vision*. Boston: 1960.

Zolberg, Aristide. *Creating Political Order*. Chicago: 1966.

ARTICLES

Almond, Gabriel. "Comparative Political Systems." In *Comparative Politics: Notes and Readings*, edited by Roy C. Macridis and Bernard E. Brown. Homewood, Ill.: 1961.

Apter, David E. "Ghana." In *Political Parties and National Integration in Tropical Africa*, edited by James S. Coleman and Carl G. Rosberg, Jr. Berkeley and Los Angeles: 1964.

———. "Ideology and Discontent." In *Ideology and Discontent*, edited by David E. Apter. New York: 1964.

Bachrach, Peter, and Morton Baratz. "Two Faces of Power." *American Political Science Review* 57 (September 1963): 632–642.

Barnes, Samuel. "Leadership Style and Political Competence," In *Political Leadership in Industrialized Societies*, edited by Lewis J. Edinger. New York: 1967.

Becker, Howard S. "Notes on the Concept of Commitment." In *The Making of Decisions*, edited by William J. Gore and J. W. Dyson. New York: 1964.

Bendix, Reinhard. "Tradition and Modernity Reconsidered." *Comparative Studies in Society and History* 9 (April 1967): 292–346.

Binder, Leonard. "National Integration and Political Development." *American Political Science Review* 58 (September 1964): 622–631.

Deutsch, Karl. "The Price of Integration." In *The Integration of Political Communities*, edited by Philip E. Jacob and James V. Toscano. New York: 1964.

———. "Social Mobilization and Political Development." *American Political Science Review* 55 (September 1961): 493–514.

Etzioni, Amitai. "A Paradigm for the Study of Political Unification." *World Politics* 15 (October 1962): 44–74.

Fishbein, Martin. "A Consideration of Beliefs, Attitudes, and Their Relationship." In *Current Studies in Social Psychology*, edited by Ivan D. Steiner and Martin Fishbein. New York: 1965.

Frey, Frederick. "Political Development, Power, and Communications in Turkey." In *Communications and Political Development*, edited by Lucian Pye. Princeton: 1963.

Geertz, Clifford. "Ideology as a Cultural System." In *Ideology and Discontent*, edited by David E. Apter. New York: 1964.

Gerschenkron, Alexander. "Economic Backwardness in Historical Perspective." In *Economic Backwardness in Historical Perspective*, edited by Alexander Gerschenkron. Cambridge, Mass.: 1962.

Gonzalez-Casanova, Pablo. "Internal Colonialism and National Development." In *Latin American Radicalism*, edited by Irving Louis Horowitz *et al.* New York: 1969.

Gouldner, Alvin W. "Cosmopolitans and Locals: Toward an Analysis of Latent Social Roles — I, II." *Administrative Science Quarterly* 2 (1957–1958): 281.

Gregor, A. James. "African Socialisms, Socialism and Fascism: An Appraisal." *Review of Politics* 29 (July 1967): 324–353.

Haas, Ernst B. "International Integration: The European and the Universal Process." In *International Political Communities: An Anthology*. New York: 1966.

Heaphey, James. "The Organization of Egypt: Inadequacies of a Non-Political Model for Nation-Building." *World Politics* 18 (January 1966): 177–193.

Hoffmann, Stanley. "Obstinate or Obsolete? The Fate of the Nation-State and the Case of Western Europe." *Daedalus* 95 (Summer 1966): 862–915.

———. "Paradoxes of the French Political Community." In *In Search of France*, edited by Stanley Hoffmann, Charles P. Kindleberger, Laurence Wylie, Jesse R. Pitts, Jean-Baptiste Duroselle, and Francois Goguel. New York: 1963.

Horowitz, Irving Louis. "Consensus, Conflict, and Cooperation: A Sociological Inventory." *Social Forces* 41 (December 1962): 177–188.

Huntington, Samuel P. "Political Development and Political Decay." In *Political Modernization*, edited by Claude E. Welch, Jr. Belmont, Calif.: 1967.

Karpat, Kemal. "Society, Economics and Politics in Contemporary Turkey." *World Politics*, 17 (October 1964): 50–74.

Kirchheimer, Otto. "Confining Conditions and Revolutionary Breakthroughs." *American Political Science Review* 59 (December 1965): 964–974.

Kling, Merle. "Towards a Theory of Power and Political Instability in Latin America." In *Political Change in Underdeveloped Countries*, edited by John Kautsky. New York: 1962.

Kothari, Rajni. "Tradition and Modernity Revisited." *Government and Opposition* 3 (Summer 1968): 273–293.

Legum, Colin. "Socialism in Ghana: A Political Interpretation." In *African Socialism*, edited by William H. Friedland and Carl G. Rosberg, Jr. Stanford: 1964.

Lenczowski, George. "Radical Régimes in Egypt, Syria, and Iraq: Some

Comparative Observations on Ideologies and Practices." *Journal of Politics* 28 (February 1966): 29–57. (Reprint No. 31, Department of Political Science, University of California, Berkeley, pp. 29–56.)

Lindblom, Charles E. "Has India an Economic Future?" *Foreign Affairs* 44 (January 1966): 239–252.

——. "The 'Science' of Muddling Through." *Public Administration Review* 19 (September 1959): 79–88.

Linz, Juan. "An Authoritarian Regime: Spain." In *Cleavages, Ideologies, and Party Systems,* edited by Erik Allardt and Yrjo Littunen. Helsinki: 1964.

Moore, Clement Henry. "Tunisia After Bourguiba: Liberalization or Political Degeneration?" In *Political Modernization in the Near East and North Africa.* Princeton University Conference, 1966. (Reprint No. 37, Department of Political Science, University of California, Berkeley.)

Morse, Richard. "The Heritage of Latin America." In *The Founding of New Societies,* edited by Louis Hartz. New York: 1964.

Navarro, Moises Gonzalez. "Mexico: The Lop-Sided Revolution." In *Obstacles to Change in Latin America,* edited by Claudio Veliz.

Nettl, J. P. and Roland Robertson. "Industrialization, Development, or Modernization." *British Journal of Sociology* 17 (September 1966): 274–291.

Organski, A. F. K. "Fascism and Modernization." In *The Nature of Fascism,* edited by S. J. Woolf. New York: 1969.

Ozbudun, Ergun. "Established Revolution vs. Unfinished Revolution: Contrasting Patterns of Democratization in Mexico and Turkey." In *Authoritarian Politics in Modern Society,* edited by Samuel P. Huntington and Clement H. Moore. New York: 1970.

Payaslioglu, Arif T. "Turkey." In *Political Modernization in Japan and Turkey,* edited by Robert E. Ward and Dankwart A. Rustow. Princeton: 1964.

Polsby, Nelson. "The Institutionalization of the U.S. House of Representatives." *American Political Science Review* 62 (March 1968): 143–169.

Presthus, Robert V. "Authority in Organizations." In *Concepts and Issues in Administrative Behavior,* edited by Sydney Mailick and Edward H. Van Ness. Englewood Cliffs, N.J.: 1962.

Pye, Lucian. "Introduction: Political Culture and Political Development." In *Political Culture and Political Development*, edited by Lucian Pye and Sidney Verba. Princeton: 1965.

Rhodes, Robert I. "Mexico — A Model for Development?" *Science & Society* 34 (Spring 1970): 61–77.

Roth, Guenther. "Personal Rulership, Patrimonialism, and Empire-Building in the New States." *World Politics* 20 (January 1968): 194–207.

Rustow, Dankwart A. "The Development of Parties in Turkey." In *Political Parties and Political Development*, edited by Joseph LaPalombara and Myron Weiner. Princeton: 1966.

Sugar, Peter F. "Economic and Political Modernization in Turkey." In *Poltical Modernization in Japan and Turkey*, edited by Robert E. Ward and Dankwart A. Rustow. Princeton: 1964.

Thompson, James D. and Arthur Tuden. "Strategies, Structures, and Processes of Organizational Decision." In *Comparative Studies in Administration*, edited by James D. Thompson, Peter B. Hammond, Robert W. Hawkes, Buford H. Junker, and Arthur Tuden. Pittsburgh: 1959.

Van Neste, Dominique. "La Turquie et le problème d'intégration." *World Today* 22 (June 1966): 242–252.

Vatikiotis, P. J. "Egypt 1966: The Assessment of a Revolution." *The World Today* (June 1966): 242–252.

Wolin, Sheldon S. "Violence and the Western Political Tradition." *American Journal of Orthopsychiatry* 33 (January 1963): 15–28.

Womack, John, Jr. "The Spoils of the Mexican Revolution." *Foreign Affairs* 48 (July 1970): 677–688.

Zolberg, Aristide. "Ivory Coast." In *Political Parties and National Integration in Tropical Africa*, edited by James S. Coleman and Carl G. Rosberg, Jr. Berkeley and Los Angeles: 1964.

———. "Patterns of National Integration." *Journal of Modern African Studies* 5 (December 1967): 449–468.

Studies of Communist Systems

BOOKS

Azrael, Jeremy. *Managerial Power and Soviet Politics*. Cambridge, Mass.: 1966.

Blackner, Donald L. M. *Unity in Diversity: Italian Communism and the Communist World*. Cambridge, Mass.: 1968.

Brown, J. F. *Bulgaria Under Communist Rule*. New York: 1970.

Brzezinski, Zbigniew. *Ideology and Power in Soviet Politics*. New York: 1962.

———. *The Soviet Bloc*. Cambridge, Mass.: 1967.

Conquest, Robert. *Power and Policy in the U.S.S.R.* New York: 1961.

Dallin, Alexander (ed.). *Diversity in International Communism*. New York: 1963.

Debray, Regis. *Revolution in the Revolution?* New York: 1967.

Djilas, Milovan. *The New Class*. New York: 1957.

———. *The Unperfect Society: Beyond the New Class*. New York: 1969.

Draper, Theodore. *Castroism: Theory and Practice*. New York: 1965.

———. *Castro's Revolution: Myths and Realities*. New York: 1962.

DuBois, Jules. *Fidel Castro*. New York: 1959.

Erlich, V. *The Soviet Industrialization Debate: 1924–1928*. Cambridge, Mass.: 1960.

Fagen, Richard. *Transformation of Political Culture in Cuba*. Stanford: 1969.

Fainsod, Merle. *Smolensk Under Soviet Rule*. New York: 1963.

Gray, Richard. *Jose Marti: Cuban Patriot*. Gainesville, Fla.: 1962.

Griffith, William E. *Sino–Soviet Relations, 1964–1965*. Cambridge, Mass.: 1967.

Guevara, Che. *Guerrilla Warfare*. New York: 1961.

Hoffman, George W. and Fred Warner Neal. *Yugoslavia and the New Communism*. New York: 1962.

Hudson, G. F., Richard Lowenthal and Roderick MacFarquhar (eds.). *The Sino-Soviet Dispute*. New York: 1961.

Iglesias, Jose. *In the Fist of the Revolution*. New York: 1969.

Johnson, Chalmers A. *Peasant Nationalism and Communist Power*. Stanford: 1966.

Koestler, Arthur. *Darkness at Noon*. New York: 1941.

Lenin, V. I. *Left Wing Communism, An Infantile Disorder*. New York: 1940.

———. *State and Revolution*. New York: 1932.

Linden, Carl. *Khrushchev and the Soviet Leadership: 1957–1964*. Baltimore: 1966.

Lowenthal, Richard. *World Communism: The Disintegration of a Secular Faith*. New York: 1964.

Macartney, C. A. and A. W. Palmer. *Independent Eastern Europe*. New York: 1962.

MacGaffey, Wyatt and C. Barnett. *Cuba: Its Peoples, Its Society, Its Culture*. New Haven: 1962.

Maclean, Fitzroy. *Tito*. New York: 1957.

Mills, C. Wright. *Listen Yankee*. New York: 1960.

Mnachko, Ladislav. *The Seventh Night*. New York: 1969.

———. *The Taste of Power*. New York: 1967.

Pipes, Richard. *The Formation of the Soviet Union*. Cambridge, Mass.: 1964.

Richman, Barry, *Industrial Society in Communist China*. New York: 1969.

Roberts, Henry. *Russia and America*. New York: 1956.

Rush, Myron. *Political Succession in the USSR*. New York: 1965.

Schram, Stuart R. *The Political Thought of Mao Tse-tung*. New York: 1964.

Schurmann, Franz. *Ideology and Organization in Communist China*. Berkeley and Los Angeles: 1966.

Seers, Dudley (ed.). *Cuba: The Economic and Social Revolution*. Chapel Hill: 1964.

Seton-Watson, Hugh. *Eastern Europe Between the Wars, 1918–1941*. Hamden, Conn.: 1962.

Simmonds, George (ed.). *Soviet Leaders*. New York: 1967.

Stalin, J. V. *The Foundations of Leninism*. Peking: 1965.

Tatu, Michel. *Power in the Kremlin from Khrushchev to Kosygin*. New York: 1968.

Townsend, James R. *Political Participation in Communist China*. Berkeley and Los Angeles: 1967.

Von Rauch, Georg. *A History of Soviet Russia*. New York: 1967.

Ward, Benjamin. *The Socialist Economy*. New York: 1967.

Wilber, Charles K. *The Soviet Model and Underdeveloped Countries*. Chapel Hill: 1969.

Zagoria, Janet D., ed. *Power and the Soviet Elite: "The Letter of an Old Bolshevik" and Other Essays by Boris I. Nicolaevsky*. New York: 1965.

ARTICLES

Armstrong, John A. "Party Bifurcation and Elite Interests." *Soviet Studies* 17 (April 1966): 417–431.

Bass, Robert. "The Post-Stalin Era in Eastern Europe." *Problems of Communism* 12 (March–April 1963): 68–76.

Czechoslovak Press Survey. "Czechoslovak Action Program." *Radio Free Europe*, May 20, 1968.

Dallin, Alexander and George Breslauer. "Political Terror." In *Change in Communist Systems*, edited by Chalmers A. Johnson. Stanford: 1970.

Deutsch, Karl. "Cracks in the Monolith: Possibilities and Patterns of Disintegration in Totalitarian Systems." In *Comparative Politics: A Reader*, edited by Harry Eckstein and David E. Apter. New York: 1963.

Fainsod, Merle. "Bureaucracy and Modernization: The Russian and Soviet Case." In *Bureaucracy and Political Development*, edited by Joseph LaPalombara. Princeton: 1963.

Feldmesser, Robert A. "Social Classes and Political Structure." In *The Transformation of Russian Society*, edited by Cyril Black. Cambridge, Mass.: 1960.

Inkeles, Alex. "The Totalitarian Mystique: Some Impressions of the Dynamics of Totalitarian Society." In *Comparative Politics: A Reader*, edited by Harry Eckstein and David E. Apter. New York: 1963.

Johnson, Chalmers A. "Building of a Communist Nation in China." In *The Communist Revolution in Asia*, edited by Robert A. Scalapino. Englewood Cliffs, N.J.: 1965. (Reprint No. 190, Center for Chinese Studies, Institute of International Studies, University of California, Berkeley.)

Kotyk, V. "Some Aspects of the History of Relations Among Socialist Countries." *Radio Free Europe*, October 30, 1967.

Laird, Roy D. "Some Characteristics of the Soviet Leadership System: A Maturing Totalitarian System." *Midwest Journal of Political Science* 10 (February 1966): 29–38.

Lee, Chong-Sik. "Stalinism in the East." In *The Communist Revolution in Asia*, edited by Robert A. Scalapino. Englewood Cliffs, N.J.: 1965.

Lee, Chong-Sik, and Oh, Ki-Wan. "The Russian Faction in North Korea. *Asian Survey* 2 (April 1968): 270–288.

Lowenthal, Richard. "The End of an Illusion." *Problems of Communism* 12 (January–February 1963): 1–9.

Meyer, Alfred. "Authority in Communist Political Systems." In *Political Leadership in Industrialized Societies*, edited by Lewis J. Edinger. New York: 1967.

Nove, Alec. "Soviet Political Organization and Development." In *Politics and Change in Developing Countries*, edited by Colin Leys. Cambridge, Mass.: 1969.

———. "Was Stalin Really Necessary?" In *Economic Rationality and Soviet Politics*, edited by Alec Nove. New York: 1964.

Paige, Glenn. "North Korea and the Emulation of Russian and Chinese Behavior." In *Communist Strategies in Asia,* edited by A. Doak Barnett. New York: 1963.

Revai, Jozsef. "On the Character of Our People's Democracy." In *Readings on Contemporary Eastern Europe,* edited by C. E. Black. New York: 1953.

Schöpflin, George A. "National Minorities Under Communism in Eastern Europe." In *Eastern Europe in Transition,* edited by Kurt London. Baltimore: 1966.

Schurmann, Franz. "Mao Tse-tung." Unpublished manuscript, University of California, Berkeley, 1965.

————. "Politics and Economics in Russia and China." In *Soviet and Chinese Communism,* edited by Donald W. Treadgold. Seattle: 1967.

Shoup, Paul. "Communism, Nationalism, and the Growth of the Communist Community of Nations After World War II." *American Political Science Review* 56 (December 1962): 886–898.

————. "Comparing Communist Nations, Prospects for an Empirical Approach." *American Political Science Review* 62 (March 1968): 186.

Slusser, Robert. "Alexei Alexeevich Yepishev." In *Soviet Leaders,* edited by George Simmonds. New York: 1967.

Stalin, Joseph. "Industrialization of the Country and the Right Deviation." In *Foundations of Soviet Strategy for Economic Growth,* edited by Nicolas Spulber. Bloomington, Ind.: 1964.

Tomasevich, Jozo. "Yugoslavia During the Second World War." In *Contemporary Yugoslavia,* edited by Wayne S. Vucinich. Berkeley and Los Angeles: 1969.

Vucinich, Wayne S. "Interwar Yugoslavia." In *Contemporary Yugoslavia,* edited by Wayne S. Vucinich. Berkeley and Los Angeles: 1969.

Wiatr, Jerzy. "State and Nation." *Polish Perspectives* 11 (March 1968): 16–25.

Works on Romania

BOOKS

Dumitriu, Petru. *Incognito.* New York: 1964.

————. *Meeting at the Last Judgment.* New York: 1962.

Fischer-Galati, Stephen. *The New Rumania: From People's Democracy to Socialist Republic.* Cambridge, Mass.: 1967.

———. (ed.). *Romania*. New York: 1957.

———. *The Socialist Republic of Rumania*. Baltimore: 1969.

———. *20th Century Rumania*. New York: 1970.

Floyd, David. *Rumania: Russia's Dissident Ally*. New York: 1965.

Ionescu, Ghita. *Communism in Rumania*. New York: 1964.

Montias, John Michael. *Economic Development in Communist Rumania*. Cambridge, Mass.: 1967.

Roberts, Henry. *Rumania: Political Problems of an Agrarian State*. New Haven: 1951.

Seton-Watson, Robert. *History of the Roumanians*. London: 1934.

Smultea, Ilie J. "Political Development and Bureaucracy in Romania Prior to World War II." Ph.D. dissertation, University of California, Berkeley, 1968.

ARTICLES

Boila, Romulus. "Press and Radio." In *Captive Romania*, edited by Alexander Cretzianu. New York: 1956.

Bossy, George H. "Transportation and Communications." In *Romania*, edited by Stephen Fischer-Galati. New York: 1957.

Braham, R. L. "Rumania: Onto the Separate Path." *Problems of Communism* 13 (May–June 1964): 14–24.

Brown, J. F. "Eastern Europe." *Survey* 64 (January 1965): 65–89.

———. "Rumania Steps Out of Line." *Survey* 49 (October 1963): 19–35.

Burks, R. V. "The Rumanian National Deviation: An Accounting." In *Eastern Europe in Transition*, edited by Kurt London. Baltimore: 1966.

Ciurea, Emil. "Religious Life." In *Captive Romania*, edited by Alexander Cretzianu. New York: 1956.

Dumitriu, Petru. "The Two New Classes." *East Europe* 10 (September 1961): 3.

Fischer-Galati, Stephen. "Rumania." In *East Central Europe and the World: Developments in the Post-Stalin Era*, edited by Stephen D. Kertesz. Notre Dame, Ind.: 1962.

———. "Rumania." In *Eastern European Government and Politics*, edited by V. Benes, A. Gyorgy and G. Stambuk. New York: 1966.

———. "Rumania and the Sino-Soviet Split." In *Eastern Europe in Transition*, edited by Kurt London. Baltimore: 1966.

Gross, George. "Rumania: The Fruits of Autonomy." *Problems of Communism* 15 (January–February 1966): 16–28.

Ionescu, Ghita. "Social Structure: Rumania Under Communism." *Annals of the American Academy of Political and Social Science* 317 (May 1958): 53–62.

Montias, John Michael. "Backgrounds and Origins of the Rumanian Dispute with Comecon." *Soviet Studies* (October 1964): 125–152.

———. "Rumania's Foreign Trade in the Postwar Period." *Slavic Review* 25 (September 1966): 421–442.

Plessia, Radu. "Financial Policy." In *Captive Romania*, edited by Alexander Cretzianu. New York: 1956.

Roberts, Henry. "Politics in a Small State: The Balkan Example." In *The Balkans in Transition*, edited by Charles and Barbara Jelavich. Berkeley and Los Angeles: 1963.

Spulber, Nicolas. "Changes in the Economic Structures of the Balkans, 1860–1960." In *The Balkans in Transition*, edited by Charles and Barbara Jelavich. Berkeley and Los Angeles: 1963.

Stoianovich, Traian. "The Social Foundations of Balkan Politics, 1750–1941." In *The Balkans in Transition*, edited by Charles and Barbara Jelavich. Berkeley and Los Angeles: 1963.

Tatu, Michel. Articles in *Le Monde*, November 11–14, 1967.

Tomasic, D. A. "The Romanian Communist Leadership." *Slavic Review* 20 (October 1961): 477–494.

Weber, Eugen. "The Men of the Archangel." *Journal of Contemporary History* 1, no. 1 (1966): 101–127.

———. "Romania." In *The European Right*, edited by Hans Rogger and Eugen Weber. Berkeley and Los Angeles: 1966.

Romanian Sources

Bălcescu, Nicolae. *Istoria românilor sub Michaiu Vodă Vitezul.* București: 1878.

Ceaușescu, Nicolae. *Congresul al II-lea al Partidului Muncitoresc Romîn.* [speech] București: 1956.

———. *România pe drumul desăîrșirii construcției socialiste.* Vols. 1–4. București: 1968–1970.

Gheorghiu-Dej, Gheorghe. *Articles and Speeches.* București: 1963.

———. *Articole și Cuvîntări.* București: 1951.

———. *Articole și Cuvîntări.* București: 1961.

———. *Articole și Cuvîntări.* București: 1962.

———. *The Plan of the Rumanian People's Republic for 1949.* [Report

to the Grand National Assembly by Gh. Gheorghiu-Dej.] București: 1949.

————. *Rapport d'activité du Comité Central du Parti Ouvrier Roumain présenté au II Congrès du Parti.* București: 1956.

Agerpress

Lumea

Lupta de clasă: organ teoretic și politic al CC al PMR.

Probleme economice

Romanian Journal of Sociology [in English]

Scînteia

Studii, revistă de istorie

Anale istorie

Index